Reclaiming Social Policy

Reclaiming Social Policy

Globalization, Social Exclusion and New Poverty Reduction Strategies

Arjan de Haan
Social Development Adviser,
UK Department for International Development, China

First published 2007 by
PALGRAVE MACMILLAN
Houndmills, Basingstoke, Hampshire RG21 6XS and
175 Fifth Avenue, New York, N.Y. 10010
Companies and representatives throughout the world

PALGRAVE MACMILLAN is the global academic imprint of the Palgrave Macmillan division of St. Martin's Press, LLC and of Palgrave Macmillan Ltd. Macmillan® is a registered trademark in the United States, United Kingdom and other countries. Palgrave is a registered trademark in the European Union and other countries.

ISBN-13: 978-0-230-00781-9   hardback
ISBN-10: 0230007813   hardback

This book is printed on paper suitable for recycling and made from fully managed and sustained forest sources. Logging, pulping and manufacturing processes are expected to conform to the environmental regulations of the country of origin.

A catalogue record for this book is available from the British Library.

Library of Congress Cataloging-in-Publication Data

Haan, Arjan de.
    Reclaiming social policy: globalization, social exclusion, and new poverty reduction strategies / Arjan de Haan.
        p. cm.
    Includes bibliographical references and index.
    ISBN 0-230-00781-3 (cloth)
        1. Social policy. 2. Developing countries–Social policy.
    3. Globalization–Social aspects. 4. Marginality, Social.
    5. Poverty–Government policy. 6. Structural adjustment (Economic policy)–Social aspects. I. Title.
HN18.3.H33 2007
320.609172′4–dc22

2006048883

10   9   8   7   6   5   4   3   2   1
16   15   14   13   12   11   10   09   08   07

Printed and bound in Great Britain by
Antony Rowe Ltd, Chippenham and Eastbourne

Contents

List of Tables and Figures

Tables

Figure

Foreword

This book re-evaluates the importance of social policies in the shaping of well-being and combating exclusion, and develops a critical understanding of how these policies are constituted in a globalizing world. Written from a practitioner's perspective, the core concern of the book is the capacity of policy-making to protect groups from becoming excluded, to promote inclusion and to avoid the sharpening of trends towards marginalization.

There were two key arguments for writing this book. First, globalization, and its perceived and material impacts, urge a better understanding of the policies that impact economic and social processes. This has been widely documented with reference to economic policies in a globalizing world; this book attempts to fill a lacuna with respect to the social policies – health, education, social security and social integration – that play a constitutive role in national development, but have often been described merely in terms of residual safety nets.

Second, development studies has tended to neglect the study of the processes around the making of such social policies. Dominant poverty studies have tended to focus on outcome indicators, while the 'social development' literature has paid insufficient attention to policy processes at macro level. This book contributes to a strand of literature that has emphasized the integration of economic and social policies, an idea launched by the UN in the 1970s, and only recently taken up by UNRISD and others, still leaving significant gaps in the analysis of public policies, particularly in the poorest countries.

The book's central hypothesis is that national social policy is becoming increasingly important with globalization. A core theme of the book is the analysis of the relevance of social policies in the shaping of well-being across nations, including in the world's most marginalized countries. This is illustrated through a comparative approach, analysing the histories of social policy-making during periods of opening up, the varied impact of globalization and the social as well as economic forces underlying the realities and possibilities of public policy-making. Across these objectives runs a concern to bring together poverty debates in North and South, while emphasizing the context- and path-dependence of patterns and policies of inclusion and exclusion.

The book concludes with a normative and practical framework for supporting social policy-making. Departing from a rights approach, emphasizing national traditions, norms and values, it calls for grounding public policies in a conception of the state's responsibility to develop people's capabilities. It provides a practical guide to assessing social policy frameworks, regarding access, quality, relevance and participation.

This publication brings together development theory and practice, and in this way contributes to the recent studies on social policy in a development context. Written from the perspective of a practitioner in a development agency, it contributes to the critique of residual approaches to social policy, to the literature that has focused on poor people's needs and livelihoods, while its main purpose revolves around the strengthening of national systems for policy-making.

Acknowledgements

The motivation to write this book has built up over almost a decade of working in international development, and I am thus indebted to large numbers of colleagues and friends. The relevance of debates on social policy was highlighted for me while I was at the Poverty Research Unit at the University of Sussex, through the calls for proposals for research by DFID, under the guidance of Rosalind Eyben and Andy Norton, who became mentors when I moved to DFID.

This book has been written on the basis of my experience as adviser at the UK Department for International Development since 1998. The number of colleagues at DFID who in different ways have contributed to my thoughts is large, and the following alphabetical list is probably incomplete: Nick Amin, Phil Evans, Max Everest-Phillips, Rosalind Eyben, Shantanu Mitra, Jillian Popkins, Christian Rogg and colleagues in Pro-Poor Growth and Agriculture teams, Gita Sabharwal, Amarjeet Sinha and Judy Walker all contributed, in very different ways, sometimes possibly even unawares. Dennis Pain has been a great source of inspiration.

Colleagues in other international agencies have shown much interest in and encouraged my writing. Insights by Anis Dani and Caroline Kende-Robb at the World Bank have informed my thinking greatly, and I benefited much from working with Anis on the project New Frontiers of Social Policy. Encouraging comments were received from Wouter van Ginneken, Rolph van der Hoeven and Gerry Rodgers at the ILO, and Bob Huber and Sergei Zelenev at UNDESA. Shahin Yaqub provided detailed comments while at the Human Development Report Office, and has continued to ask supportive questions since our time at Sussex.

Engagement with the academic community in the UK has been very important. Michael Lipton's commitment to poverty research has remained an inspiration. David Hulme provided early encouragement, and Simon Maxwell and Bob Deacon were very enthusiastic about the idea while providing helpful suggestions. I benefited a great deal from the work of Armando Barrientos on social protection, and the CPPRC conference on the theme. David Lewis and John Farrington both gave very valuable feedback on early thoughts. I am grateful to Ian Gough for feedback on a draft, and to Geoff Wood for inspiration through the innovative research programme at the University of Bath.

The book was written during a one-year period of leave from DFID, and I am grateful to the Department for making this possible, as well as to the University of Guelph for hosting me, and particularly the undergraduate students who kept reminding me about the importance of the questions in this book, even though the answers may not always convince them.

Writing a book inevitably puts a burden on family and friends, particularly when it is written in periods of transition and travels across continents. The idea for writing the book was formed in the now unimaginably quiet period before our son Sohail was born, and much of the writing has been done with his and his younger sister Nanaki's noises in the background. I am thus deeply indebted to Paramjit, for her companionship and critical reflection on international development practices.

1
Introduction: Why Focus on Social Policy?

Since the late 1970s, with the advent of conservative policies in OECD countries, and of structural adjustment in the South, the state has been under pressure. Social policies have been particularly under stress, with an emphasis on reducing budget deficits and increased targeting of benefits provided by the state. With the critique of structural adjustment, and global pressure towards debt relief, poverty reduction has become core to much of the international development debate. Since 2000 strong commitments to increased aid financing have been articulated, and the trend in aid flows is indeed fairly rapidly upwards. But global inequalities continue to rise, and there are major questions regarding the success of development efforts.

This book re-evaluates the importance of social policies in the shaping of well-being and combating exclusion and will enhance critical understanding of how these policies are constituted in a globalizing world. Written from a practitioner's perspective, the core concern of the book is the capacity for policy-making to protect groups from becoming excluded, to promote inclusion and to avoid the sharpening of trends towards marginalization. The book's central argument is that national social policy is more, not less, as commonly argued, important in a globalized world and more open economies and societies. It therefore emphasizes the need for strengthened analysis of social policies, and its role in the shaping of well-being across nations, and particularly in the world's most marginalized countries where social policy analysis has remained underdeveloped.

The term 'social policy' is used in an ambitious sense. It is seen as an essential complement to economic policies, and not just in a 'residual' fashion, such as the interventions that deal with the unintended consequences of economic trends and policies. The perspective is cross-sectoral, arguing that international development debates need to be based in a better understanding of the inter-related nature of sectoral policies. Moreover, the perspective adopted here highlights the political dynamics of public policies, which, for example, can prioritize one set of policies over the other, often at the cost of reduced impacts on poverty.

This introductory chapter discusses why strengthening national social policies is of crucial importance for poverty reduction. The chapter first provides a working definition of social policy. It then highlights the changes in social policy approaches with the advent of structural adjustment, and how the role of social policy has changed under globalization and economic integration. The fourth section discusses the way social policy has been dealt with in the development studies literature, and whether a notion of social policy which emphasizes national path-dependence and principles of social integration can be usefully applied to the very different contexts in North and South. Section 5 presents the structure of the book.

1.1   What is social policy?

Different people have different understandings of social policies, as do governments and development agencies. Social policy analysis in the European tradition suffers from a 'dependent variable problem', and definitions and measurements have varied considerably (Gough, 2005). This section discusses some of the key questions in these debates, proposing a working definition relevant for the context of countries in the South.[1]

Social policies are a subset of public policies. But even the nature of public policies and how they are understood are not undisputed, and very much depends on disciplines and ideological backgrounds. Economists tend to focus on the role of the state in the provision of goods and services that are in the public interest but not provided through markets, and as creator of enabling environments for and regulator of these markets. Political scientists tend to focus on public policies as outcomes of political struggles, in the broad sense of the term, and the result of differences in interests.

The way public policies and the role of the state is understood in this book is based on Karl Polanyi's study of nineteenth-century political economy. He emphasized the 'clash of the organizing principles of economic liberalism and social protection which led to a deep-seated institutional strain', interacting with the conflict of classes which turned this crisis into a catastrophe (Polanyi, 1968: 134).[2] His framework focused on the inter-action between the expansion of market forces and social institutions that try to steer these markets, and the way policies are embedded in institutional contexts.[3] Against the deep social and economic crisis of the 1930s, Polanyi emphasized the central role of the state in organizing the market, as an institution, and the shaping of nation states through the extension of citizens' social rights, or as Esping-Andersen put it 'an alternative to the supposedly disembodied treatment of economic life typical of mainstream economics' (Esping-Andersen, 1999: 11). The market is a political and social construct, and neatly separable domains of a 'market' free from 'politics' or 'social concerns' do not exist (also Chang, 2003, 2004). The interaction between social and economic policies is of key importance, as will be discussed in Chapter 3, and in the discussion of social policy this book focuses on the diversity of actors and institutional areas, and interactions of state, market, communities and households.

With respect to social policy, a number of definitions are available. At the London School of Economics, social policy is introduced as

> an interdisciplinary and applied subject concerned with the analysis of societies' responses to social need ... focused on those aspects of the economy, society and polity that are necessary to human existence and the means by which they can be provided. These basic human needs include: food and shelter, a sustainable and safe environment, the promotion of health and treatment of the sick, the care and support of those unable to live a fully independent life, the education and training of individuals to a level that enables them fully to participate in their society. The study of Social Policy is designed to reflect on the ways in which different societies have developed ways of meeting these needs ... Some societies rely on informal or family institutions, some on private markets and individual actions, some on governmental actions through what is often termed the welfare state.[4]

Social policy, understood in this way, is thus broader than a notion of the welfare state, relevant in most OECD countries. According to Cox (1998), the idea of the welfare state has four common elements. First, welfare is – or used to be – an entitlement, based on citizenship, a main theme in T.H. Marshall's work of 1950 (the relevance of this in the context of the South will be discussed in the fourth and concluding chapters). Second, income maintenance was the core of the welfare state, which developed mainly in a period of economic growth with full employment. Third, central planning and coordination was a key mechanism of welfare state operations. Finally, the approach was based on an assumption that the welfare state would bring out the best in human nature. Such a definition of welfare state is much more restricted than what is to be understood as social policy relevant for conditions in the South.

The definition of social policy is thus also wider than that of, and incorporates, social security, as defined for example by the ILO: 'the protection that a society provides to individuals and households to ensure access to health care and to guarantee income security, particularly in cases of old age, unemployment, sickness, invalidity, work injury, maternity or loss of a breadwinner.'[5] While notions of the 'public management of social risks' (Esping-Andersen, 1999: 36) and social protection are part of the social policies discussed, the focus in this book is on a cross-sectoral view of public policies.

A broad definition is mirrored in the research programme on social policy in the South at the University of Bath, which highlighted four elements (Gough, 2004: 22; see also Wood and Gough, 2006). First, social policy is a *policy*, an intentional action within the public sphere to achieve certain goals. Second, it is oriented to welfare goals. Third, it operates through a wide variety of policy instruments and sectors, such as land reform, work programmes, food subsidies, tax expenditures, health, education and social protection. Finally – and consistent with Esping-Andersen's (1999: 34–5) emphasis on – 'the combined, inter-dependent way in which welfare is produced and allocated between state, market, and family' and a non-profit sector – it is formulated and implemented by various collective actors, not confined to the nation-state, but includes regions, localities, associations, and transnational and global actors.[6] In the research programme, mainly through the work of Ian Gough (2000), the concept of 'welfare regimes' has been used and expanded, as a way of helping to understand the complexity of social policy arrangements, the leading principles of solidarity that determine public policy interventions, emphasizing countries' histories and ideologies.[7] This research programme, too, continued to struggle with terminology, particularly the critique that notions of welfare states and social policy are derived from Northern debates and hence are of limited analytical value in the South.

The scope of social policy

Despite similarities in definitions, a key question in the literature and the pre-eminent underlying issue in many policy debates relates to the proactive nature of social policy. There are disagreements regarding whether social policy should be 'merely concerned with the correction of malfunctions in the operation of society (and particularly of the economy) or involve some overall and logically prior concern with welfare in society, and about the extent to which welfare should be regarded as a key state responsibility.'[8] Titmuss favoured a narrow definition: 'the study of a range of social needs and functioning, in conditions of scarcity, of human organisation, traditionally called social welfare systems, to meet those needs', and focused on the social services, lying 'outside or on the fringes of the so-called free market' (in Lavalette and Pratt, 1997: 2). The comparative work on liberalization led by Lance Taylor similarly defines social policy as 'an important tool that can in principle be used by governments to *cushion some of the adverse effects* of external liberalization' (Taylor, 2001: 7 – my italics).[9] Similar differences continue to inform debates around labour markets and public policy, whether the state should merely manage the 'market failures', or play an active role in shaping the working and outcomes of labour markets.[10] The position taken in this book, and justified, for example, in the discussion on safety nets, is that a social policy focus includes core welfare responsibilities, and a concept of interrelationship with market processes, striving to move away from a 'ghettoization' of social policy. Social policies are seen as constitutive complements to economic policies, and creating conditions for market functioning.[11]

A second question, less prominent in the academic literature but central to poverty concerns about adjustment programmes, is whether social policy analysis should be concerned with the welfare and poverty impacts of other policies, for example the impact of trade liberalization or devaluation, of infrastructure projects or fuel subsidies and other projects or policies without an evident direct relation to poverty.[12] The position taken in this book is that this is a key concern, and deserves a publication in its own right, but it will not be central in the discussion here. This is partly a pragmatic choice, as it would greatly expand the scope of the book. Moreover the book focuses on specific policy instruments, the policies and actors that directly and *deliberately* shape well-being and processes of inclusion, while emphasizing the interrelationships between social policy instruments and other types of policies and market processes.

It is important to be clear about the term 'policy'.[13] The emphasis on deliberate action implies a focus not on the policy *outcomes* (though these are crucial, of course), but on policies to achieve these outcomes.[14] In this context, the fragmentation of social policy formulation, particularly in Africa, is of key importance. For example, Ghana 'continues to lack a unified or well-articulated social policy [though] social programmes have existed in a variety of sectors since Independence.'[15] Second, the book has an institutional approach, by concentrating on 'actual' policies as much as policy intentions, and the constraints on the scope of institutions and actors as much as policy objectives. Such constraints include formal and informal rules (for example, in India constraints imposed by caste 'rules and norms'), commitment as well as capacity to deliver policies, and the unintended outcomes of public policies (for example, reinforcement of caste identities as a result of affirmative action). Policies thus are shaped by politics, and this book tries to contribute to the strand of literature that tries to 'put the politics back into development' (for example, Hickey, 2005, with reference to Uganda).

A third question regarding the definition of social policy concerns its coverage of sectors. There is merit in defining social policy more widely than social protection or safety nets (and conversely, it is important to avoid the temptation to define social protection too broadly). It should also not be restricted to the area of 'poverty alleviation'. Targeted pro-grammes for poverty reduction do have a place in the field of social policy, but universal provisions are central even in situations of fiscal constraints, including those due to public pressure, and in the shaping of solidarity and national identity. Thus the working definition of social policy used in this book relates to the policies for enhancement of human develop-ment, health and education (which can have a more productivist as well as a welfarist orientation, as discussed in Chapter 4), preferential policies such as 'reservation' in India, the range of poverty alleviation schemes such as integrated development projects and micro-finance, and social protec-tion instruments such as employment schemes and welfare transfers to the poorest, the people unable to create their own livelihood.

This book builds on the definition of social policy provided by Aina (1999), which is mirrored in recent African Union discussions, partly because this is formulated in an attempt to recapture the active nature of social policy, in the context of structural adjustment that has tended to undermine national autonomy towards such efforts, particularly in Africa. His definition focuses on the

> systematic and deliberate interventions in the social life of a country to ensure the satisfaction of the basic needs and the well being of the majority of its citizens. This is seen as an expression of socially desirable goals through legislation, institutions, and administrative programs and practices.... [and] is thus a broader concept than ... social work and social welfare.[16]

The approach to social policy adopted in this book is also in line with Drèze and Sen's *Hunger and Public Action* (1989), which argues that the provision of social security in developing countries needs to be viewed from a broad perspective, and as an objective to be pursued through public means rather than as a narrowly defined set of particular strategies, and builds on – but cuts across – their distinction between 'growth-mediated security' and support-led security' (Drèze and Sen 1989, 1991).[17] But it goes beyond the conclusion of Atkinson and Hills (1991), who argue that, while there are many lessons from comparative research about the methods of social policy analysis, there are few lessons concerning policy recommendations: the framework proposed here is directly relevant for policy analysis and advice.

In defining the scope and objectives of social policy, this book bases itself on the agreements of the Copenhagen Summit for Social Development – which contains the most important international agreements with respect to social policies – and subsequent work by, *inter alia*, the World Bank[18] and DFID.[19] It is against the background of these objectives that this book studies social policies, as the means and institutions through which they are achieved. The inclusion of the aim regarding social integration also highlights that the interest in social policy is not merely related to achieving certain outcomes, such as 'halving poverty' or 'education for all', but equally about the social and institutional processes responsible for such outcomes.

The definition of social policy adopted thus has a strong normative element. In practice, many social policies have not been equitable or participatory. South Africa's Apartheid was a form of social policy, with an interventionist state that redistributed on the basis of racist principles. Both Hitler and Mussolini expanded state intervention, and affirmative action in Rwanda became part of the extremely violent inter-ethnic strife (Mamdani, 2001). Regressive social policy approaches during the colonial period are illustrated in a statement by the then Southern Rhodesia's Prime Minister: 'I shall do all I can do to develop the native if I am allowed to protect my own race in our own areas and, if I am not, I will not do anything' (quoted in Osei-Hwedie and Bar-on, 1999: 92). The resulting dualism in the provision of social services and rights, reinforced by post-colonial modernization projects, still strongly influence many social policies across the South: for example, Zimbabwe's social policies of the 1980s had a strong focus on reducing racial disparities (Davies and Rattsø, 2001). The normative element of the social policy approach adopted here is discussed in the concluding chapter, with an emphasis on social rights which has been central to Northern social policy debate, but relevant in the South too.[20]

The normative emphasis chosen in the book is combined with a focus on the path- and context-dependent nature of social policies, particularly around principles of solidarity enshrined within the delivery of national policies. Social policy-making is not a technocratic exercise, but embedded in political economy. Social policy 'can be seen as an intensely political project ... in which competing ideologies can clash' (Lavalette and Pratt, 1997).[21] They are the result of struggles of interest groups and the working classes, but also evolve from elites' attempts to defuse power struggles and reduce political tension (as the Social Fund PAMSCAD in Ghana aimed to; Gayi, 1995), attempts to undercut trade union power (as in Bismarck's social policy), or aims to create a productive labour force (predominant in East Asian policies).

It is therefore essential to look at the interaction between the formulation and implementation of social policies on the one hand, and democratization and empowerment on the other. Lindert (2004) highlights the simultaneous evolution of social spending with both economic growth and the extension of democracy or political voice (thus pointing to a paradox that social spending is least likely to happen where it is most required). Analysis of the nature of policy processes in post-communist countries shows that responsive states are nurtured by increasing wealth (Johanssen, 2005). However, this should not lead to deterministic conclusions, and the perspective adopted here focuses on the interplay of social policy formulation and forms of political contestation and representation. For example, the non-contributory pension schemes in Brazil and South Africa, now playing an important redistributive and anti-poverty role, originated under autocratic rule, and included motivations to stem migration to urban areas (HelpAge International, 2003: 20). Similarly, anti-poverty schemes – such as the Maharastra Employment Guarantee Scheme – are both the outcome of political negotiation and grounds for advocacy on behalf of poor people (Joshi, 2005).

Understanding the formulation and implementation of social (and other public) policies of course requires an understanding of the tax or other funding base. Among OECD countries, there are large differences in levels of taxation and public funding. For poorer countries, the tax base is often low, did not increase with the expansion of public finances in the 1960s, and raising tax revenue is usually seen as a technical problem rather than as part of the development of a social contract. Moreover, particularly in aid-dependent countries, donors have tended to fund countries' social spending. The result of these combined forces has been low levels of accountability. The interest in taxation in this book is not from a technical perspective, but seen as an important and oft-neglected entry point for analysis of the underlying social contract. This has two components. First, with Independence states generally received international legitimacy, without underlying pressures of war and inter-state competition that were decisive in European nation-building processes, forcing states to raise taxes and strike deals with its citizens.[22] Second, aid dependence has greatly influenced the social contract, generally by reducing the need for taxation, as well as accountability in terms of service provision. Whether new aid modalities like PRSPs have changed this will be the subject of discussion in Chapter 6.

The proposed scope of discussion under the term 'social policy' is thus broad. This is justified on the basis that it is important to conceptualize public policy-making across a range of sectors, and to emphasize the interaction between social and economic policies. This broadens the focus beyond a strand of analysis that defines social policy merely in a residual fashion, and reverses the trend of the last decades in which the proactive role of social policies has been underemphasized. The next section provides a brief genealogy of the debate in a developmental context.

1.2   Social policy before and after structural adjustment

Across the world, North and South, the economic crisis and subsequent reforms of the 1970s have been seen as a breakpoint for the social policies that had prevailed since the Second World War and Independence. Globalization has been seen as a crucial factor in this divide. Even if globalization is not historically unique, and may be reversed (Brawley, 2003: 195), a key difference with earlier waves of globalization is that, 'from the standpoint of the welfare state the financial openness of economies is an entirely new and significant development' (Mishra, 1999: 5).[23] Globalization has been considered as a threat to the functioning of the economic models of the welfare state, the fiscal and monetary policies of Keynesianism, and interventions to achieve full employment, mass education and industrial relations. In the South, the fiscal constraints were accompanied by increasing influence of international organizations, which stressed approaches to social policy mirroring the concerns in the North. This section briefly situates current social policies historically, through their creation during the colonial period, the optimism of the early period of Independence and crisis of the 1970s and 1980s and the advent of structural adjustment.

From colonialism, to Independence, to structural adjustment

While colonialism involved mainly a highly exploitative integration of the South into the global economy, concerns over citizens' welfare were not absent. However, the social policies that emerged during the colonial period, with large differences between countries and colonial powers, showed very narrow interpretations of social welfare, and were largely determined by colonial objectives. The narrow definition of social policy was particularly important, as colonialism often changed social networks and informal support, and taxation policies contributed to commercialization of the economy, in turn creating demands on social policy interventions.

The main actors of colonial social policy were colonial officials, volunteer agencies, missionaries, foreign economic interests and various local groups. In Africa policies were 'selective, discriminatory, and exclusionary, geared to protecting and advancing colonial interests and those of white settlers' (Aina, 1999: 76).[24] Colonial social policies were focused on the elite, spatially restrictive and usually urban biased, providing only minimum services to the majority of the population, and often focused on the security of colonial officials. The provision of social services was often closely related to colonial interests, such as education in Eastern India for the purpose of creating an administrative elite, a legacy that possibly can still be traced in the emphasis on higher education. The divisive nature of engagement with elites has been highlighted by subsequent violence in Rwanda (Mamdani, 2001). Health provisions or interventions were often related to the need for healthy workers, and defined in utilitarian terms. In the late colonial period, and often under international pressure, protective legislation and limited social policies were introduced for workers in the large, usually export-oriented manufacturing and mining enterprises.

Independence and the nationalist governments that came to power in Asia and Africa brought great expectations and promises regarding provision of services to the entire population under a social contract to end the injustice of colonialism (Manji, 2000: 12). Optimism was fuelled by the growing world economy of the 1960s, including growing demand for primary commodities, and in the early 1970s by the financial measures that helped to weaken the impact of the 1973 oil crisis. Socialism dominated as an ideology, in many parts of Africa, China of course and even in India under the democratic Gandhi–Nehru compromise. The ideology led to nationalization of the means of production, justified by promises that this would benefit the entire population, and to increasing employment provided in the civil service and public sector enterprises.[25] Donors tended to be favorably disposed towards state investment in social sectors (Manji, 2000: 12). The impact that the social contracts have had on the population can still be traced, for example in India where research shows that poor people still turn out in large numbers to vote, and expect services to be provided by the state, and not NGOs for example (Kumar, 2001). Understanding social policy in the South, similar to the shaping of welfare states in the North where social provisions and nation building went hand in hand, implies recognition of the intertwining of ideologies of nationalism and entitlements to state-provided services.

The approach to social policy was pro-active, rather than reactive, with remarkable improvements in human development indicators – but for a short period of less than two decades. Though social security provisions remained limited to civil service and some other 'formal sector' employees, governments very rapidly expanded provisions. In Mozambique, for example, primary school enrolment rose by 122 per cent between 1975 and 1979 (to fall in the subsequent decade, marked by civil war; Morgan, 1991: 423). Many of the social policies introduced during the Tanzanian and Chinese experiments with socialism have been of lasting importance. Latin America since the 1930s has been marked by expansion of social policy, in many cases prompted by massive rural–urban migrations. In principle, labour and education, health and other social policies were universalistic, but in practice universalism – for example, in Chile and Argentina – was 'stratified' (see Chapter 4).

The crisis in the dominant approach to social policy in the early period of Independence was caused by a number of factors. The turning point can probably best be situated in 1973, with the fall of Allende in Chile and the advent of the 'Chicago Boys" . . . neo-liberal structural adjustment, as '[n]owhere else in Latin America (or elsewhere) was the program adopted so completely and with so much doctrinal purity' (Mason, 1997: 79). For social policy this implied a radical shift from a search for a welfare state to a neo-liberal model highlighting reductions in social spending, targeting, decentralization and private administration and delivery of services (Raczynski, 2001).[26] This highlights a combination of internal economic and political crises, the impact of rising oil prices and declining commodity prices, and the interventionist US policies that often overtly supported authoritarian regimes, and with that neo-liberal policies, and safeguarding foreign interests.

In Africa and elsewhere, the expansion of infrastructure for social services had proceeded fast, arguably too fast and with too much optimism regarding the possibility of building accountability into the system, and many nationalist leaders considered policy and resources as elements of patronage. Much of the expansion was donor funded, and in a project mode which tended to neglect the wider policy environment (sector-wide approaches resulted from this, as discussed in Chapter 6). The financial and economic crisis of the 1970s and 1980s in Africa forced many countries to adjust their public funding (Adesina, 2006),[27] and similar pressure came to bear on public policies in India during the 1990s although they did not experience economic or similarly severe fiscal crises. Finally, civil unrest and wars in many countries brought an effective end to the experiments of the early years of Independence. Thus, 'newly constructed schools, clinics and hospitals could no longer be maintained. For the same reason, transportation, water delivery, and electricity supplies also stagnated or, more often, degenerated ... large numbers of trained personnel left for greener pastures, undermining the delivery of existing services and the development of new initiatives' (Osei-Hwedie and Bar-on, 1999: 98).

Social policy in the 1980s

Particularly in the aid-dependent countries, social policy approaches during the 1980s and 1990s have been greatly influenced – or imposed – by the approach to structural adjustment during the Reagan/Thatcher period and similar changes in the North. The impact of adjustment, the focus on the types of social policies that emerged and their merits and shortcomings have been widely disputed. At the risk of overgeneralization social policy approaches acquired the following dominant, interrelated characteristics.

First, driven by economic crises and the re-emergence of conservative ideologies in large parts of the North, emphasis was put on alleviating the impacts of crises and shocks, particularly – at least in theory – on poor people. The 'social funds' as developed particularly by the World Bank and regional development banks, and the lack of linkages with sectors or ministries of human development within those agencies, is a prime example of how the social policy approach turned 'residual'. This is discussed in detail in Chapter 5.

Second, fiscal constraints have dominated the social policy debate, for example in discussions on pensions in Chile and Poland, in OECD countries regarding unemployment benefits, and in discussions on user fees in Africa.[28] Affordability became the most important concern, combined with concerns about allocative efficiency, with little serious discussion of possibilities to enhance fiscal resources. An emphasis on the contribution of human development to economic growth is an extension of this, as it retains an instrumentalist vision of human development, with less emphasis on entitlements and the intrinsic value pertaining to development of people's capabilities.[29]

Third, social policy debates since structural adjustment have had a strong focus on targeting, as Chapter 5 emphasizes. This has been seen as a means of both reducing public expenditure and ensuring that benefits reach the most needy people. Examples of this can be found in many of the analyses in the context of structural adjustment programmes, in India for example in the reform of the Public Distribution System to a Targeted Public Distribution System, as well as in most OECD countries, though significant national variations remain.[30]

Fourth, social policy approaches now are embedded in radically different approaches to public policy and 'governance'. While the early period after

Independence had a strong focus on, and faith in state control, production and provision of public goods, newer approaches emphasize decentralization, partnerships ('public–private'), participation and involvement of civil society in at least the implementation of public policies. The new governance agenda also puts strong emphasis on the performance of the public sector, and ways of measuring this, including through 'outcomes' (the Millennium Development Goals are an instance of this). Strengthening of consultative mechanisms, across different parts of government and outside, is considered important. Good governance is now generally recognized as a precondition of economic growth and poverty reduction: 'the past two decades have been a watershed of policy and institutional reform in many developing countries' (Grindle, 2002; Fanelli, 2004).

Recent writings on the 'post-Washington Consensus' (see Chapter 6), suggest new approaches to economic policies, with a wider role for public policies. This stresses, as before, the complementary role of the state vis-à-vis the market, economic growth as a precondition of poverty reduction, and the role of the private sector and trade. It also recognizes, from the perspective of international organizations, that national ownership of the development agenda is crucial. Empowerment of people, and basic health and education are seen as essential ingredients for development and poverty reduction, and the new consensus pays much more attention to the role of governance and institutions (Stern, 2002). Again Chile can be seen as the marker of the shift, where the successive post-dictator governments of *Concertación*, while not changing the macroeconomic focus on global markets, focused on increased access to opportunities for all, with specific programmes for the most marginalized – contributing to drastic reductions in poverty in the 1990s.[31]

Thus approaches to public policy have moved from the optimism of the period immediately after Independence, via the market approach of the 1980s, to a renewed emphasis on the importance of public intervention, in terms of enhancing welfare as well as correcting 'market failures' more generally.

1.3 Why does social policy matter during globalization?

An emphasis on social policy-making is thus well in line with recent changes in thinking about development, the current emphasis on institutions that drive policy and outcomes in terms of growth, poverty reduction and human development. But there is a critical edge to this, which has clearly emerged during the debates on globalization. One of the critiques of notions of social policy or 'welfare regimes', as discussed below, is the potentially imperialist implication of application of a notion that originated in the North,[32] and its spread during a period of global 'adjustment' thought to be responsible for spreading the same notion. These critiques are important for this book which conceptualizes the strengthening of national policies, taking into account path dependence, and it is thus essential to answer the question of the importance of social policy during a period of globalization.

A first argument concerning why social policy considerations are important in the context of the South relates to countries' public expenditure, discussed in Chapter 2 as a simple indicator for state intervention. This may be low per capita, but as a proportion of GDP it is far from insignificant. On average in low-income countries *total* government expenditure is 18 per cent of GDP, compared to about 27 per cent in high-income countries, but in some of the African countries – as diverse as South Africa, Kenya and Zimbabwe – the proportion is as high or higher than the average for high-income countries.[33] There is little evidence that these proportions have been declining during adjustment or globalization, and as we will see later *social* spending fairly consistently is and remains a high proportion of overall spending. This is not to pass a judgement on the quality or desirability of high government spending in poor countries, or its composition, but an argument that a priori government interventions need serious consideration, including during globalization.

A second argument for a social policy notion is a normative one. There is considerable evidence that state intervention, of various kinds, is more and not less urgent at low levels than at higher levels of economic development. Though empirical evidence suggests the reverse – that is, state intervention tends to expand with economic growth – the state has a crucial role to play in social policy areas such as the provision of basic education, public health, and famine relief, as well as the economic areas of agricultural research, infrastructure and regulation (as a precondition of economic development). The inefficiency and inequity of many governments in these areas is an area for study, not an argument for neglecting them. With the opening up of economies this argument is at least as important as in more closed economies, because of increased demands on basic provisions, and the risks – though not necessity – of the marginalization of groups in the process.

The third argument relates to the question: who sets the agenda? In countries in the South there is a common perception that social policy agendas have been set by international agencies, are part of an agenda of global neo-liberalism, and have moved the primary concerns from equity and justice to market efficiency. First, as argued by Aina (1999: 70), for example, 'state-led social provisioning was one of the earliest victims of the IFIs' [International Financial Institutions] solutions to the economic crisis ... [and] ... social policy was seen as wasteful and negative, contributing little or nothing to economic growth and national revenues ...' Or according to Poku, 'African governments have capitulated to the will of the World Bank and International Monetary Fund (IMF) in formulating the continent's health and social policy (Poku, 2002: 531).[34] Subsequent social policies and inventions – such as social funds (see Chapter 5) – have often not been considered as equal alternatives, but as a continuation of external imposition. Finally, attempts by UN agencies to redefine an international social policy agenda have often been resisted as attempts by the North to impose new conditionalities.[35]

Such perceptions regarding agenda setting do not square entirely with the practices of policy making, or the content of resulting policies. For example, while it is often argued that structural adjustment policies implied a reduction in social sector funding, the reality has often been different. In India, it is often argued that the targeting of the public distribution system happened under pressure from the IMF and World Bank (after the 1991 crisis); however, these reforms and approaches to targeting more generally were as much home grown as they were externally imposed. The important point, however, is that perceptions matter: the concerns over external imposition are real, and have become more urgent under globalization where information becomes more widely available, including critiques of official policies. This book provides a framework for assessing social policy trends in the context of globalization.

Moreover, these critiques highlight a continuing gap, a discrepancy between globalization, that has mostly taken an economic form, and the desirability of social regulation or policies. As Chapter 2 argues, there is no general demise of the state, yet state policies – and social policies amongst them – are challenged by a number of trends associated with globalization. With increased opportunities for investment and trade across borders, states' possibilities for taxation have been challenged – and in many poor countries these capacities were never well developed, and aid dependence has not improved them. Increased capital mobility has changed the possibilities of fiscal policies. Post-war ways of regulating production, labour conditions and redistribution have become increasingly unpopular. Finally, labour (as well as capital) mobility across borders, and the emergence of a global market in health, education and social insurance may contribute to undermining welfare provisions within countries.

The key point is the following. The aspects of globalization discussed here have been driven by, or are primarily market forces. In a period where redistribution as an ideology generally has lost popularity, and dominant policy thinking has an anti-statist bias, the search for social policy approaches is an urgent priority because there is a need to combat real and potential exclusionary processes, to address the roots of political dissent (as in Korea and Indonesia), and because – as discussed in Chapter 3 – economic integration makes social policies more, not less important.

1.4   Social policy in the development studies literature

'Reclaiming social policy' is an ambitious project, in more ways than one. It is ambitious in an analytical sense, as it draws on different academic disciplines, and it puts forward the idea that consideration of public policy needs to cut across sectors. It thus goes against the grain of some of the ways of working of international development studies. Second, the idea also takes sides in debates between strands of theories that have deep ideological and political roots, particularly the way in which analysis of economic policies has been separated from, and has been given priority over that of other public policies. Finally, it is ambitious because it contains thoughts about and a critique of common practices of international development agencies, particularly how they have segmented different types of policies or sectors, and how they have approached development in a technical sense without sufficient explicit realization of how deeply political policy formulation and implementation are.

Social policy, it is the contention in this book, has remained understudied in development studies.[36] The reasons for this are complex, and critiques of the notion of social policy are very relevant; it is not my intention to simplify them. The primary intention of this book is to help strengthen social policy-making and analysis thereof, in a variety of contexts, and for that purpose it is essential to understand and incorporate the critiques raised against the notion. The contribution of this book lies in the intersection of a number of strands of literature, which this section touches on briefly: the literature on public expenditure management and governance, the project-oriented social development literature, and critical analysis of globalization.

Governance

This book complements, from a human or social development perspective, the literature that has focused on 'good governance', including the relatively new literature that has emphasized the importance of institutions for economic growth, and pro-poor growth (Resnick and Birner, 2006). In the dominant international approaches, in a way, good governance has come in through the back door, and – as Nick Stern, quoted above, acknowledges – its neglect during the 1980s and 1990s has come with hard lessons. And it is far from certain that the lessons have been learned all around, and evidence suggests, for example, that adjustment lending by the World Bank privileges fiscal adjustment over strengthening institutions, engages predominantly with finance ministries and departments neglecting other policy institutions, considers social spending as costs and not also as investment, and insufficiently integrates lessons from social sector work and policies into structural adjustment conditionality.[37] The analysis emphasizing the importance of institutions for economic growth (Rodrik, 2003) has broadened the debates on growth and distribution; this book, while written from a different background, aims to contribute to this, particularly looking at the policies that have tried to alter patterns of inequality, while considering the importance of these social policies for overall growth patterns.

The book also provides a social development perspective on the public-expenditure management literature, which has had a predominantly technical focus.[38] This includes, in particular, an understanding of the 'stories behind' the budget allocations to various sectors (described in Chapter 4), and a widening of the debate beyond both the need for higher allocations (in the 20/20 goals, for example, or the emphasis on the lack of a link between expenditure and development 'outcomes'). Subsequent chapters provide guidance regarding ways in which public policies and policy reform can be shaped to attain welfare goals, emphasizing the political and path-dependent nature of public policy-making, the need to base reforms in an understanding of political economy, and the interrelated or cross-sectoral linkages which determine long-term well-being (see Chapter 3).

Public expenditure reviews are a key instrument in the international development debate, and at this stage it may be worth highlighting what these do and do not do. The literature on public expenditure management has a strong focus on the technical and procedural aspects of the budget process, and reform. Over time, the agenda has moved towards an emphasis on how systems deliver results, in particular for enhancing well-being and poverty reduction (Roberts, 2003a). One strand of literature has emphasized the need and options for broadening the space of public debate on these issues, and for the participation of non-state actors (Norton and Elson, 2002). However, this literature has not focused on the question of how important state interventions should be, norms regarding relative importance of sectors, and the political context and contestation that drives public spending and taxation.[39]

Further, there has been much emphasis on economic or statistical regressions that have analysed linkages between globalization and poverty reduction, and a number of policy variables have been introduced in these analyses. Chapter 2 draws lessons from these debates, but also points to the limitations of the studies. The key point is that these quantitative studies are no substitute for understanding public policy-making and the way policies impact the process of human development or poverty reduction, or indeed economic growth,[40] as they are limited in their understanding of the reasons why policies came into being, and therefore are limited in the extent to which they can help to formulate policy alternatives.[41]

Social development literature: project focus

In the social development literature only a few attempts exist to relate to the literature on poverty at macro-level, or to the reform and public-expenditure management literature. On the other hand, much of the writings on reform go without reference to reforms of social sectors and policy (for example, Fanelli, 2004). Significant work has been undertaken from a gender perspective, with analysis of the gender implications of macro-policies,[42] and with a focus on budget analysis that has aimed to challenge macroeconomic theories and policy-making.[43] Studies on social policy have focused on social protection, and operational inputs to PRSP processes. At the World Bank, social development specialists have limited engagement with social policy issues, as the 2004 Social Development Strategy, for example, shows. By and large, engagement with macro-policy issues has remained limited – and often highlighted as a gap, despite intentions to move 'up-stream' – in most bilateral agencies.

Much influential poverty analysis has focused on 'outcomes', and has been concerned with the measurement of characteristics of the poor, numbers and proportions of poor people, and poverty 'profiles'. Studies on human development, particularly those that have focused on the human development or similar indices, while expanding the narrow confines of the 'money-metric' approach, equally have focused on measuring outcomes. Thus, as David Booth has argued convincingly, poverty analysis has suffered from a 'missing middle', which in the case of poverty reduction strategies implies a conceptual gap between poverty analysis and the public policies that influence well-being, directly or indirectly.[44] The theme of social policy developed in this book emphasizes the social relations and institutions that lie beneath measured outcome indicators, building on alternative conceptualizations of poverty that emphasize context-dependent ideologies and practices of 'social exclusion' and 'inclusion'.

The literature on participation also has not closed the gap in the conceptualization of ways in which social policies have been constituted. A main contribution of participatory poverty studies has been to complement quantitative studies with different and 'subjective' perceptions and interpretation of poverty, which usually has not been linked to analyses of policy-making processes.[45] In a background paper for the IDS research project on social policy, Cornwall and Gaventa (2000) make a determined effort to link debates around participation and social policy. They describe how contexts of decentralization, privatization of provisioning and globalization challenge traditional approaches to participation in social policy, but also that concepts and approaches of participation need to be re-situated, taking into account constraints as well as new opportunities for participation. They emphasize that 'social policy must see citizens not only as users or choosers, but as active participants in shaping and implementing social policy and social provisioning.' Further, more recent work on participation has focused on what the *IDS Bulletin* of April 2004 labels 'new democratic spaces' (Cornwall, 2004), the ways and reasons participatory processes are invited into and become part of mainstream public policies. A large agenda remains, however, to link studies of bottom-up approaches or grassroots policy initiatives to an understanding of how macro-policy is shaped and can be influenced.[46] This book builds on the expanding literature on participatory budgets, and integrates this in a wider view of public policy-making.

While many international agencies have tried to move away from project approaches to support for up-stream policy processes, the social development literature has continued to focus on project approaches, often not distinguishing sufficiently the social 'dimensions' of development from social 'policy'.[47] The World Bank is a prime example of this: above we quoted the social policy principles which were an attempt to follow up the Social Summit declaration, to develop standards regarding principles in social policy making. A few years later, however, the social development strategy showed no trace of these social policy principles, despite much work 'up-stream' in the context of PRSPs. According to Steen Jorgensen (verbal communication), the lack of macro-policy engagement by social development specialists is related, *inter alia*, to a continued focus on safeguards for World Bank projects, and a lack of coordination of social development inputs with the Bank's own human development agenda (which includes work on social funds).[48]

Many academics and practitioners have actively argued against the application of a notion of social policy;[49] research by UNRISD (discussed below) provides the main exception. At the forefront of critiquing the notion has been the research programme on social policy at IDS Sussex. Quoting Baltodano (1999)[50] who emphasized that the concept of social policy is intimately linked with the evolution of modern Western society along a capitalist trajectory and the perceived need for policy interventions to protect the working population from the vagaries of the market place, Naila Kabeer (2004) explains how the IDS program was organized around the sustainable livelihoods framework which had been developed precisely to address the conditions prevailing in poorer southern countries, and on the institutional configuration of social provisioning which prevailed in different contexts.[51] It was thus 'detached' from 'its moorings in particular sectors, programmes and projects and [widened] to encompass the purposive efforts made by a range of public actors...' The programme, while emphasizing the limitations of state-driven welfare systems, argued for a notion of social policy that recognizes that policy goals are shared by a wider range of institutional actors than previously acknowledged, namely families, social networks, private sector or civil society organizations as well as bilateral and multilateral development agencies.[52]

The research programme at Bath, while explicit in trying to apply a notion of social policy, also remained skeptical of its value. Above we quoted concerns that attempts to use a notion of social policy would be seen as imperialistic or Western-centric. Gough in particular used Esping-Andersen's categorization of welfare regimes in OECD countries (liberal, conservative, social democratic – discussed in Chapter 4) for identifying patterns of social policy in the South, in an effort to highlight potential lessons from Western experience, but acknowledges the difficulties in applying concepts of welfare regimes. The reasons for this are manifold. The welfare state as the outcome of a political settlement, the state as regulator of labour markets and as guarantor of benefits, are conditions that do not apply in most of the South (Gough and Wood, 2004). Processes of decommodification and the interaction between states, markets and households are different in countries with, for example, large agricultural populations (Gough, 2000), or in Bangladesh where, according to Davis (2004), a welfare regime approach needs to take account of a wider range of actors, NGOs, donors and customary cultural institutions, and the international influence on the national politics driving welfare provisions. In short, the state as core social policy actor, as described by Esping-Andersen, was thought to be of limited relevance in the South, and both international and national community-level institutions and informal arrangements need to be more central to the analysis.

In summary, the critiques have raised important objections against a particular notion of social policy. They have warned against the transfer of concepts from the North. They emphasize the gap between rhetoric and the reality of state-led policies in the South, and the low coverage of social policy (particularly 'social security') provisions, and focus on formal labour markets that exclude the large majority of people in many countries, particularly women. The critiques point to the problems with a sectoral,[53] and more generally a state-centric approach that a social policy concept brings along, and concomitant neglect of non-state actors in, and informal mechanisms of welfare provisions.

The concerns over the transfer of concepts are valid, but some of the more ardent critiques have thrown the baby out with the bath water. First, by not assessing existing policies, histories, politics and impacts (for example, by ignoring the attention given in social policy debates to diversity in institutions providing services), the critique has inadvertently widened the gap in the understanding of the policies that do impact populations' well-being, and the reasons for the failure of such policies. I would include under this the relative neglect of attention to labour market issues, and the assumption that because of the relative size of the informal sector, classic social policy concerns are not relevant;[54] I would argue instead that labour market policies have been key to the way labour markets have manifested themselves in the South – including the sharp policy-induced division between the formal and informal sectors. Second, the critiques tend to be theoretically naïve, as northern concerns anyway are mirrored in development debates: for example, the dominant emphasis on residual social policy and the (newer) approaches to partnership and participation have become increasingly popular in North and South, and even colonial traditions continue to exert influence on the way public policies are structured.

Globalization

The third set of literature to which this book provides a contribution is formed by the critical approaches to globalization. As discussed in Chapter 2, the literature on globalization is voluminous. Much of the literature has a focus on economics and economic policy-making; the present book complements this by a focus on social policy-making in the context of globalizing economies and societies. In doing so, it will broaden the scope of the book edited by Lance Taylor (2001) which discusses impacts of liberalization and the varied social policy responses across nine case studies, by providing a practitioner-oriented framework for understanding public policy in a wider and proactive sense. The literature that addresses public policies has had a strong focus on global institutions (as have the protests against globalization), and has tended to pay little attention to national policy-making processes (Nayyar, 2002). This book thus complements a stream of work that has focused on the global dimensions of social policy, for example the work by Deacon and others that has been framed as a reaction to the emergence of perceived hegemonic neo-liberal global policies, and possibly a weakening of national entitlements and rights.[55] Complementing these, the book will reassert the importance of national public policy from an empirical point of view by showing that states are important and carry national histories of social integration, and from a normative point of view as possible and essential for the realization of the rights of its citizens.[56]

Often with reference to the theme of globalization and the increased volatility of the economy as experienced during the late 1990s crises in East Asia and Latin America, development policy and the literature have devoted much attention to the theme and concept of social protection.[57] This book, while drawing on strands of work in this field, distinguishes itself by emphasizing a wider definition of social policy, and the interrelationship between different aspects or sectors of public policy. Similarly, the approach advocated here aims to be wider but to build on ILO work on social security, particularly related to new forms of universalistic social protection (www.ilo.org/ses), and the seminal work on social security in developing countries (Ahmed et al., 1991).

In developing this broader understanding of social policy in the context of globalization, the book draws on a range of publications that have made national policy processes central in attempts to understand the processes leading to inclusion and exclusion. Studies in the publication edited by Taylor have already been mentioned. Further, the IDRC-funded project in the late 1990s on transnational social policy, as published by Morales-Gómez (1999) provides a range of national perspectives on the evolution of social policy approaches. The UNRISD research programme on Social Policy in a Development Context has been the most explicit recent attempt to bring a policy perspective into the social and human development debate, aiming to 'move (thinking) away from social policy as a safety net ... towards a conception of active social policy as a powerful instrument for development working in tandem with economic policy'.[58] Central to conceptualizing the approach was Mkandawire (2000, 2004), which incorporated lessons from the 'late industrializers' among current OECD countries for understanding the importance of social policy, taking issue with views regarding the primacy of economic policy over social policy, and helping to move the debate away from a residual social policy approach.

1.5   Structure of the book

The book is structured around the themes of globalization, the role of social policies in shaping the well-being of populations, and the need to revive a more pro-active and holistic approach to social policy in international development. It draws on material from about twenty countries in Africa, Asia and Latin America. The choice of these countries illustrates different approaches to social policy, and their very different histories, though, as we will see in Chapter 2, many have rising inequalities. For example, China has undergone a transition from a socialist model to much more emphasis on private enterprise, and rapidly rising inequalities, without a loss of basic state responsibility; while India has undergone a much more gradual transition, with a presumed decline in state responsibility for the poor, but elections in 2004 reversed that trend.

After this introductory chapter, this book contains six chapters. Chapter 2 discusses trends of global well-being and inequality. While cross-country economic and econometric studies show that the opening up of economies usually benefits countries and often most people within them, generalizations about the effects of globalization are not meaningful. Even in successful countries, some groups have lost out, and impacts depend on the type of well-being indicator looked at, the unit of analysis and the starting position of countries opening up. The analysis focuses on the interaction between globalizing and national forces and processes, illustrated by policy changes in India during the 1990s, and contrasted with cases of globalization where the policy agenda was more strongly determined by external forces. Processes of opening up are generally not, and should not, be accompanied by less state intervention. Countries with more integrated markets, including during periods of adjustment, do not spend less, and often more on social sectors – ideas about the 'demise of the nation-state' thus appear misplaced. Higher social spending may be related to the need to mitigate the risks associated with more open economies; proactive social policies are required to help prepare populations for more competitive markets; and regulation becomes key when service provisions are privatized and opened up to international markets.

The third chapter describes how social policies relate to economic growth and macroeconomic policies. It reviews a key fault-line in the debate around social policies: are they concerned merely with correcting malfunctions in the operation of society and economy, or are they proactive interventions shaping those institutions? The period of adjustment has give prominence to the first, residual definition of social policy; however, the key hypothesis of this chapter is that social policies do – intentionally or unintentionally, and as shown convincingly in the gendered analyses of economic policies and budgets – play a constitutive role in creating patterns of inclusion and exclusion, and directly and indirectly shape the conditions for market functioning. The chapter will analyse the ways in which social policies impact on economic growth: the negative impact of expanding state finances, and the moral hazard caused by state transfers; the importance of health, nutrition and education policies for economic growth; the importance of policies related to redistribution and social inclusion for economic growth, and difficulties posed by sharp social divisions for the possibility of carrying out economic reforms; and the importance of social security in helping to address adverse long-term consequences of economic shocks, and in allowing people to take risks.

Chapter 4 looks at national social policies from an historical perspective, which is essential for understanding the ways in which social policies come into being – including specific forms of private–public mix, statutory or community-based approaches, and social insurance or security versus national service approaches – and the political dynamics behind the policies. It starts with a quantitative overview of public expenditure, as an indication of how different state intervention, and the commitment to social or human development can be across countries, and reviews studies on the impact of public funding on development indicators. Building on writings by Esping-Andersen, Gough and Silver, Chapter 4 develops a typology of 'social policy regimes' (with a discussion of the pros and cons of using typologies as heuristic tools, emphasizing principles of solidarity). With roots in the late colonial period, and shaped during the post-colonial period of inward-oriented economic development, social policies in some countries attained a strongly *dualistic* character, with inclusive social policies for a small section of the population, targeted programmes for the large majority of poor people, and 'reservation' policies for marginalized groups. East Asian policies have tended to be *production oriented* and *inclusive*, not generally targeted on the poor, and shaped to enable the entire population to participate in economic growth and mainstream development. Latin American social policies can possibly be characterized as state *corporatist* – in which pressure group bargaining rather than the rights of citizens have dominated the policy-making process – moving towards a more liberal regime.

Chapter 5 discusses in detail the contested theme of 'residual' social policies, targeted safety nets and social funds, which have dominated the social policy debate since the 1980s. The chapter first explores the role of poverty analysis, providing a short genealogy of poverty analysis that has formed the intellectual basis for such residual approaches to social policy-making. Dominant approaches to poverty analysis, with a focus on 'outcomes', have reinforced residual approaches to social policies. Social funds are an example of such a residual approach to social policy. With the rise of structural adjustment policies, and the need to provide these with a 'human face', donors have experimented with instruments to ame-liorate the worst effects of crises and adjustment. While these social funds have had successes, they have not sufficiently contributed to strength-ening mainstream policy-making for social and economic development. The third section discusses approaches to social protection, rapidly gain-ing in popularity after crises like East Asia's in 1997, and the recent emphasis on conditional and unconditional cash transfers, asking the question whether these social policies are associated merely with mecha-nisms for dealing with the unintended consequences of economic change and crises, and whether they thus reinforce the marginalization of social policy.

Chapter 6 describes recent trends in international development strat-egies for poverty reduction. It elaborates on the theoretical approach of the post-Washington consensus, the progress that this entails in terms of broad-based and comprehensive approaches to development and poverty reduc-tion, and attention to institutions in reform debates. The chapter critically appraises two development approaches that gained popularity during the 1990s: sector-wide approaches developed to improve policy-making and the environment for service delivery, particularly in health and education; and the Poverty Reduction Strategy Papers developed for HIPC countries, to combine debt relief with a focus on poverty reduction in development strategies. While progress has been made towards more integrated strate-gies for poverty reduction, the evidence suggests that development prac-tices still fall short in a number of respects, relating to strengthening cross-sectoral capacity for social policy formulation, and integrating an understanding of the political nature of public policies. While poverty reduction strategies have managed to bring deprivation to the core of the international development agenda, international development perspectives need to be broadened beyond the confines of addressing 'poverty', better understand the political economy that underlies policy-making for the poor but also the non-poor, and position itself strategic-ally in terms of inclusive social policies.

Chapter 7 concludes, providing a framework for supporting social policy-making, from an international development perspective. The framework has a normative and rights-based element, departing from international agreements, particularly the declaration of the Social Summit. It empha-sizes the path-dependent character of social policy-making, the ways social policies shape patterns of provision and of exclusion and inclusion, and the context-dependent ways in which international agreements are and can be translated into welfare outcomes. This has a practical perspective, focus-ing on entry points into the strengthening of integrated policy-making for development and poverty reduction. It emphasizes a strengthened analysis of social policy in the development of poverty reduction strategies, and incorporating debates on safety nets and social protection into wider processes of national policy-making, including their politicized nature. It suggests a framework for assessing cross-sectoral social policies, on the basis of access, quality and relevance, and participation.

2

Globalization, Inequality and the Demise of the State?

This chapter places the main thesis of this book in the context of two of the main development trends of the end of the twentieth century: the liberalization of economies that in the South is often expressed as structural adjustment and reforms imposed by World Bank and IMF, and the phenomenon of globalization, the increasing interconnectedness of economic, political and social-cultural processes. These interrelated processes have contributed to gains in economic welfare, but have also been associated with rapidly rising inequalities, between but also within countries.

The chapter starts by synthesizing evidence regarding trends in well-being, whether inequality has been rising, both between and within countries. This shows that while conclusions about inequality trends (more so than poverty trends) are very sensitive to the indicators and measures chosen, it is very clear that the increases in wealth in recent decades (if not centuries) have not been shared equally, and that both globally and nationally increasing inequalities pose new challenges to public policies.

The second section focuses on globalization, particularly the impact of increased integration of trade and production systems. It first defines globalization more precisely, and then looks at whether the trends described in the first section can be explained by these economic processes. Cross-country economic studies show that opening up of economies has benefited many countries, and many people within them. But generalizations about the effects of globalization have limited relevance, as a focus on averages tends to neglect that some countries, regions and groups do lose out. Conclusions about the impact of structural adjustment, similarly, show that few generalizations can stand scrutiny. Instead, the chapter argues, what is required is context-specific understanding of such processes, their starting position and specific outcomes and policies.

The chapter then reviews the debate on the 'demise of the state', the impact that this would have on social exclusion, in both North and South, including the concern for increasingly dual structures of social services, and the role of fiscal crises in opening up. Its core argument is that the process of opening up is generally not – and should not be – accompanied by less state intervention. Countries with more integrated markets do not spend less, and often spend more on social sectors, and during periods of adjustment social sector spending is not necessarily reduced. Open economies tend to have more pro-active social policies, to mitigate risks, prepare populations for more competitive markets and improve quality of regulation.

2.1   Global inequality trends: 'divergence, big time'

Few topics in the development studies literature have been more controversial than the question of whether globalization has increased inequality, whether it has reduced or increased poverty, and for what reasons. On the one hand, a large contingent of analysts and activists stress the negative impacts of globalization. For example, Munck (2005) emphasizes how globalization deepens inequities and social exclusion, and Joseph Stiglitz (2002) stresses that 'globalization today is not working ... for many of the world's poor'. On the other hand, many economists have pointed to the positive benefits, and how the successful economies have been the ones that have integrated themselves into world markets. Sachs (2005), for example, while acknowledging the importance of the anti-globalization protests, argues that it would be wrong to blame globalization for many problems of poverty in the South.[1] In an Issues Brief, the IMF (2000) stresses that outward-oriented policies brought prosperity to East Asia, while inward-oriented policies in Latin America and Africa led to economic stagnation, inflation and increased poverty.

Clearly, there is no simple answer to questions about the impact of globalization. With respect to measurement issues, Kanbur (2001), for example, has argued that the debate is often split between different camps that make little effort to understand each other, and Basu (2001) notes the 'curious feature about the debate on globalization ... that those who favor it see no negative fallout from globalization and those who oppose it see no silver lining'. Ravallion has shown very convincingly that even within the fairly narrow domain of money-metric poverty analysis results depend on the indicators and units of analysis chosen.[2] When measurement of trends in poverty and inequality causes such big differences, it should come as no surprise that there are large differences in the analysis of the causes of these trends. Taking into account those questions, this section describes what inequality trends have emerged. It focuses on the last 25 years, the period generally associated with economic down-turn in some parts of the world, globalization and adjustment, and increasing inequalities in many countries, and globally.

Inequalities: global trends

It is now commonly accepted that the period since the 1950s has brought historically unprecedented rates of economic growth and poverty reduction. It is often stated that, in terms of economic growth, during the last 50 years more progress may have been made than in the thousand years preceding them.[3] Progress in many human development indicators, too, has been very substantial.

But this progress has not been shared evenly. Although data are limited, long-term studies show that the incomes of the richest and poorest countries have constantly diverged, and that progress in poverty reduction in one part of the world has been accompanied by stagnation elsewhere. Pritchett (1995) noted that, despite expectations around 'conditional convergence' – the tendency for economies with lower income levels to grow faster – there has been massive absolute divergence in the distribution of incomes across countries, not less than sixfold between 1870 and 1985. In terms of inter-country inequality, the long-term trend according to Pritchett was 'diver-gence, big time'. Bourguignon and Morrisson (2002) also show a steadily increasing global inequality, over an even longer period (1820–1992).

Trends depend crucially on the concepts and units of analysis used. Ravallion (2003b) concluded there was no convincing sign of a significant change in overall inequality over the last 20 years, but that such assess-ments suffer from significant measurement problems.[4] According to the 2006 *World Development Report* (p. 62ff) too, inter-country inequality measured by the Gini coefficient has been increasing, especially since 1980. However, if the measure of inequality is weighted for population, the picture changes radically, and the trend would be of a fairly steady *decline* in the Gini coefficient since the 1960s.[5] The difference between the two trends is largely accounted for by the rapid progress in India and China (if India and China are excluded, the two trends are parallel). A large part of global inequality is due to differences between countries, and the progress in India and China has tempered the long-term trend significantly – without reducing the differences between the world's poorest and richest countries or people. Furthermore, the Gini coefficient, showing a steady decrease, is a relative measure. If an absolute measure of inequality is chosen, inequality has been steadily rising since 1970.[6]

What about non-income dimensions of poverty? *World Development Report 2006* (Chapter 3) provides an excellent overview of global inequalities in health and education.[7] Long-term trends in life expectancy show tremendous progress, more than doubling in the last 200 years. Since the 1960s, there has been a global convergence ('vanishing twin peaks'). However, there were enormous losses in Sub-Saharan Africa during the 1990s, mainly caused by HIV/AIDS, making the gap with the North in 2000 higher than in 1950 (World Development Report [WDR], 2006: 58). Health inequalities within countries, too, remain substantial, as will be illustrated below. Only a small proportion of the inequalities can be explained by differences in income growth (Deaton, cited in WDR, 2006: 59).

Cornia and Menchini (2005), using DHS data, emphasize that health improvements slowed down during the 1990s compared to previous decades, *and* global progress became more uneven, which can only partly be explained by the negative trends in Sub-Saharan Africa and Eastern Europe. Within-country progress was frequently uneven, too. The causes of these trends, according to Cornia and Menchini, need further investigation, but the authors highlight the following: the spread of HIV/AIDS was partly responsible for worsening trends in most of Africa and some Caribbean countries; while health spending is not seen as a key variable to explain trends, progress in extension of primary health care is thought to be a key variable; local conflicts and natural disasters; erosion of traditional family structures and support; and finally slower, and more volatility in, growth, and rising income inequality.

Since the 1960s, the global distribution of education (in terms of years of schooling) has also become less unequal. Many of the poorest countries saw large increases in enrolments, and inequality has steadily decreased. But large variations within countries, and between men and women, continue to exist (Human Development Report, 2005). Also, differences in achievement appear to remain significant, and larger than the differences in attainment (Pritchett, 2004, in WDR, 2006: 61–2).

Thus, while definitions and units of analysis matter for conclusions about trends, a crucial part of the story lies behind the national averages and many countries show clear trends of increasing inequalities. This is illustrated below with reference to (mainly) income inequality in a select number of countries, with some focus on India and China, as these countries have been so important for global trends.

Country trends

As highlighted by Ravallion (2003b), it is important to keep in mind that whatever trends the global or regional analyses show, they refer to averages, and thus hide inter and intra-country differences. This and the next sub-section describe trends of inequalities within countries, showing that in a substantial number of countries significant changes in inequality have occurred, over periods of half decades or more (in the following sections we will come back to many of these trends and highlight their causes, including public policy interventions). According to Cornia (2004), inequality rose in no fewer than 53 of the 73 countries he analysed. Table 2.1 below shows trends for the countries in the South which feature as case studies in this book.

In a number of OECD countries, notably the US, the UK and New Zealand, there have been significant increases of inequalities of earnings. In America in 1980 the salary of CEOs was 40 times that of the average production worker, but by 2003 this had risen to about 200 times; and the share of income going to the richest 1 per cent doubled from 8 per cent to 16 per cent between 1980 and 2005.[8] Some Eastern European and former FSU countries, particularly Russia, have experienced rising income differences over the last decade, from initially low levels. Based on the Luxembourg Income Study of 30 richer countries, Smeeding (2005) highlights that, after Russia and Mexico, income inequality in the United States is higher than anywhere else, but also that since the late 1970s there have been very different trends among OECD countries, with the Gini rising in the US, the UK, the Netherlands, Belgium and Norway (still very equal), but not, for example, in Canada, Italy and France.[9]

Latin America has traditionally had high levels of inequality, possibly largely reflecting its colonial history. Over the last four decades the Gini coefficient has remained fairly stable (around .50), and may on average have increased slightly in the last decade. But trends varied across countries. Recently, Argentina showed a large increase in inequality, from .45 to .52 (possibly related to the macroeconomic instability, discussed later), and inequality may have increased marginally in Peru. Income inequality in Brazil rose from a Gini of 0.57 in 1981, to 0.63 in 1989, then fell back to 0.56 in 2004 (making it the world's tenth most unequal country) (Ferreira et al., 2006).[10] Income inequality in Mexico, too, declined, though wage inequality increased, possibly associated with liberalization, and the southern part of the country fell further behind (Andalón and Lopez-Calva, 2002).

Human development indicators have improved consistently in the region. Inequality in education fell in most countries during the 1990s, though gaps between the top and bottom increased more often. But here too the trends differ across countries. Peru has particularly high inequalities in terms of health outcomes and access to health facilities, even for its

Table 2.1 Level and trends in income inequalities in selected countries

	Levels of inequality and poverty				Trends in income inequality – Gini coefficients			
	Year of income survey	Gini coefficient income inequality	Income ratio top 10 to bottom 10%	Poverty ($1/day)	Gini coefficient land inequality	Years of survey	Gini year 1	Gini year 2
Argentina	2001	.51	13.7	3.3	.83	1992–2001	.45	.52
Bangladesh	2000	.31	3.9	36	.62	1989–2000	.38	.42
Bolivia	2002	.58	29.7	14.4	–	1996–1999	.58	.58
Chile	2000	.51	10.7	<2	–	1990–2000	.56	.57
China	2001	.45	–	16.6	–	1981–2000	.29	.46
Ghana	1999	.41	7.3	44.8	–	1991/92–1998/98	.37	.39
India	1999–00	.33	–	35.3	.46	1984–2000	.32	.33
Indonesia	2000	.34	–	7.5	–	1970–2002	.35	.33
Kenya	1997	.44	6.6	22.8	.34			
Korea, Rep	1998	.32	–	<2	.52			
Malawi	1997–98	.50	–	41.7	–			
Malaysia	1997	.49	–	<2	–	1970–2002	.52	.46
Mexico	2002	.49	11.9	9.9	–	1992–2000	.56	.55
Pakistan	2001	.27	3.1	17	.57	1979–2002	.37	.40
Peru	2000	.48	14.6	18.1	.86		.49	.49
South Africa	2000	.58	16.9	10.7	–			
Tanzania	2001	.35	4.9	48.5	.47			
Thailand	2002	.40	5.6	<2	.59			
Uganda		–	–	–	–	1992–2003	.38	.43
Vietnam	2002	.35	4.73	–	.53	1993–2002	.34	.42
Zambia	1998	.53	–	63.7	–	1991–1998	.56	.52
Zimbabwe	1995	.57	–	56.1	–			

Notes: Comparisons of inequality are notably difficult (WDR, 2006). Different data on Vietnam, for example, show that a very different picture would emerge if a measure of consumption was used. Inequality data for Argentina refer to urban areas only.

Sources: First part Table WDR (2006): 278–81, trends for Latin America, Medranot et al. (2006); Asia, Balisacan and Ducanes (2006) (Malaysia trend quoted in Yusof, 2005, Indonesia in Timmer, 2004) and Africa, Okojie and Shimeles (2006) (Ghana in Aryeetey and McKay, 2005).

level of economic development (Medrano et al., 2006). A Peruvian child born in the poorest quintile is nearly five times more likely not to reach the age of 5 compared to a child in the richest quintile. The economic crisis of the late 1980s may have widened disparities,[11] while subsequent expansion of funding for health may have reduced these somewhat.

In Africa, inequality has generally been considered less of an issue (unlike ethnic diversity or fractionalization), but recent interest has shown that on average levels of income inequality are almost as high in Africa as in Latin America, but also with much more variation.[12] 'Results from recent surveys reported by a number of countries in sub-Saharan Africa confirmed the fear that income inequality is indeed considerably higher than had been thought initially in Africa despite the low level of per capita income and predominantly homogeneous livelihood systems' (Okojie, 2006). During the 1990s, the Gini coefficient was as high as .75 in Niger, .61 in South Africa, with Zimbabwe at similarly high levels. Tanzania, Burundi and Rwanda showed very low levels of inequality, with a Gini around .30.[13] Ghana and Uganda fall into a middle category with a Gini around .40. Christiaensen et al. (2002) showed that among eight African countries levels of inequality were very diverse, and that the Gini coefficient masks significant socioeconomic and regional disparities (Ghana is a case in point, where a relatively low Gini is accompanied by deep-rooted disparities between North and South; Shepherd and Gyimah-Boadi, 2004).

Data on non-income dimensions by and large confirm the picture of significant polarization on the African continent. Using unit record data for 12 countries, Sahn and Stiefl (quoted in Okojie, 2006) show severe inequality in terms of assets and human capabilities. The Gini coefficient for asset-ownership varied from a high of .75 in Niger to a low of .43 in Tanzania. Asset inequality in Africa was found to be higher in rural areas than in urban areas. Booysen et al.'s (quoted in Okojie, 2006) indicator of asset inequality using DHS data for seven African countries shows low inequality in Ghana (.38), followed by Senegal and Zimbabwe (.5), Kenya and Mali (.57), Tanzania (.59), and Zambia (.63). Also, asset inequality tended to be lower in urban areas than in rural areas.

Comparable data on trends are not widely available for Africa, but for some countries information is available. The 'Operationalizing Pro-Poor Growth' research programme highlighted some modest short-term increases in income inequality in Ghana (1992–9) and Senegal (1992–2001), and somewhat more in Uganda. Christiaensen et al. (2002) – who observed very little change in the Gini in eight countries – showed a modest increase in Ethiopia during 1994–7. There was a more substantial increase in inequality in Uganda between 1992 and 2002, which accompanied substantial economic growth and poverty reduction, and has been largely attributed to unbalanced growth between sectors (Okidi et al., 2005). In Kenya it is reported that inequality has been rising over the last ten years, during a period of economic stagnation, rapidly declining human development indicators, and while institutions have been weakening.[14] Declines in inequality are hardly ever observed, except for Zambia during 1991–8, during a period of decline in GDP. In South Africa, one of the most unequal countries on the continent, despite large policy changes since the end of Apartheid, the Gini coefficient has not changed significantly (Gelb, 2003; Jenkins and Thomas, 2004).

Levels of income inequality in Asia have traditionally been low, by comparison, probably to a great extent due to much more equal distribution of land. But in many countries, inequalities have been rising too, notably in China, Bangladesh, Vietnam and Thailand.[15] But generalizations across Asia, too, would be misleading, as South Korea has continued to have very low levels of income inequality (in fact decreasing during the 1980s; You and Lee, 2001: 298), Indonesia perhaps has the most impressive record in reducing poverty without growing inequality, while Malaysia's levels of inequality have been much higher though slowly declining since the introduction of the New Economic Policy in 1970.

China in the 1970s had very low levels of income inequality, but these have shown an enormous increase since the reforms of the late 1970s,[16] accompanying very high rates of economic growth and poverty reduction. Zhang and Kanbur (2003) highlight that disparities in health and education too have increased since the reforms began. According to Ravallion and Chen (2004), while rural economic growth was mainly responsible for poverty reduction, rising inequality within the rural sector hampered poverty reduction. China's Gini coefficient now is .45, and after a period where increases in equality were publicly accepted, fairly recently public policy has become concerned with these rises, possibly because of the threats posed to public health or threats of social unrest.[17]

Significant rises in inequality have occurred in Thailand, Vietnam and Bangladesh too. Thailand's inequality rose steadily between 1975 and 1998, alongside rapid economic growth. The increase in inequality has been associated with disparities in regional growth, and a shift from agricultural to non-agricultural activities.[18] Vietnam's recent inequality trends show similarities with China's,[19] with high rates of 'pro-poor growth', based on conditions created by past policies and communist ideology, and recent reforms in rice and land policies (Klump and Bonschab, 2005). During the 1990s, poverty declined rapidly, but better-off households benefited more (Glewwe et al., 2000). While the measure of inequality is disputed (jump of the income Gini from .34 to .42 during 1993–2002, but no increase in inequality if consumption measure is used), the observed rising inequality seems to be largely a regional phenomenon, and particularly affects ethnic minorities. Most recent data suggest that poverty rates are declining relatively rapidly in the poorer Northern areas.[20] Provisional data for 2004 suggest that the rise in overall income inequality has been halted, though the ratio of top to bottom quintile continues to increase.

Data on Bangladesh have been disputed but inequality seems to have been increasing since the 1990s, and the bottom 20 per cent may have profited very little during the period of liberalization and economic growth. In terms of human development indicators, Bangladesh has done very well over the last two decades. A recent study found no evidence that Bangladesh's liberalization had an impact on wage inequality between skilled and unskilled workers (Durevall and Munshi, 2006).

Much is known about trends in economic growth, poverty and inequality in India, which has a long series of comparable surveys dating back to about 1960. This shows that over the long run, India has experienced substantial rates of economic growth and poverty reduction. But research also shows large intra-country variation in both rates of economic growth, and the rate at which the poor benefit from economic growth (and the public policies that influence this, which we discuss later). A stable Gini coefficient also marks significant diverging trends, in income and human development indicators, across and within states, and pervasive gaps between social groups that show little sign of closing.[21] Moreover, the annual surveys (considered less reliable) showed important fluctuations, for example an increase in poverty during 1992, a year after the main 'globalizing reforms', sparking a sharp public debate and increased public policy attention around the effects of increases in food prices and cutbacks in public expenditure.[22]

Finally, income poverty has been reduced very rapidly in Indonesia since the late 1960s – though with significant setbacks in the late 1990s because of the economic crisis, and of course under a politically repressive regime. According to Timmer (2004) economic growth has been very 'pro-poor': the poor have benefited from economic growth and suffered during declines. The income Gini has remained low, and health and education spread relatively equally – public policies as described in Chapter 4 were key to this.

This brief overview of trends in a small number of countries indicates that, while considerable diversity exists, there are probably more cases of rising than of decreasing inequality, as Cornia and others have pointed out too. Also, while Latin America has been recognized as the continent where inequality has been extremely high – reducing, for example, the impact of economic growth on poverty reduction – recent research indicates that Africa has average levels of inequality almost as high as Latin America. And while inequality is generally lower in Asia, quite a few countries are rapidly moving towards the status of middle-inequality countries. The next section looks at main 'contributors' to inequality, both with significant policy implications: regional and social disparities.

Beyond the averages: spatial and social disparities

This section looks at issues that underlie the above-described trends of overall inequality, both regional and those of social groups, including gender. This focuses on a small selection of issues within some of the countries described earlier. Some economic literature asks the question of the 'contribution' of regional or group inequality to overall inequality, but from a social policy perspective the questions of regional and group inequalities are important in their own right and are particularly acute when deprived groups are concentrated in poor regions.

Examples of convergence in terms of regional income disparities among OECD countries include the US, which has shown convergence over an extended period of time. Indonesia's provinces too have experienced convergence of income over time.[23] In other cases, trends have been more diverse. In the case of Mexico a long-run trend of convergence shifted to divergence from the late 1980s onwards (WDR, 2006: 204). Vietnam's rising overall inequality is largely linked to increasing regional inequalities. Economic growth in Thailand has been concentrated in the better-off areas of Bangkok and the Centre (Richter, 2006). Rising inequality in China is determined by a combination of rural–urban and regional disparities, possibly in opposite directions, as we discuss below. In the case of Ghana, underneath a fairly stable indicator of overall income inequality, inequalities between North and South have been increasing, as declines in poverty have been concentrated in Accra metropolitan area and the rural forest zone (Aryeetey and McKay, 2004).

Similar to Ghana, in India overall income inequality as measured through the national household survey has remained by and large stable, but this masks significant spatial changes. In 1992, for example, rural poverty varied from 15 per cent in Punjab to 60 per cent or more in Maharashtra and Bihar, and in 1999/2000 the state variation was from 6 per cent in Punjab to 47 per cent in Orissa.[24] The variation across 'NSS regions' is even larger: in 1992 the variation was between 9 per cent in

Himalayan Uttar Pradesh, to 77 per cent in Southern Orissa; in 1999/2000 differences were between 5 per cent in the northern part of Punjab, to over 80 per cent in southern Orissa.[25]

In countries where overall inequality has grown fastest, rural–urban inequality has usually increased too, despite expectations that price liberalization would reduce such differences (Eastwood and Lipton, 2004). But experiences have varied in this respect, too. Balioumune-Lutz and Lutz (2004) looked at rates of growth in rural and urban areas (rather than measures of income and poverty) in Africa and found that sectoral inequalities were on average increasing, but rural–urban disparities were decreasing, and similar issues and off-setting trends are relevant in China too.

Across these countries, inequalities based on ethnic or racial differences are crucially important. In Latin America, on average, about 20 per cent of the population identify themselves as Afro-descendants, and 10 per cent as indigenous – of course this varies enormously across countries (World Bank, 2003: Chapter 3). Buvinic and Mazza (2005) summarize how excluded populations suffer from invisibility, higher rates of income poverty, which tends to be permanent rather than transitory, and stigma and discrimination.[26] In Peru, for example, Andino's represent 45 per cent of their total population but 60 per cent of the population in poverty, their levels of income and human development deprivation are much higher than the average, and gaps are not necessarily closing (Figueroa and Barrón, 2005: 13). While the position of Latin American women has improved markedly over recent decades, women from marginalized groups suffer from multiple forms of deprivation.

While for Latin America studies of group deprivation provide a fairly clear picture, and one that can be traced to colonial history, no such picture emerges from the literature on Africa. Ethnic diversity is generally seen as the main cause of political and national instability, and the colonial origins and role of colonial power in politicizing social differences have been extensively discussed by Mamdani and others.[27] As highlighted above, a significant number of countries have high levels of income inequality, and these are concentrated in the 'settler' regions in the southern part of the continent, notably but not only South Africa (where affirmative action has become central to the post-Apartheid social contract). Elsewhere, such as in Ghana and Nigeria, ethnic diversity has been an integral part of political and administrative settlements. Both Rwanda (before the 1994 genocide) and Tanzania have had low levels of income inequality: in the case of Rwanda this masked extreme levels of social differences; while in the case of Tanzania social integration has by and large been maintained as a result of explicit nation-building policies under the post-colonial socialist regime.

Asia is no less diverse than Africa, though perhaps overall this diversity has had less impact on national unity and development. In Vietnam, India and China remaining poverty and increased disparities have very clear social group dimensions that overlap with regional concentration; 'chronic poverty' as defined by the Centre for Chronic Poverty Research may increasingly be the face of deprivation in these areas.[28] In Vietnam, increasingly, poverty is concentrated in upland and forest areas, and among ethnic minorities, with a poverty incidence of about 75 per cent compared to 31 per cent among the Kinh majority, and the gaps appear to be widening. In India too, it appears that the face of poverty is increasingly marked by overlapping regional, social and gender dimensions, as illustrated in the following box, with a focus on Orissa.

Box 2.1: Inequality traps in India

In India, overall income inequalities have remained low, throughout the period of liberalization. However, studies show stark social disparities, and they overlap to a large extent with regional disparities, which appear to be increasing. Average per capita income of so-called Scheduled Castes (SC) and Scheduled Tribes (ST) at the all-India level is about one-third lower than that of non-deprived groups. Headcount poverty in 1999/2000 among non-deprived was 16 per cent, while it was 30 per cent for minorities (largely Muslims), 36 per cent for SC and 44 per cent for ST. Over time, and despite public debates showing concerns over inequalities, these disparities have shown very few signs of being reduced, particularly with respect to the ST categories (and agricultural and urban casual labourers). Deprived groups suffer from equal human development disparities: data for 1998/99 showed that 88 per cent of ST women, 73 per cent of SC women, and (a still very substantial) 44 per cent of women from other groups were illiterate. Rankings on neonatal, post-neonatal, infant, child and under-5 mortality indicators for socially excluded groups are similar to those of other indicators: for example, infant mortality for SC and ST was about 84, compared to 62 for non-deprived groups.

Beyond those averages, state level analysis for Orissa suggests that these social disparities are at least as severe in India's poorest regions, and that the various forms of disparities overlap and mutually reinforce each other. In the case of Orissa, which had the highest level of poverty among India's major states in 1999/2000, inter-state regional disparities are extremely high, and social group and (most) gender disparities higher than the Indian average. The quantitative data reflect extreme disparities, and possible 'log-jams of disadvantage' for people in the tribal upland (in itself highly unequal) versus a coastal and higher caste elite. Long-standing inequalities in access to natural resources impact on disparities between social groups and gender relations (for example as a result of deforestation). The socio-economic disparities are reflected in highly unequal access to public policies and institutions, reflected, for example, in very inefficient implementation of centrally-sponsored schemes, including the special scheme for the 'KBK region', the poorest area in 'tribal' southern Orissa, and the much-criticized IFAD supported rural development programme. The region, while considered 'remote', is not disconnected from the global economy: continued and often violent disputes around mining and displacement suggests that globalization comes with many potential negative consequences, particularly in the poorest regions.

Sources: Sundaram and Tendulkar (2003); de Haan and Dubey (2003); de Haan (2004d).

Conclusion: how and why disparities matter

The key message of the short overview of geographical and social disparities, and how the two interlink, is that public policy debates cannot shy away from addressing these questions. Globalization often changes the composition of inequalities but does not make the questions less urgent; similarly donor engagement is likely to have an impact on the manifestation of inequalities, as for example in Rwanda and Nepal. In many countries, and we will come back to this in Chapter 4, the social differences have been key to the social contract that underlies many of the public policies, and these policies in turn have changed the manifestation of these differences.

This highlights the importance of looking beyond average trends in poverty reduction and inequalities. While there is firm cross-country evidence that the poor do, on average, benefit from economic growth, and that there may not be a systematic correlation between economic growth and inequality, focusing on existing and emerging disparities is important for at least four reasons. First, there are enough cases of increasing inequalities during the last two decades to make this a key concern. Second, the correlations are based on averages, which imply there may be – and in fact are – large number of cases of groups or regions that do fall behind. Third, public policy-making at national level has been forced to consider disparities of different kinds: for example, both the recent Chinese concerns, and long-standing concerns about distribution and political representation in African states show that inequality, in different forms, matters, under processes of growth as well as economic stagnation. And finally, 'initial' inequalities can play a role in reducing economic growth and may affect government spending (further discussed in Chapter 3). The next section considers the role of globalization in creating or reducing these disparities.

2.2   Opening of markets and well-being: cross-country regressions and local narratives

This section tries to give farther insight into the trends described in section 2.1, namely whether they can be ascribed to processes of globalization and economic reform. Globalization is, of course, a complex phenomenon, and it is important to highlight its many dimensions, as each may have different, and sometimes contradictory, impacts on national trends in well-being and governments' scope and needs in formulating social policies. According to Cornia, for example, while recent trends of increased global inequality are attributable to contemporary globalization effects, these include such a wide variety of forces as technological change, policy reform measures, trade and financial liberalization, and changes in labour institutions and the redistributive role of the state.[29] Birdsall (2005: 22ff) also notes that globalization has been disequalizing, and that this can be because markets work, because markets fail (particularly for the poor), or because existing rules benefit the better-off.

Elements of globalization
Conceptually, structural adjustment needs to be clearly distinguished from globalization – though in practice, and particularly when adjustment implies reducing barriers for international economic exchange, the two may be undistinguishable, and in any case imply a drastic turn away from the earlier regimes of state control and import substitution industrialization. In the South, in the 1980s adjustment implied a focus on fiscal and monetary restraints and realignment of exchange rates. This was followed by reductions in trade barriers and domestic and external financial liberalization (Berg and Taylor, 2001: 12). Of course, the composition and timing

of these reforms varied. For example, India – unlike Argentina and South Korea – kept strong restrictions on currency convertibility (protecting it from the effects of the financial crisis in 1997), but liberalized current accounts and controls on technology imports, and started to dismantle industrial licensing. Mexico underwent massive restructuring after the 1982 debt crisis till NAFTA came into effect in 1994, and the financial crisis of 1994 led to strong devaluation. Zimbabwe remained closed until the early 1990s, partly because of externally imposed import-restriction in the 1960s, which continued during the 1980s.

In at least three spheres globalization has been important, each with potential implications for poverty and inequality trends, and scope for public policies: economic, political and socio-cultural.[30] In the economic sphere, four sets of processes have been important.[31] First, financial flows across borders have increased significantly in recent decades. Foreign exchange, negligible in the 1950s, reached a trillion dollars a day in the early 1990s. International capital flows reached $600 billion, twice the size of current account imbalances (Brawley, 2003: 81). This has been associated with deregulation of financial markets, increased capital mobility, and the rise of mergers, international acquisitions and some degree of globalization of shareholding (Yeates, 2001). These international flows have not detracted from investment in the North (Brawley, 2003): a strong 'home bias' continues to exist in investment, and equity capital held by individuals is still concentrated in domestic firms. But capital mobility has been associated with international financial crises. While many authors consider capital control obsolete, the examples of Malaysia and Chile show that they have been used in recent times, not without success (Brawley, 2003: 86–7). As discussed below financial crises have had a considerable impact on well-being and distribution of income.

A second element of globalization refers to foreign direct investment, integration of markets, business strategies and competition. Numbers of multinational companies have shown rapid growth over recent decades. But they are by no means 'footloose'. Investment remains concentrated in economically advanced countries, and the poorest countries may be ignored rather than swamped by international investors (Brawley, 2003: 87–8). A globalization index presented in *Foreign Policy*[32] shows that the most globalized countries are in the North, while countries like China, Indonesia and India belong to the least globalized countries.[33] A simple regression by Sachs (2005: 354) shows that richer countries tend to have more foreign direct investment. Nevertheless FDI was more important for lower income countries (about 15 per cent of GDP) than richer countries (about 9 per cent) (UN Statistics, in Brawley, 2003: 88).

The third and perhaps most visible element of economic globalization refers to trade flows, including services. Trade has risen faster than overall economic output every year since the Second World War. While much of this has been between developed countries – partly due to liberalizing agreements under GATT – trade dependency is much higher in Africa than in OECD countries.[34] Some of the assessment of the opening of markets and positive impacts in effect refers to *successful* opening up (that is, volumes of trade or investment), thereby begging the question of how this success is achieved.

Movement of labour across borders is the fourth main element associated with the economic processes of globalization. As with other elements, it is often assumed that international migration has increased, but quantitative evidence does not show this to be the case, at least not as much as usually assumed. If anything, the late nineteenth century was the period of global movement of labour, and the early years after the Second World War saw large flows of unskilled labourers. Also, as with international investment, much of the movement remains regional. What has changed is the nature of international migration, with a shift towards more skilled migration, at least in the category of legal migrants.[35] International remittances have grown substantially, now at US$ 200 billion or so, far ahead of official aid flows.

Financial liberalization has been associated with an increase in volatility, and volatility is a particular concern for small and poor countries.[36] There may have been about 70 financial crises during the last two decades, many with an international dimension, and often short-run.[37] The East Asia crisis and other crises during the second half of the 1990s, such as those in Mexico, Russia and Brazil, started with increases in the current account deficit, often also accompanied by fiscal deficits. Fears of default or devaluation stopped the capital inflows that financed the deficits, thus making it imperative for the country to reduce expenditure, which led to recession, and to switch demand and production, and depreciate the currency.[38] The crises depressed the living standards of many groups, usually including the poor. The potential long-term impacts, particularly for the poor, have been serious and coping strategies are potentially damaging in the long run – though there have been policy interventions, as we discuss later, that have managed to mitigate these impacts.

In the political sphere, globalization has been associated with a political unification of the world. A state-centred analysis has given way to a focus on a global political and economic system, led by a core power, which exerts enormous influence over the global institutions. Roles of national governments and powers are often thought to have diminished regulatory capabilities and governance is increasingly subject to global norms, and the focus has been increasingly on the generation of rules and institutions for global governance (with questions about the unequal division of capacities).[39]

The term 'globalization' is also used – and as such disputed – as a means of justifying a certain type of economic policy, mainly neo-liberal. This ideology 'claims that the world has moved permanently into a new and promising era; that the growing density of market relations allows more stable as well as faster growth [and] that a single set of policies – liberalization of markets for goods and finance, small government and fiscal discipline – is best for capturing the benefits of globalization' (Wade, quoted in Harriss, 2001). In economic and social policy-making in poor countries, reference to global institutions has become an integral part of politics, including in attempts to build regional economic and political blocks, most recently in the form of the African Union and NEPAD, to harness resistance to forces of globalization.

Finally, in the social-cultural sphere the world has become more interconnected, too. Culture, modes of life and consumption patterns have become more globalized. Communication technologies and media have played an important role in this. Perceptions and consciousness of events elsewhere have increased, and as Sen emphasized protests against globalization are an integral part of globalization itself. Ferguson (quoted in Dow, 2003), for example, observed:

> I dare say that one of the evident social disruptions caused by adjustment and globalization is a popular perception, particularly among the young, that we are not in control, that we have no role in defining our reality, that the immense sacrifices that are being borne by the vast majority of our peoples are at the behest of external forces and reward only a few, primarily foreign interests. The upshot is growing incidences of social alienation.

For the purposes of this book, globalization is perceived as a dynamic process, where national political agency has changed dramatically, but is as much present as it was before. Liberalization and privatization, for example, in the words of Rodrik and Subramanian (2004), are institutional transitions, and successes in liberalization are accompanied by efficiency-enhancing institutions adapted to specific initial conditions, in India for example building on already strong institutions, and innovative forms of ownership such as China's town village enterprises. And the impacts, as described next, have been diverse.

Impacts

Given the complexity and multi-dimensionality of globalization processes it is unlikely that simple conclusions about impact will emerge. Moreover, external factors strongly affect outcomes in terms of economic growth and well-being, as do fiscal possibilities, political commitment and public pressure to introduce social policies. The debate on the impacts of globalization has been heavily influenced by economic studies, particularly cross-country regressions, and assessments of links between economic integration, economic growth, and poverty reduction and inequality. The evidence from these studies is very ambiguous. There are major questions about the robustness of the type of analysis, the appropriate indicators, the relevance of cross-country regression for the experience of individual countries, whether gendered effects are captured (Elson and Çagatay, 2000, 2003), and the problem of comparing countries with very different starting positions.

Cross-country regressions commonly divide the question about the impact of globalization into questions about the impact of integration on growth, that of growth on poverty reduction, and the combined effect. As for the first question, the literature suggests a positive relationship between openness and economic growth. But the *period* of globalization was less successful in terms of economic growth than the preceding two decades (though this does not show any causality).[40] The link may well be a virtuous circle rather than direct causality: openness may lead to faster growth, which in turn generates larger trade.[41] Moreover, as Milanovic (2003) stresses, in important cases like China and India economic growth *preceded* the opening up (and even now opening up is limited); in India there was no marked increase in growth during the period of opening up in the early 1990s.[42] Even if on balance open trade policies lead to better growth performance, 'the positive openness–growth link is neither automatically guaranteed nor universally observable' (Nissanke and Thorbecke, 2005: 7). Finally, the volatility that has been associated with liberalization may hamper economic growth because of declines in investment in human capital, falling investor confidence, and uncertainty may undermine the support required to implement structural reforms.

The second main question refers to the impact of growth on poverty reduction. It is undeniable (almost tautological) that economic growth is necessary for sustained poverty reduction, and economic crises have led to increases in poverty and falls in human development indicators.[43] Cross-country analysis has shown little evidence of the existence of the classic Kuznets curve (high inequality in Africa similarly contradicts the idea of a Kuznets curve; Milanovic, 2003b), and that aggregate inequalities change only very slowly. On average, economic growth is not associated with rising inequalities.[44] The growth–poverty analyses that mushroomed after comparable data sets became available have emphasized that there is no significant link between levels or trends in economic growth and levels or trends in inequality. Income distributions change only very slowly, and appear to have a great deal of path dependence.

However, empirical findings that on average growth is roughly distribution neutral are consistent with the fact that it increases half the time during spells of growth (Ravallion, 2001). The Pro-Poor Growth research shows a number of countries where recent and new episodes of growth (in the 1990s) were associated with rising inequalities. And the extent to which growth contributes to poverty reduction has been shown to vary enormously (White and Anderson, 2000). Poverty elasticities have been found to vary between 0.6 per cent and 3.5 per cent (Dollar and Kraay, 2002, in Nissanke and Thorbecke, 2005: 10). Similar differences have been found within countries too, particularly in India, because of public policies and spending.[45]

Using household data for seventeen Latin American countries, Behrman et al. estimate that the financial sector liberalization reforms that took place during the 1990s negatively affected income distribution.[46] Within a cross-country framework, Dollar and Kraay (2002) found that financial development negatively affects inequality. The deterioration in income distribution in Argentina mentioned above was partly the result of its macroeconomic instability,[47] often regarded as an important result of liberalization. But changes in income distribution were not attributed to globalization alone, or directly: inflation was found to contribute significantly to increasing poverty, particularly during the late 1980s (Gaspirini, 2004: 20); during the 1990s both unemployment and wage dispersion contributed to increased household income inequality; and the impact of both liberalization and the substantial privatization on inequality was found to be relatively small (Gasparini, 2004; Berg and Taylor, 2001: 39).

Crises affect the poor in many ways (Ferreira et al., undated). Poor people do not necessarily lose more than others in absolute terms, but the impact of such losses is usually bigger for poor people who have less means to cushion themselves. Impacts on women can also be different from those on men. Relative price changes, related to exchange rate depreciation, international price fluctuations, trade reforms and subsidy or tax changes, can affect relative wages and employment. Labour demand and hence employment changes following decreases in demand for goods and services, and lay-offs in the public and private sectors. Crises can affect returns on physical assets and capital, which is mostly not relevant for poor households. Cuts in public transfers can have a big impact, particularly when those to the non-poor are not protected. Finally, traditional ties and networks may be disrupted by economic hardship and by the conflict and increasing criminality that often accompany crises.

The impacts of trade liberalization appear even more varied that those of financial liberalization (Lopez, 2004; Ravallion, 2003a). Some studies using cross-country analysis find that trade openness increases income inequality,[48] others find a decrease, and yet others find there is no impact, or emphasize the problems of attributing these changes to economic or policy variables (Ravallion, 2003b). In an extensive overview, Winters et al. (2002) concluded that there are no general conclusions about whether trade liberalization will increase or reduce poverty, that impacts on poverty will differ across countries, and that the effects of liberalization depend on countries' starting positions. As mentioned with respect to Bangladesh, opening up to trade in many cases does not lead to narrowing of wage gaps between skilled and unskilled labour (as some theories predict). Trade liberalization might reduce wage differentials, but if unskilled labour was protected in a pre-liberalization regime, trade liberalization is more likely to have a negative impact.[49]

The literature on trade liberalization hints at the difference between necessary and sufficient conditions for economic policies to benefit the population. For example, reduction of import tariffs and quotas may undermine a country's industrial capacity faster than it creates incentives and possibilities to shift production towards new export sectors. Factors that have been found to matter include: macro-stability and fiscal discipline, private property rights and primary education (Dollar and Kraay, 2002); the poor's access to land, credit and primary education (Bussolo and Sollignac Lecomte, 1999); and even local knowledge and participatory political systems can matter for market performance (Rodrik, 2000).

Micro-research illustrates the complexity. Research in Kenya (Bigsten and Yurevall, 2006) and Mexico (Borraz and López-Córdova, 2004) has shown that economic integration can reduce wage or income inequality, for example because Mexican states that have more firms with foreign participation were found to have more job opportunities for unskilled women. Whereas macro-evidence shows rising inequalities in Vietnam and Bangladesh during periods of opening up of markets, IDS-based research in Bangladesh and Vietnam shows that women do gain from globalization, through expansion of women's labour market opportunities and remittances to families – but against disadvantages of long working hours and poor working conditions.[50] Research by the Universities of East Anglia and Sussex shows economic restructuring as a result of globalization created new employment in export industries, but also led to job losses in previously protected industries. Impacts of job losses varied across countries because of differences in social protection provided to workers (for example, in South Africa and Vietnam; Jenkins, 2003). Assessment of the impact of globalization is further complicated because of the combined impact of opening up and technological development.

Underneath changes in Gini coefficients there may be different and even opposing trends, formed by different causal factors. Inequality in China consists mainly of rural–urban and inland–coastal disparities, and analysis by Kanbur and Zhang (2004) shows how different factors, policies and policy phases impinge on these. Pre-reform, rural–urban disparities were large, which was clearly policy-induced through the promotion of heavy industry and restrictions on labour mobility (the latter is slowly being reformed, but land ownership has remained restricted). Reforms diminished the importance of policy-induced inequalities, but increased openness with decentralization contributed to increases in disparities between coastal and inland areas over the last two decades.[51] As highlighted earlier, in Africa, where there is very little research on the impact of globalization on inequalities, the picture that emerges is of increasing disparities across sectors, while rural–urban inequalities often are reducing (Balioumune-Lutz and Lutz, 2004). In both Uganda and India the economic growth during the 1990s led to substantial poverty reduction, but growth rates varied strongly across sectors.

There is a common fear that the increased competition may lead to a race to the bottom, and increasing trade to many losers, but the evidence is very mixed. Cross-country regression by Cigno et al. (2002) indicates that globalization may not have raised the incidence of child labour. Following Rodrik's work, Burgoon (2001) suggests that states that compensate those whose interests are damaged by trade are improving competitiveness in the long run. Moreover, pressure for competitiveness may lead to the creation of political institutions that help reduce corruption – shown for example in Japan and Italy. But none of these impacts are automatic.

Impacts of international labour mobility similarly are heavily disputed.[52] On the one hand, labour mobility almost by definition leads to reduced global inequality, and cross-country analyses show that larger numbers of migrants are associated with lower rates of poverty (significantly, the size of the country is an important determinant). On the other hand, such findings are subject to major criticism. Perhaps most important for the discussion here, international migration is increasingly dominated by better skilled people, thus reducing the potential for reduction of inequality within countries of origin. The increased skill levels also imply higher investments in education in home countries, the costs of which need to be off-set against gains in assessments of 'impacts' of migration.

Thus, the impact of globalization on any indicator of well-being, and even on economic growth is due to a large number of factors, and generalizations do not appear meaningful.[53] Specific groups can and will suffer from globalization, and many of the structural reforms that accompany this. Significantly, however, government action matters, and the political settings in which globalization and its impacts take place are crucial (Brawley, 2003: 94). Public policies often hurt poorer groups, and globalization can reinforce these effects: inflation, biases against the poor in taxation and spending policies,[54] adding to the risks and costs poor people face in attempting to escape poverty (for example, through migration); or control over natural resources on which the poor depend. According to Ravallion (2003: 20–1), apart from redressing these biases, there are many things governments can do to enhance positive impacts:

> combining growth-promoting economic reforms with the right policies to help assure that the poor can participate fully in the opportunities unleashed by growth ... Redressing the antecedent inequalities of opportunity within developing countries as they open up to external trade is crucial to realizing the poverty-reducing *potential* of globalization.

This highlights the issue of public policy commitment and capacity, the last particularly in the world's poorest parts and smaller countries. The next section will look at how capacities of states have been influenced by globalization, and an oft-neglected and paradoxical question: in increasingly integrated economies and societies stronger (and perhaps larger) states are required; at the same time, as pressure for state involvement increases, the ability of the state to raise taxes and to formulate public policies may be reduced with globalization.

2.3 Social policies when countries open up: theories and evidence

What is the impact of globalization on the state's capacity to design and implement social policies? Public policies – social policies amongst them – are being challenged by a number of trends that are the prime movers of globalization: increased investment and trade across borders challenges states' traditional possibilities for taxation; increased capital mobility alters the possibilities of fiscal policies and introduces additional insecurity; regulation of production and labour conditions and redistribution have become increasingly unpopular; and labour and capital mobility across borders, and the emergence of a global market in health, education and social insurance may contribute to undermining welfare provisions within countries. This section briefly reviews the debate on the 'demise of the state', the impact that this might have on social exclusion, including the concern for increasingly dual structures of social services, and the role of fiscal crises in precipitating opening up. Its core argument is that the process of opening up is generally not, and should not, be accompanied by less state intervention. A quantitative picture of social spending indicates that countries with more integrated markets do not spend less, and often spend more on social sectors.

Demise of the state? Review of the debate

The academic literature is divided over the question of whether globalization undermines nation states, or whether it restructures and transforms them. Many authors have held the first position, and emphasize how economic globalization, in the opinion of Hirst and Thompson, 'realizes the ideals of the mid-nineteenth century free trade liberals'.[55] According to the Report of the World Commission on the Social Dimension of Globalization, global unemployment and the lack of a future for children

> are largely the result of deep-seated and persistent imbalances in the current workings of the global economy which are both 'ethically unacceptable and politically unsustainable' ... we have reached a crisis stage in the legitimacy of our political institutions, whether national or international ... The unfairness of key rules of trade and finance reflect a serious 'democratic deficit' at the heart of the system ... market-opening measures and financial and economic considerations have consistently predominated over social ones, including measures compatible with the prerogatives of international human rights law and the principles of international solidarity.
> (http://www.ilo.org/public/english/fairglobalization/report/index.htm)

The political scientist John Gray claims passionately that globalization, as the great American project, has not only led to 'an astonishing growth of economic inequalities of all kinds' but has also destroyed the stability of post-welfare capitalism and undermined social cohesion (quoted in Ghosh, 1999). The instability created by the new global markets, and, for example, the fact that the annual turnover of multinational companies outstrips the GNP of many smaller poor countries, have been considered as constraining national governments' policies, and as instigating a 'race to the bottom' in taxation as well as different forms of regulation, monetary policies and subsidies in social sectors.[56] With respect to social spending and the impact of globalization, Tanzi (2000) concludes that

> globalization will affect governments' ability to continue providing social protection at the level of recent decades. Specifically, tax competition among jurisdictions, ballooning electronic commerce, and increased mobility of the factors of production will likely cause significant falls in tax revenue in future years while increasing competition will reduce the scope for some forms of regulations ... countries need to look for new ways to provide social protection.

As highlighted by Yeates (2001), whose work has focused on the integration of a global perspective in the study of OECD social policy, different frameworks have been adopted to analyse the impact of globalization on national policies. A first approach is labeled the 'strong' globalization hypothesis, which sees globalization as 'an economic, external phenomenon which is largely passively perceived by states, welfare states and populations', and focuses on the erosion of state sovereignty, capacities and social standards (Yeates, 2001: 32). With a focus on South Africa, Abedian and Biggs (1998) indicate that economic globalization narrows the scope for economic policy-making (and increases the need for transnational policy coordination) through increased pressures to reduce budget deficits and reduced freedom to exercise conventional fiscal powers, as well as through a global policy convergence, norms around increased private funding and partnerships, and reform of budgeting systems.

A second approach focuses on globalization as, at least partly, a creation of states, and therefore as partly under the control of states (Yeates, 2001).[57] This highlights the adaptive and proactive capacities of states, including 'the centrality of social politics [sic] in determining the timing, course and pace of globalization and the diversity of political responses and outcomes' (ibid.), an approach illustrated by UNRISD research. Brawley (2003) emphasizes how globalization engenders particular political models, but this process is mediated through national politics and preferences (for example, regarding core government services).

A third approach focuses on political agency at the transnational level, and the institutions and structures that increasingly influence social policy formulation and implementation (Yeates, 2001); in a way, as Amartya Sen has emphasized, global civil society – often very critical of globalization – is a core part of the very process of globalization. Bob Deacon's work is a prime example of this: he has highlighted the risks to or changes in social standards – for example, the emergence of a global health market alongside privatization of social services[58] – under globalization, but also notes the possibility of influencing this change. Social policy itself has been globalized, while global policies are socialized through the emergence of poverty and social policy approaches within IFIs, OECD, WTO, and most recently also the African Union (2006).

The approach in this book falls under the second approach, while emphasizing the different positioning of states, and perceptions thereof, in the global system. In the North globalization is perceived as a threat to the Keynesian economic model of fiscal, monetary and employment policies (and job losses are associated with globalization), as governments have to be increasingly concerned with policies affecting decisions by domestic capital and competition for international investors.[59] China's and India's size, state capacities and extent of aid and other forms of dependency make a lot of difference:[60] both countries, though with very different political processes, have continued to carefully manage the processes of global integration. Especially in Africa, authors associate globalization with declining national policy-making capacity, structural adjustment with 'a growing process of transnationalization of social policy' (Aina, 1999: 85), and states are seen to have lost authority over social policy, to the WTO, the IMF and multinationals, and through externally imposed constraints on social policies, liberalization and dismantling of state enterprises. Structural adjustment and globalization – often seen as synonymous (Manji, 2000: 18) – are associated with neo-liberal ideologies and a long-term project for restructuring the world economy and dismantling the public sector, and with major implications for the formulation of social and economic policies. Initiatives like NEPAD and the strengthening of the African Union are attempts at regional integration to harness the continent against global forces.

Within this differentiated approach, the analysis of social policies here is embedded in a proactive perspective on state–global interaction. Many of the assertions above are in principle subject to empirical analysis – though too little of this exists, particularly in the South. The fall in tax revenue, for example, can be analysed empirically, and as shown below the evidence is that overall states have *not* been shrinking – though ways of taxation are changing.[61] As indicated above, increased competition does not necessarily lead to a fall in labour standards, suggesting that the state's role in regulation remains of prime importance. As with impacts on well-being, different aspects of globalization are likely to have varied effects on states: for example, Garrett's statistical analysis suggests that liberalization of capital markets created downward pressure on government spending, but higher levels of trade did not, and the impact of capital mobility was lessened or even reversed when political factors were taken into account.[62]

A global convergence of practices in public administration – if this exists – can mean different things: Brawley (2003: 66) emphasizes that globalization reshapes how domestic and international politics function, which may imply declining acceptance of politically sanctioned rents, and Budd (2004) suggests that globalization may (though does not necessarily) help transform the patrimonial character of state intervention. Globalization results from both deliberate and unintended processes, can entail greater privateness, but also can be 'quintessentially about enhanced publicness – about more accessible and transparent national policy domains, public policy convergence, and greater inter-dependence as people experience the effects of others' management of cross-border spillovers' (Kaul and Conceição, 2006: 9).

Finally, analysis of the impact of globalization on states needs to take account of policy-makers' and elites' perceptions and public pressure around redistribution. Atkinson's (1999) analysis of inequality trends in OECD countries emphasizes that rising wage inequality is not only due to globalization and competition from low wage countries, but is also socially generated, and related to a shift away from redistributive norms. China's social policies since the 1970s have been marked by an often open recognition – with little public debate, reflected in the way health insurance was abolished – that inequality needed to increase. And in India, where liberalization was introduced by stealth during a period of political-religious turmoil in the early 1990s, many perceived a retreat of state responsibility towards marginalized groups during that decade.

Convergence?

The literature on social policy in the South has generally shied away from study of public spending. None of the major research programmes on social policies quoted earlier included substantial studies on spending, and the subject was criticized for being absent during the Arusha social policy conference. UNRISD only recently started to look at social spending, and a recent IFPRI overview of studies on governance found only two studies that focus on social expenditure and poverty, with differing results.[63] The next chapters will discuss social spending in more detail; this section summarizes some quantitative evidence on public and social spending under globalization.

A simple overview of government spending globally during the 1990s, based on World Development Indicators, is presented in Table 2.2. Problems with interpreting such data are manifold, and much more study than

Table 2.2 Government revenue and spending as a percentage of GDP

	Current revenue		Total expenditure	
	1990	2000	1990	2000
World average	22.7	24.7	25.8	25.8
Low-income	15.5	15	18.4	18.3
Middle-income	17.3	17.7	22.1	21.3
High-income	23.8	n.a.	26.6	n.a.

Source: World Bank, *World Development Indicators 2003*.

the present book can offer is required, but the following patterns can be highlighted. The data show no downward (or upward, for that matter) trend in the share of the state in national GDP during the 1990s, generally considered as the period of globalization.[64] High income countries have on average larger states: government revenue in high income countries is about 24 per cent of their GDP, while it is about 15 per cent in low income countries.[65] However, the variation within these categories is very large, larger than between them. As will be discussed in more detail later, state revenue and expenditure, for example, in communist China or in post-reform Ghana, are much lower than in Kenya, South Africa or Malaysia. Moreover, public spending in poor countries is low, but as highlighted by Siebrits (1998: 309), 'public outlays appear to be increasing more rapidly in today's developing countries than was the case in the high-income countries during the corresponding phase of their development'.

Chapter 4 focuses on differences across countries, and how government spending is divided across sectors, showing even larger variations. The central message is that there are neither signs of a demise of the state, nor convergence towards a minimalist state. While these data need much more scrutiny, this conclusion is consistent with a range of studies. Evidence quoted in Brawley (2003: 63) suggests that levels of government spending in OECD countries have not been converging, and taxes on capital remain varied. There has been wide variety in the role different governments have played in their economies since the crisis of Keynesianism (Brawley, 2003: 44). Analysis of the influence of globalization over 30 years on OECD countries' tax and expenditure policies shows 'few economic variables robustly influence tax rates – probably because decisions to change taxes are dominated by political considerations' (Dreher, 2006: 197). Finally, Rothgang et al. (2006) show reduction in variability, but an upward trend in spending, through a catching up by low spending countries.

Levels of social spending are also discussed in more detail below, but at this stage it is important to emphasize that there has been no general downward trend in social spending as a proportion of government spending or of GDP (Mishra, 1999: 50). Globalization leads to contradictory pressures on state intervention (Tanzi, 2000). On the one hand, the ability of the state to raise taxes may be reduced with globalization, and the welfare states of late industrializers were smaller.[66] But on the other hand, the pressure for state involvement may be increasing. As summarized in Gough (2005), as early as 1978 it was concluded by Cameron that social expenditure in the OECD was positively correlated with openness to trade.[67] In OECD countries, the welfare state formed a precondition for economic liberalization because 'only social policy could assume the social protection functions previously provided by tariffs and quotas ... [and] only when national individuated rights to social benefits had been established could states seriously dismantle trade protection and open up domestic markets to foreign competition'.[68]

Research on OECD countries (for example, Scharpf and Schmidt and Pierson et al. quoted in Gough, 2005), which initially also expected a downward pressure on state provisions, has emphasized the importance of national differences in responses to globalization: 'countries reacted differently to common international challenges according to their domestic institutions: countries were moving on different employment and welfare system trajectories'.[69] This finding is in line with work on welfare regimes as articulated by Esping-Andersen to which we return in Chapter 4, suggesting that the logics of national trajectories reproduce themselves also when countries open up. 'The conclusion ... is that economic globalization pressures are usually mediated by domestic and international institutions, interests and ideas' (Gough, 2005). Finally, Bowles (2000: 20) concludes that both states and trade unions as 'traditional vehicles of egalitarian aspirations ... have a different but no less important role to play in a highly competitive world than in closed economies'.

This argument has been tested mostly in the OECD context, and its relevance in the context of the South remains an empirical question. Deacon (2000) emphasizes that particularly in small weak states it is unlikely that similar patterns will be found. Existing studies show that patterns are diverse. Examples of social spending during liberalization summarized in Taylor show cases where social spending did increase during liberalization (South Korea, though from very low levels), countries that could not increase spending (for example, Zimbabwe), and countries that chose not to (including India). Moreover, structural adjustment did not, on the whole, reduce social expenditure.[70] While the politics of social policy in the South play out very differently, often there has also been an upward pressure on social spending, as shown later.

This brings us to a paradoxical conclusion – though the history of the expansion of social policies in the North shows this is less of a paradox than one might assume. On the one hand, the period of globalization and opening up of national economies has been associated with liberal ideologies and conservative social policies, and increasing importance of international influence on ways of policy formulation. The way this general trend has expressed itself has been different in each country, but the limited evidence that we have does *not* suggest a downward convergence in the importance of the state, including in social spending. Countries with more integrated markets do not spend less, and often spend more on social sectors, including on education to enhance competitiveness and on social protection, which tends to expand during crises. During periods of adjustment social sector spending is not necessarily reduced.

This paradox highlights at least three areas for further discussion and social policy research. First, attention to the quantity of spending, as public expenditure specialists have emphasized, needs to be accompanied by a focus on quality of spending, particularly where social spending has been increasing as a proportion of total government spending, often without concomitant rises in internal revenue generation, thus posing crucial questions regarding accountability. Second, from a development-oriented perspective this points to the importance of strengthening national processes of policy-making: state intervention, including, for example, regulation when service provision is privatized and opened up to international markets, has become more, not less, important, and increasingly challenging. Finally, this highlights the need to understand the politics and social processes that determine the specific and context-dependent ways in which social policies are evolving at the beginning of the twenty-first century.

2.4   Conclusion

The debate about benefits and losses from globalization will continue. This chapter has stressed how much conclusions depend on definitions and units of analyses. It is possible to substantiate both that recent decades have been beneficial for the South (for example, China's progress leading to reduced global income inequality and rapid declines in poverty), and that the differences between the poorest and the richest countries and people have continued to increase. In terms of health and education, while tremendous absolute progress has been made, disparities in some cases have been growing (for example, in life expectancy, because of AIDS), remain very substantial within countries (as shown for India), and simple measures of years of education may mask significant differences in achievement. The chapter has emphasized the importance of interpreting cross-country analysis with care because of methodological limitations, and because they refer to averages and may mask substantial variations, as highlighted by the enormous differences in growth–poverty elasticities.

The evidence reviewed in this chapter highlights two main issues. First, globalization – even if defined in a fairly narrow sense – in itself cannot account for trends in inequalities. Despite strong correlations, there are huge differences across countries, in the extent to which economic growth reduces poverty and the extent to which globalization increases economic growth. Generalized conclusions about increasing disparities or convergence, and policy responses to these cannot be sustained: for example, in China increasing inequality has been close to an open policy objective since the 1970s reform (until recently); while the public debate in India has continued to exert pressure to keep inequalities in check; and in adjusting countries, social spending trends have not generally been downward.

A range of factors determines what type of economic growth is generated by globalization, and which sections of the population benefit from different types of economic growth. For example, the sectoral composition of growth, which liberalization often influences, has been shown to matter, as do initial conditions relating to human resources, infrastructure, labour market institutions, transfer systems and even norms governing redistribution. A growing body of literature analyses the gendered effects of liberalization, showing varied impacts, such as changes in female labour force participation. Finally, the reason that globalization does not lead to increased child labour appears to be related to national policies increasing the levels of education and public health expenditure.

Second, globalization has also not led to the demise of the state: quantitative evidence suggests that states expand with economic growth, and that globalization exerts contradictory pressures on state intervention (often initiated by economic shocks), of which the outcomes are crucially mediated through national institutions. In the case of aid dependent countries, a key question – which we will explore further when discussing PRSPs – remains around the state's capacity and public pressure to mediate international exposure; but in any case the newly emerging international social policy debate has not in general reduced the importance of social spending and programmes, as will be shown later in this book.

Historical experiences of countries that have *successfully* integrated into global markets highlight the role that states have played in managing integration and market processes. Large and successful countries like China and India integrate into the world markets in well-designed and paced manners, to allow for potential political opposition, for example. The East Asian experience has shown that public institutions played a key role, not only in terms of social policies but also in helping markets adapt to changing circumstances, through assisting technology transfers, for example. What kinds of reforms are and can be implemented of course depends on the strength of the government and its public support: in China in the 1970s health insurance reforms were implemented undemocratically, while India's liberalization is a process of steps backward and forward, prompted by the foreign exchange crisis of 1991, while policy attention focused on religious and communal tensions. The key message is that the state matters as much as it used to, and maybe even more. The following chapters therefore explore further the role of social policies as integral elements of broader public policy processes.

3
Integrating Social and Economic Policies

While economic growth is essential for sustainable poverty reduction, economic growth in itself is not enough. The reasons for this are manifold, even if we restrict ourselves to a narrow income-based definition of poverty: the figures on the relationship between economic growth and poverty reduction are averages, the deviations from these averages are large, and inequalities are important and in many cases rising. Moreover, and a core concern in this chapter, economic growth is the result of a range of public policies and private actions. Many economic policies have been shown to impact distribution – or are perceived to do so, which may be equally important for public policy-making. On the other hand, social policies impact both growth and distribution.

This chapter describes the relationship between social and economic policies, and social or human development outcomes and economic growth. The chapter first provides conceptual grounding for this debate, particularly the different ways in which the distinction and integration of the social and economic have been conceptualized, including the debate on whether social policy is merely a correction of malfunctions in the economy or proactive intervention shaping those institutions. This is followed by a discussion of the role of the state and a description of public funding trends, which underlies many of the questions around links between public policies, particularly regarding the potential negative impact of a large state sector and the 'crowding-out' of private transfers. The following sections describe some of the interactions between 'the social' and 'the economic': the importance of health, nutrition and education for economic growth, the importance of vulnerability and the role of social security spending, while the last section describes the recently re-emerged question of redistribution, and the importance of social inclusion for economic growth.

3.1 Why 'integrate' social and economic policies?

'Integration' of social and economic policies was a subject of discussion in the early 1970s through the publications of UNDESA in 1971 and inputs from Myrdal. The idea disappeared from the radar screen with the advent of structural adjustment, but has more recently become an international and national policy commitment. In Chile, the 'articulation of mutually reinforcing social and economic policies' has been described as one of the distinctive priorities of the *Concertación* governments, alongside a strengthened social strategy, decentralization and private sector participation in social programmes (Raczynski, 2001: 215). The Copenhagen Declaration and Programme of Action, which was ratified by heads of state and governments at the UN Summit on Social Development in 1995, included a commitment to 'integrate economic, cultural and social policies so that they become mutually supportive, and acknowledge the interdependence of public and private spheres of activity'. During the Copenhagen+5 meeting, ECOSOC and the Commission for Social Development (which monitors the implementation of the Copenhagen Summit) were asked to facilitate sharing experiences in the development of such policies to promote the goals of the Summit.[1] Recently, the African Union (2006) emphasized the need for a cross-sectoral perspective on public policies.

There are different reasons why social and economic policies should be considered in conjunction, from both academic and advocacy points of view. It can be seen as both a process (enhancing the balance between policy areas) and a substantive objective (that is, to resolve contradictions between goals).[2]

One of the arguments around integration focuses on the outcome of statistical analysis, particularly cross-country regressions, which emphasizes the importance of investment in health and education for economic growth. Authors like Robert Lucas and Robert Barro have emphasized the importance of human capital, particularly educational attainment, as a critical determinant of economic progress: greater educational attainment means more skilled and more productive workers, higher output of goods and services, and easier absorption of new technology.[3] Research on East Asia (Birdsall et al., 1995) has argued that rapid growth has been associated with *prior* spread of access to education and land. Some of the details of this are discussed below.

A further concern has been the impact and 'social dimensions' of economic policies. Fuelled by concerns about the impact of structural adjustment and responses to economic and financial crises, many have argued for (*ex ante*) review of the impact of such economic policies on social and human development outcomes. Following years of criticism, the International Financial Institutions now recognize that contributing to the achievement of the Millennium Development Goals implies reviewing the role of macroeconomic policies, and incorporating social and political aspects within, for example, the IMF Poverty Reduction and Growth Facility (PRGF).[4] This highlights the possibility of structuring stabilization policies in different ways, so as to incorporate social and poverty consideration. An approach called Poverty and Social Impact Analysis (PSIA) has been institutionalized by the IMF and the World Bank. This analyses the positive and negative distributional impacts of policy changes on the well-being of different groups in society, focusing on the poor and vulnerable (Robb, 2003). While, for example, Harris (IMF) and Kende-Robb (World Bank) (2005) emphasize the need for integrating social and economic policies, the emphasis has remained on the impact of economic policies (even if these are understood as broader than just macroeconomic stability) on poverty or social *outcomes*.[5]

The existing literature on the social aspects of economic policies shows a mixed picture – unsurprisingly perhaps, but often not in line with the optimistic predictions of the advocates of adjustment, nor of the people and organizations who have criticized adjustment.[6] For example, tax reforms impact both the revenue and expenditure side, and in many poor countries depend on capacity for taxation and complicated tax regimes. The impact of taxation depends on exact design, type of tax (for example, VAT versus sales tax), and exemptions.[7] Assessment is complicated by the fact that individuals and enterprises not currently taxed also usually do not qualify for state benefits and are often subject to demands for bribes from officials. Second, fiscal deficits can impact economic growth, but costs and benefits to the poor of deficits and attempts to reduce these depend on their composition (including the ratio between current spending on non-wage goods and services – tending to rise faster – and capital spending), and the benefits that accrue from existing government expenditure.[8] Third, expenditure policies and budget prioritization have a direct impact on different groups, but again the impact is complex. Sectoral distributions do not directly match benefits for particular income groups and the division between social and economic objectives crosscuts poverty or distributional dimensions. Finally, pressure to reduce support to domestic economic development may result in increased unemployment and growing informal sectors, and is often followed by pressure to pursue active labour market interventions to compensate for losses of markets.

That economic policies and, for example, budgets (as a reflection of government choices) have a social content has been argued most forcefully by gender analysts and advocates: 'there is now widespread recognition of the need to integrate macroeconomic policy and social policy, but the mainstream approach is one of adding on social policy' (Elson and Çagatay, 2000). Macroeconomic policies, in their view, have three sets of biases which affect women negatively: a deflationary bias impacting women through the labour market (reduction in formal sector employment); a male breadwinner bias which assumes women take responsibility for social reproduction affecting, for example, claims on the state; and a commodification or marketization bias and reduction of social provisions which increase the burden on women. According to Elson and Çagatay integrating the economic and social is a question of both policy type and processes of policy-making, and gender budget initiatives provide examples of practices in which the 'social' and the 'economic' are integrated.

While gender advocacy has focused on the biases within macroeconomic policies, recent literature that focuses on social policy in a development context makes the argument that social policies were key in many successful economic policies and growth models, perhaps *particularly* in cases of successful integration into global markets. As highlighted by Chang (2004), East Asian countries used a wide range of social policies – broadly defined, including attempts to redress social and political conflict – alongside economic policies. These included public works in Korea, state pensions in Singapore, land reform in Japan, but also repressive policies against trade unions in many countries of the region. In Japan, '[r]esponses to poverty ... many of which are key elements of contemporary welfare states, were closely linked to efforts to manage the pattern of industrialization and growth' (Milly, 1999: 3) – economic priorities dominated social priorities, but policy choices were embedded in a normative predilection for equality.[9]

The emphasis on successful cases should also make us consider the link between social and economic policies in less successful cases. For example, Kerala's 'model', widely considered a human development success story, has not been accompanied by sustained economic growth (Véron, 2001). Similarly, though more directly influenced by the economic crisis of the 1980s, Zimbabwe and Tanzania's progress in education after Independence was not followed by sustained growth. This does not contradict findings suggesting the positive contribution of human development policies for economic growth, as such analyses emphasize that these impacts work only under certain conditions. Moreover, as we will see in Chapter 4, there is no evidence of *relative* underinvestment in African countries, as public social sector investment in Asia has remained relatively low. The point that remains, however, is that for an analytical and operational view the inter-linkage between social and economic policies is of central importance.

Peter Lindert's (2004) historical study of the growth of the welfare state in OECD countries provides interesting lessons about how economic and social policies interact. Advances in social spending since the 1880s were partly the result of increased political voice (including the self-interest of elites), and partly went alongside economic expansion and income, plus demographic changes such as aging (Vol. 1, p. 24). Lindert's conclusions about the costs of social spending for economic growth are discussed below; the key point and lesson from his work is the emphasis on the political economy of links between the social and the economic, which can help to conceptualize the very different political constellations that determine these interactions in the South, as discussed in the next chapter.

The debate on the integration of social and economic policies highlights the continued strength of the theoretical separation, and abstraction, of the economic and the social, as well as the perceived dominance of economic analysis and policy-making.[10] Within this paradigm, social policy continues to be perceived as existing outside economic policy, and vice versa. The political-economy perspective adopted in this book, however, stresses how in practice the two are inseparable, concurring, for example, with Shin (2000) who in the context of the globalization debate focuses on 'the real policy-making process where social policy is not decided in a state of isolation from economic policy. In practice, economic and social policies are inextricably intertwined in the policy-making process, reciprocally affecting the form and content of each other in direct or indirect ways.'

To summarize, the need for an analytical view that incorporates economic and social policy in an integral manner – and *not* in a way in which the first is the domain of economists and the second of 'non-economist social scientists' – can be argued from different perspectives. A normative perspective highlights that social outcomes need to – and can – be considered when designing macroeconomic policies. An analytical point of view stresses that economic and social policies are closely interlinked, and that we ignore the links at our peril. But it also highlights how arguments around entitlement and rights are interlinked with an understanding of the power structures through which realization of rights is articulated. Thus, and thirdly, the interlinkage of public policies also needs to be considered from the perspective of politics and ideologies. The separation of economic from social policies – as under the 'Washington Consensus' – itself is a political project articulating an ideology or public policy priorities, and politicians consciously use 'social issues' as opposed to harder economic questions to mobilize political support.

The argument around integration is by no means new, but it has obtained renewed significance. Politically, new policy experiments after the adjustment period show new ways in which the social and economic are articulated, which need more accurate interpretations than frameworks of neo-liberalism. Moreover we need a broader understanding of the politics that drives these public policy models, including the global context in which policy formulation is embedded.

3.2 The state as hindrance or precondition – the role of public funding

Underneath the debate on economic and social policies lie different perceptions of the role of the state, including whether the state is a hindrance to private sector activity or a necessary precondition. This section looks at a part of this discussion, particularly the evidence around whether the size of the state sector has an impact on economic growth, and the possibility that state transfers crowd-out private transactions.

While during the post-war period a proactive state was seen as essential in particular to avoid severe economic crises such as in the 1930s, and Keynesian economics dominated research and policy-making, during the 1970s and 1980s an increasing number of publications focused on the constraints imposed by state intervention. In 1981, the World Bank Report *Accelerated Development in Sub-Saharan Africa* stressed the policies that resulted in economic decline:

> Statist policies fostered excessive government intervention in domestic markets, bloated and profligate public sectors, protectionism and restrictive investment regimes, and a widespread bias against agriculture. Common recourse to overvalued exchange rates, price controls, subsidies, uncontrolled spending, and heedless foreign borrowing created debilitating economic distortions. Cumbersome administrative regulations stifled trade and investment.[11]

By the early 1980s, the state was no longer seen as a solution, as was the case in the first decades after Independence, but had come to be regarded as part of the problem, and some seemed to have given up hope that the state could play a useful developmental role.[12]

The literature since the late 1980s has reflected a new optimism. In a 'Third Wave' of democracy, in the words of Samuel Huntington, authoritarian regimes began to experiment with new political frameworks. In Africa, as in Latin America, the number of military coups and the amount of violence declined, political opposition became more common, and regimes began to democratize and elevated popular expectations that reform would improve living conditions. The literature on the political transitions emphasized the new potential of state–society interaction, and the benefits this might have for sustainable development. African reform, it was argued, had three pillars: not only a market orientation, but also liberal democracy and social pluralism (Sandbrook, 1996: 2). Reforms would include 'basic civil and political liberties, the end of arbitrary regulation and state exaction, and greater transparency and accountability in public decision making' (Bratton and van de Walle, 1992: 440) – though many authors stressed the fragility of these changes. The 1990s also witnessed new optimism in a number of cases – notably Uganda and Ghana – about sustained political reforms and possibilities of constructive donor partnerships.

In Asia, similarly, there has been a vigorous debate about the role of the state in economic development. The idea that the East Asian economic success happened under laissez-faire policies has been heavily criticized. The 1997 East Asia crisis highlighted many institutional failures, but the region bounced back remarkably quickly, while coming under pressure to expand social services (see Chapter 4). There is now much evidence that governance in support of market and economic development – even though corruption was endemic in many countries in East Asia too – was the key to success. According to Birdsall, (2005 WIDER Annual Lecture) behind East Asia's high rates of investment, productivity growth, macroeconomic stability and emphasis on exports 'were other factors rooted in equally amazing and rapid changes ... [which] included unprecedented gains in small farmers' agricultural productivity, high demand for schooling including of girls, and declines in fertility....' In these economies, public investment in education, agricultural extension (and redistribution of land in the northern parts of East Asia) reached households in rural areas.[13]

Public spending – why does it matter?

In descriptions of OECD social policy experiences, spending levels for particular purposes feature centrally – levels of (social) spending are sometimes even seen as a defining characteristic of whether a country has or is a 'welfare state' or not. By contrast, development debates on social policy have shown a remarkable lack of interest in detailed analysis of public spending, except for the technical analysis of public expenditure management. There is surprisingly little systematic information about what happened to social spending, including in countries that have undergone reforms.

Various things have been responsible for this lacuna. First, the predominant sectoral approach to social policy issues.[14] Second, there are perceptions that government intervention is irrelevant or ineffective in enhancing the well-being of people in the South. Third, recent attention has focused on 'pro-poor' rather than sectoral spending, for example through the HIPC initiative, while it has been acknowledged that definitions of pro-poor vary.[15] Fourth, a largely reactive emphasis on the reduction of spending – often combined with a focus on increasing the quality of spending – has characterized most reform debates. Fifth, a predominant concern of public expenditure management specialists and others has been the process of budgeting, and concerns with civil service reforms: in my experience, specialists have resisted debates about levels of funding as they felt this might take the focus away from reform priorities (for example, reducing spending on salaries). At the same time, budgeting work inspired by social development specialists, too, has tended to focus on the process rather than the content of budgets.

In the context of the South, is it important to have an overview of how much governments spend? In particular, when governments are forced to reduce spending, is it relevant to know what existing patterns of government spending are, and what desired patterns would be? I believe the answer to these questions is yes, for the following reasons (illustrated in Box 3.1). First, as the descriptive review in this section shows, there are enormous variations in how much governments spend (as a proportion of GDP), and what they spend it on. This enormous variation cries out for explanation, whether the main objective of analysis is expenditure management, improving social policies and their outcomes, or understanding the politics of public policy. Theoretically, an overview of public spending would inform possible categorizations of social policy 'regimes', which are the subject of the next chapter.

Second, patterns of spending are at the same time a statement of public policies and the outcome of political struggles. As Addison et al. (2006: 7) conclude 'fiscal policy reveals more about a country's development strategy than probably any other area of policymaking'. In the OECD welfare state contexts, until the start of the crisis of the welfare state in the late 1970s, public spending progressively increased due to public demand and governments' desire to please voters.[16] The subsequent restructuring, while for instance in the UK not leading to dramatic decreases in spending but entailing a large shift away from spending on public housing, also shows the clear footprint of political settlements. In the case of India, which, as will be seen below, has low public spending overall and in social sectors, the increase in spending on primary education was at least partly the result of the effective lobbying of activists. And in much of Africa, donors of course have played an important – and contested – role

---

Box 3.1 The composition of budgets: does it matter during fiscal crises ?

During 2000–3, the World Bank and DFID were in policy dialogue with the state government of Orissa about its state's fiscal crisis and donor budget support or adjustment lending. The main theme of the dialogue was reducing the fiscal deficit, in particular a reduction or freeze in the number of public sector employees. Within that context, there was – in my view – remarkably little discussion of the composition of the budget. The argument of the World Bank public expenditure management specialist seems convincing: in the context of budget deficits, and when spending on salaries makes up close to 100 per cent of total spending, discussions about the composition of spending would be unwelcome, as this would risk taking the focus of attention away from the need to reduce spending. However, during one mission, and following a review by education specialists (as part of extensive engagement with the large centrally-sponsored primary education programme), the donors did argue that an increase in state education spending would be desirable, as this would help the government of Orissa to obtain more centrally-funded resources. In my own perception, the sector where increases in funding were desirable was health; the central point here, however, is that discussions about the composition of the budgets did become part of the policy dialogue (almost inevitably, and slipping in through the back door), hence it seems very important to develop more explicit guidance around this.

---

in determining patterns of public spending, including for basic social services.

A third argument for highlighting patterns of public expenditure relates to the importance of considering public policies in a cross-sectoral way. Enhancing spending on education is important, but can be justified only in a cross-sectoral public policy perspective, one that identifies needs and political and financial margins to allocate public finance across a range of sectors, on the basis of analysis of needs for investment in, for example, rural areas and infrastructure, social protection, health, and so on. The way governments and, not least, donor agencies are structured has failed to strengthen the capacity to develop such a public policy perspective.

Spending levels and trends

While for OECD countries it is possible to provide acceptable comparisons of levels and patterns of spending, for countries in the South this poses many more problems, and has generally been available only since the 1970s. Classifications can of course vary across countries, and can by themselves be problematic. Also, data on spending can refer to central government spending only, excluding state/province and local government spending (which in the case of India, for example, affects conclusions about health policies significantly). Nevertheless, studies by the IMF (Chu et al., 2000), the World Bank Social Protection sector (Besley et al., 2003), Musgrove et al. (2002) on health, and UNDP (Mehrotra, 2000) provide comparisons.

As mentioned in Chapter 2, as a proportion of GDP poorer countries' governments tend to spend less than richer countries, but spending is still substantial (and probably well above OECD countries' historical records), and has not been decreasing recently. Equally important is the fact that there is enormous diversity across the South. For example, and as Table 3.1 shows, while the average for low-income countries is 15 per cent, total government revenue as a percentage of GDP is around 10 per cent in Bangladesh, while it is about 25 per cent in equally-poor Kenya.[17] Neither can one observe a universal trend towards a shrinking public sector, though with important exceptions such as Ghana, as described below. The existing literature, to my knowledge, provides little help in explaining these differences in levels and trends.

Similar large variations exist in the proportion of government spending to the various sectors, including within the social sector. There is a wide range in terms of the percentage of government spending for education and towards health, for example India and Bangladesh give much more priority to education than to health, as does Malaysia, which overall spends much more on social sectors. Education received great priority in Thailand, but much less in India (though increasing during the 1990s) and Argentina. Public health expenditure is relatively high in Mexico, but very low in Uganda, Vietnam, Indonesia and India[18] – though in countries with a federal fiscal structure these figures are likely to underestimate total public spending.[19] Beyond this, there are large differences in the proportion of this spending on primary education: Zimbabwe and China spent 15 times more public money on tertiary education than on primary education, while Korea was one of the few countries where more public money was spent on primary than on tertiary education.

The least information is available on social security or safety net expenditures in the South, even though such expenditures are substantial (and

Table 3.1 Social spending in selected countries

| | GNI per capita (ppp) | Poverty $1/day | Inequality | Government expenditure as % of GDP | | | | |
| | | | | Total government spending | | Sectors | | |
	2004	HCI	Gini	1990	2000	Education	Health	Social security
Argentina	12,460	3.3	52.2	10.6	17.0	4.0	4.5	5.7
Bangladesh	1,980	36.0	31.8	–	12.7	2.4	0.8	–
Bolivia	7,430	14.4	44.7	–	23.8	6.3	4.2	3.5
Chile	10,500	<2	51.0	20.4	21.9	4.2	2.6	8.7
China	5,530	16.6	44.7	10.1	10.9	2.3	2.6	–
Ghana	2,280	44.8	40.8	13.2	13.2	3.2	2.3	–
India	3,100	34.7	32.5	16.3	16.7	4.1	1.3	–
Indonesia	7,550	7.5	34.3	18.4	20.5	1.2	1.2	1.0
Kenya	1,050	22.8	42.5	27.5	26.0	7	2.2	–
Korea, Rep.	20,400	<2	31.6	16.2	16.2	4.2	2.6	1.2
Malawi	620	41.7	50.3	25.4	25.4	6	4	–
Malaysia	9,630	<2	49.2	29.3	29.3	8.1	2	1.2
Mexico	9,590	9.9	54.6	17.9	16.0	5.3	3.7	2.5
Pakistan	2,160	13.4	33.0	–	23.1	1.8	1.1	0.4
Peru	5,370	18.1	49.8	20.6	19.3	3	2.2	–
South Africa	10,960	10.7	57.8	30.1	29.1	5.3	3.5	1.6
Tanzania	660	19.9	38.2	–	–	2.5	2.7	–
Thailand	8,020	<2	43.2	14.1	18.0	5.2	3.1	0.6
Uganda	1,520	–	43.0	–	20.4	1.5	2.1	–
Vietnam	2,700	–	37.0	–	23.4	2.1	1.5	–
Zambia	890	63.7	52.6	–	–	2.0	3.1	–
Zimbabwe	2,180	56.1	56.8	27.3	27.3	4.7	4.4	–

Sources: GNI WDR, 2006; poverty and inequality see Table 2.1; expenditure data World Development Indicators 2003; education and health data Human Development Report 2005 (most recent data); social security or safety net data from Besley et al. 2003, Table 1, 1972–97.

donors are important in determining patterns in low-income countries.[20] In a paper for the World Bank Social Protection group Besley et al. (2003) bring together the international data on safety net expenditures between 1972 and 1997 (which excludes many of the countries discussed in this book). This highlights the 'wide variation in the levels of expenditure on safety nets across countries', which in their view is unlikely to be explained on the basis of governments' information about 'optimal' levels of expenditure. Their benchmarking exercise relates a country's social spending levels to other countries at similar levels of income or structural factors, and of institutional development (governments can afford to spend less if their institutions are stronger and more effective), obtaining a comparison between what countries finance, given their need and ability for financing. For example, in terms of spending Sri Lanka ranks 39th in the world, India 73rd, Pakistan 75th and Bangladesh 83rd. Ranking changes substantially if structural factors are taken into account: Pakistan rises to 33rd, Bangladesh to 45th and India falls to 76th – given India's ability to finance social security, and the need for it, it performs poorly compared to its neighbours. When institutional factors are controlled for, Pakistan and Bangladesh continue to 'improve' their rankings, while India's performance remains around the same level. In Africa, Ethiopia improves its ranking significantly owing to the adverse shocks suffered in the period, while South Africa moves down after controlling for structural and institutional factors. This exercise, too, shows the enormous diversity across countries in funding social security, a diversity showing different rankings when country characteristics are taken into account, but not disappearing.

Trends in social spending

We know relatively little about levels of social spending, but knowledge about trends is also sparse. Popular discussions about structural adjustment have often emphasized the decline in social spending (often as a sign of the conservative nature of the international organizations imposing structural adjustment). However, the evidence around this question is very mixed, both regarding the trends in spending itself and the key reasons behind the trends. While on the one hand in Ghana, which has carried out structural adjustment relatively diligently for an extended period of time, state expenditure has declined significantly and social sector spending declined in the first decade of reform (Aryeetey and McKay, 2004), in many countries the state sector does not seem to have shown a declining trend (at least not during the 1990s), and the share of spending going to social sectors has not been declining either.

In a briefing paper on 'making adjustment work for the poor', Killick (1999) highlights that adjustment has not been enough for poverty reduction, usually not addressing key causes of poverty and inequality.[21] But even then, that is, before PRSPs were introduced 'SAPs have not made a decisive difference to social service provision, which has generally been among the more protected categories of government spending'. The 1990s also witnessed increased attention to social safety nets, the fastest growing sector in the World Bank in the 1990s. While non-debt spending overall has been squeezed, in many cases governments tried to protect social spending, and the heaviest cuts have tended to fall on capital budgets and economic services, and hence social spending often rose as a share of non-debt spending.

IMF research in 1998 showed that since the mid-1980s real per capita spending on education and health had increased in developing countries (while it decreased in transition economies), and that this increase occurred under IMF-supported adjustment too.[22] More recent research on 14 countries between 1985 and 2000, in response to 'many critics voicing concerns that [social sector] programs typically involve an unnecessary squeeze on social expenditures' (IMF, 2000: 7), also showed that public spending in health and education showed a slight *increase* as a percentage of GDP, and that the presence of IMF-supported programmes does not reduce spending in health or education (though this does not imply vulnerable groups are protected against economic shocks, as this depends on the targeting and timing of the spending). Wilhelm and Fiestas (2005) found that during the 1990s, while overall per capita spending declined, spending increased in defence, education and social security. Finally, recent increases in donor funding through debt relief have led to a substantial relative increase in social spending – an explicit aim as part of the process of freeing up resources for poverty reduction[23] – continuing a longer trend towards social funding and away from 'productive' activities.[24]

In his overview of case studies on social spending during liberalization, Taylor (2001) also shows diversity in trends. South Korea (like Colombia and Cuba) increased its social spending after the 1997–8 crisis, but did so from low levels and a neglect of most forms of social policy (Kwon, 2005). On the other hand, Zimbabwe, like Russia and Turkey, was forced to cut back social spending following the fiscal constraints during external liberalization. Like Argentina, India did not cut back on social spending during periods of liberalization.

The diversity in patterns and trends thus suggests that it is unlikely that we will reach easy categorizations about social policy models – even though state expansion seems to have been as likely a response during the 1990s as the shrinking of the state. East Asia's model has been widely debated but here too spending patterns have been diverse; South Asia has been marked by relatively small states; Africa has been marked by the extremes of 'adjusting' countries like Ghana on the one hand and 'non-adjusting' Kenya, Zimbabwe and South Africa on the other; while in Latin America a relatively liberal Argentina came to conform more to an interventionist model exactly during the 1990s.

Spending and growth

Do social and other forms of public spending matter for economic growth and poverty reduction? A substantial body of cross-country analysis looks at the links between government intervention and economic growth (see, for example, summary in Lofgren and Robinson, 2004). There is some evidence regarding the size of government that increased public investment may reduce growth because it is less efficient in enhancing public capital, and may compete with private capital.[25] Also, there is evidence that fiscal *deficits* (above a certain threshold) constrain growth, and that reducing reliance on domestic financing can enhance growth, but the relationship varies across countries.[26]

But the potential negative impact of larger states on growth does not necessarily apply to all forms of investment: 'how well you use it may be more important than how much you have' (the title of a 1996 NBER Working Paper by C.R. Hulten). Recent literature has focused on the kinds of investments made by government, as well as the question of whether public investment crowds in or crowds out private investment.[27] While Mehrotra (2000) at UNDP emphasizes that sustained levels of social investment have contributed to high health and education achievements, Lofgren and Robinson (2004) found in cross-country analysis for Sub-Saharan Africa that reallocation of government sources to more productive areas, particularly agriculture, would be good for growth and poverty reduction. Fan and Rao (2003) indicate that public investment in education and health has a positive effect on growth (sometimes with a lag, particularly in the case of education). Others found positive impacts of investment in infrastructure. While efficiency and trends in capital expenditure are often highlighted as concerns, in most cases, the positive relationships depend on governance indicators and 'sound' macroeconomic policy.

The findings of this research are of great importance, including vis-à-vis common assumptions about social sector spending. While the 1980s reversed the 1960–70s trend of expanding state services, this in general did *not* lead to a decrease in the *proportion* of total public finance going to social sectors (Killick, 1999). Patillo et al. (2005) show that since the mid-1980s, Sub-Saharan countries have increased their relative outlays on education and health care: it increased both as a proportion of GDP and as a share of total government spending. Second, and confirmed in Patillo's review too,[28] the quality of spending is at least as important as total funding, and donors can make improvements in quality, conditional on increased outlays. This was, for example, key to the efforts to improve education outcomes in Uganda and equally a concern in Orissa where the share of expenditure on salaries outpaced any capital investment. Third, and as highlighted particularly in research on public expenditure for agriculture and infrastructure, pro-poor outcomes greatly depend on the composition of overall expenditure across a range of sectors.

While there is too little knowledge about the role of public spending in developing countries, and questions surrounding this topic have been and will continue to be contentious, existing evidence suggests the following. For historical reasons, states in developing countries are often relatively large, and some state intervention has a negative impact on economic growth. But at the same time, many aspects of state public funding play essential roles, and the role of spending on health, education and social security are discussed further below. However, much of the debate has focused on the need for increased funding in particular sectors; a broad social policy view needs to include a consideration of 'fiscal space', the distribution across sectors, and the efficiency of spending within those sectors. Moreover, research should go beyond the dominant focus on the contribution of specific spending on, for example, growth, and *also* analyse these as outcomes of political struggles and responses, as discussed below with reference to social security, and in the next chapter in the context of social policy 'regimes'.

3.3   Social policies for growth: human development, social security and inclusion

Two earlier conclusions will be discussed in more detail here. First, that public expenditure does play a key role in the provision of services, which form entitlements in themselves, but also preconditions for processes of economic growth. Second, that the composition of spending matters, that decisions about investment in human capital are and need to be seen in the context of other investments. We discuss this with reference to health, nutrition, education, social security, and inequality and social integration.

Health and education

It is now generally recognized that health and education are central to well-being, or capabilities in Amartya Sen's terms.[29] Also, '[h]ealth care, because of its ethical weight, is ... an important arena for political organizing. Health systems, like welfare systems more broadly, once they enter the political arena, form part of the process of construction of who is a full citizen.'[30] But they are also an essential element of growth strategies. The economic literature summarized in Pattillo et al. (2005) referred to earlier shows that higher shares of spending on health and education benefit growth, with a lag, and depending on good governance and sound macroeconomic policies; and returns to education are dependent on the existence of opportunities for productive benefit.[31] Widespread education, it has often been emphasized, played a central role in the success cases of East Asia, where the state – and elites – played a role in shaping the conditions of global competition. Even in basic manufacturing – for example, in shirt and shoe factories – to be competitive basic skills have been shown to be preconditions (Owens and Wood, 1997). Econometric studies have shown that returns to education can be substantial, as argued in particular for the education of girls, the returns on which exceed those of investment in boys' education.[32] Returns to investment in basic education are often thought to be particularly high, though it has also been stressed that countries need a complete education system, and for example to educate future teachers, health workers and managers.

Similarly, health is an asset, and under-nutrition and associated problems such as ill health contribute to reducing opportunities.[33] At the individual level, malnutrition – even moderate – contributes to infectious disease mortality, particularly in the case of childhood diarrhoea and acute respiratory illnesses.[34] The continuing effects of under-nutrition of infants or during pregnancy have been well established. Ravallion (2003a, building on Dasgupta and Ray) emphasizes that unless a person obtains the minimum food energy intake needed to support bodily functions at rest it is impossible for that person to be productive, thus generating involuntary unemployment. The impact of ill health came out very strongly, also, in the large participatory research project 'Voices of the Poor' (Narayan et al., 2000).

At the macro-level, too, health has been shown to be important. Human development indicators to some extent depend on levels of economic development, but different social policies can cause large differences in outcomes at similar levels of GDP.[35] For example, Osmani (1997) shows South Asia's high levels of under-nutrition (child and maternal) compared to levels of income, including of the poor.[36] Rapid improvements in nutritional status in Vietnam were only in small part due to improved incomes.[37] But, and more relevant for the discussion here, there is also evidence that an unhealthy population may reduce economic growth. A World Bank projection indicated that GDP may fall 25 per cent over 20 years in countries heavily affected by HIV/AIDS (in USAID 2005: 41–2). Research has shown the negative impact of nutrition deficiencies on GDP,[38] and while nutrition has often been felt to be neglected in the development debate, a new consensus has now emerged that 'the returns of investment in micronutrient programs are second only to the returns of fighting HIV/AIDS among a lengthy list of ways to meet the world's development challenges' (World Bank, 2006: ix–x). 'Pathways' through which health contributes to economic development include higher labour productivity, higher educational attainment and lower fertility and mortality (WHO, 2001).[39]

Public spending clearly plays a key role in promoting health, and thus growth. Anand and Ravallion (1993: 147) conclude 'that certain components of public spending can matter greatly in enhancing human development in poor countries, and ... they matter quite independently of what they do or don't deliver in terms of reduced income poverty.' IMF research shows that 'both education and health spending have a positive and significant direct impact on the accumulation of education and health capital, and a positive and significant indirect impact on growth'.[40] But 'positive effects of both education and health spending are strongly influenced by the quality of governance', and 'reducing corruption and increasing accountability for public spending are no less important than increasing spending'.

Thus the evidence of positive economic impacts adds to capability and rights arguments for public health investment. But spending patterns globally do not reflect such a consensus, as shown in a WHO paper.[41] Public expenditure on health – as a form of public goods and services with large social benefits which private markets will not deliver adequately – is particularly important in poor countries, but on average poor countries under-invest in health. Richer countries not only spend more in total on health care, but also more as a proportion of GDP – 'arguably the opposite of the relation between total health needs and need for public spending.' In poor countries and regions, out-of-pocket spending is often very high, varying from 20 to 80 per cent of total health spending (at high incomes that share drops sharply and the variation narrows, even though absolute out-of-pocket expenditure increases with income), and as mentioned before there is much variance in terms of health spending as a percentage of GDP (Indonesia and Malaysia, for example, spend a lower proportion than Bangladesh and Vietnam), and much variation in terms of the proportion of all funding that goes to primary health care (India and Pakistan, for example, spend proportionally much less on primary care than Bangladesh or Ghana).[42] It appears that, globally, public pressure has led to increases in spending on education, but not or less so on health – though the many 'vertical' initiatives perhaps particularly in health imply that total health funding may be much higher.

From a social policy perspective this leaves important questions open. Levels of desired public funding – absolute and in relation to other forms of public investment – remain open to debate, and in policy practice heavily contested, even though in a large number of countries public spending on health is low. There is no clear guidance as to how high investments should be,[43] which proportion should go to primary as opposed to secondary and tertiary care or education, and how progressive health spending should be.[44] Moreover, there is a major unresolved debate about the role of private health spending and provisions.[45] There are concerns about the introduction of private provisions into national health care systems, which is increasing with globalization (Deacon, 2003). A key example of the public–private controversy was the question of user fees, introduced under the influence of international donors.[46] In Africa, this was introduced in the early 1980s (the first country was probably Malawi), as a response to economic crisis, with the dual purpose of generating revenue and improving allocative efficiency – demand was thought to be unresponsive to price changes.[47] This viewpoint was rapidly challenged (Cornia et al., 1987), particularly for the negative effect on access by the poor. In Zimbabwe during the 1990s it was shown that introduction of user fees, combined with economic recession and drought, led to a decline in access to health care and a reversal of human development gains of the 1980s. Nevertheless, the main problems to which user fees were thought to be a response – resource shortage and poor quality – continues to be a problem in most countries.

The debate about quality versus quantity of public funding will continue to flourish, as highlighted by Lindert in his historical study of public expenditure in OECD countries. The idea that smaller governments are better for the economy is not born out by evidence on the importance of health and education for economic growth, including under globalization. There is substantial underinvestment of public funds in health in poor countries, certainly if measured against investment needs for Millennium Development Goals (UN Millennium Project, 2005). Questions of quality and composition of spending remain: in cases like Uganda, with a strong commitment on the part of the leadership, emphasis on quality improvement before increasing funding has paid off, but with increased donor commitment (and the NGO lobby criticizing spending limits imposed by international organizations) to social spending these questions are likely to become more important.

Social security

Chapter 2 highlighted the importance of shocks: globally these have received much more attention since the crises of the late 1990s, but of course for poor people vulnerability and exposure to shocks have always been central parts of their existence. While Chapter 5 looks at the wide-ranging literature on programmes of social protection and security, this section looks at the place of providing social security in wider development policies, and particularly economic growth, which is generally more contentious than the discussion about health and education.

In a reflection on the UK White Paper on globalization, the then chief economist of DFID argued that the main arguments of the White Paper were valid, but that more emphasis needs to be placed on the institutional determinants of investment and growth, and – while highlighting the continued dominance of a residual approach to social policy[48] – the need for a clearer recognition of the complexity of the impact of increased openness on poor people, and of the need to improve systems of social protection (Wood, 2004). While this point may be generally accepted, there is very little guidance about the role of (what kind of) social security policies in relation to a country's economic growth paths and economic policies. As emphasized in an ILO paper, many of the benefits appear important but are often not quantified (Bonilla Garcia and Gruat, 2003), and, as with health and education investment, quality of spending is as important as its quantity.

Social security policies can have both negative and positive impacts on economic growth. On the negative side, first, much attention has been paid to the negative impact of high or rising public expenditure on growth. Pensions have been a prime example in this respect, and the ballooning of public spending on pensions has been core to economic reforms in Latin America and Poland, for example (though even now, in Brazil publicly provided pensions for a small group of workers form a substantial part of the government budget).

Second, existing social security provisions can be constraints on investment (Bonilla Garcia and Gruat, 2003). The desire to attract foreign investment and minimize business costs may lead to (felt) pressure to reduce social security provisions, and existing social security provisions have been considered constraints on privatization of state-owned enterprises and industrial reform. Pressure, international or otherwise, on public sector budgets may narrow the scope for general budget subsidies for social security.

A third issue relates to the possible impact of publicly provided social security on incentives, and the possibility that public transfers crowd out private ones.[49] For example, pension benefit arrangements can provide incentives for older workers to leave the labour force prematurely, and social insurance contributions as well as benefits can influence work behaviour among working age persons (particularly older workers). Social security payments may crowd out inter-generational transfers. The possible impact of benefits has been of key importance in the design of public works schemes, where successful ones have been organized in ways that minimize negative impacts on labour markets. However, such assessments usually do not capture many of the benefits of spending on social security, for example their life-time and inter-generational benefits, and spillover effects on household and community members.[50]

In an important contribution to the re-valuation of (targeted) social security transfers, Martin Ravallion states that

> the presumption of an overall trade-off between redistribution or insurance (on the one hand) and growth (on the other) has come to be questioned. It is known that a market economy can generate too much risk and inequality, judged solely from the viewpoint of aggregate output ... This theoretical possibility has given a new lease of life to targeted transfers as the main instruments for publicly-provided 'social protection' in poor countries, which is seen as being good for pro-poor growth ... by providing insurance or helping credit-constrained poor people be productive workers or take up productive opportunities for self-employment. (Ravallion, 2003a: 3)

There are a number of ways in which the provision of social security and growth can reinforce each other. Lack of security and crises can have long-term consequences in terms of human capabilities, education (providing a reason, for example, for reducing fees during crises), and early childhood. While access to adequate health care as discussed can increase worker productivity and encourage workers to invest in greater skill development, maternity benefits can help to improve the health status of the population, and social transfers generally can help enhance demand for and access to education and health services (Chapman, 2006). Unemployment benefits – while non-existent for the majority of workers in most poor economies – have the potential to facilitate longer job search, and participation in job training and thus allow workers to better utilize skills or develop new ones. Work injury programmes may enhance employers' incentive to reduce work hazards and make their workplaces safer, potentially leading to a more productive workforce and enhancing economic activity.

The positive impacts often extend beyond the individual. As highlighted by HelpAge International (2003), regular payments to older people have the potential to enhance their social standing and their health,[51] and research has shown that the elderly use their pensions to contribute towards the cost of the education of grandchildren, investments in income-generating activities and in supporting (HIV/AIDS) orphans.[52]

Further, social security provisions have the potential to 'buy social peace', and this has indeed been seen as a reason why more open and competitive economies tend to have larger welfare states. An adequate unemployment benefit programme can help to mitigate the political opposition to enterprise restructuring, thereby facilitating a shift of workers from less productive jobs to more productive jobs, and enhancing economic activity. Policies to promote growth may increase the need for effective social protection programmes to cushion the impact of labour market disruptions and guarantee portability of social insurance credits. Social protection provisions can also help to reduce wage demands.

There is also a financial market argument for well-designed social security provisions, particularly pensions. In contrast to pay-as-you-go schemes, advanced funded schemes increase rates of savings, and asset management strategies have the potential to promote financial market development – though research suggests that the link is not always there or very strong (Bonilla Garcia and Gruat, 2003). Singapore used the Central Provident Fund as an effective form of capital mobilization (Kwon, 2005a: 9).

Finally, as argued by HelpAge International in the context of social pensions, the introduction of such pension schemes can increase state accountability. Research in South Africa, Bolivia, Namibia and Nepal showed enhanced levels of local accountability and support of citizens for the working of government due to the regular transfer of income to the older poor.

Thus, social protection policies and growth, and policies for economic growth, are consistent. Particularly in poor countries (or 'low equilibrium economies'), while financing is most problematic, social security provisions can be particularly important, to enhance investment and basic security. But, as in the case of health and education policies, the question that is at least as important is *how* they are provided.[53] As highlighted in Lipton's (1998) review of anti-poverty programmes, it is key to be prepared for emergency programmes; and Cook et al. (2003: 15) similarly emphasize that economic crisis in southeast Asia demonstrated the limitations of safety nets as *ex post* responses to the crisis. From a public policy perspective, moreover, social security needs to be seen as an integral part of cross-sectoral policy-making.

Social inclusion

The importance of forms of social integration for economic growth is of course clearly illustrated by situations of conflict; indeed, a substantial number of the world's poor live in situations of conflict. This section does not look at such extremes, but at more stable contexts, and reviews evidence of the relationship between social exclusion or inequality (more easily measured) and economic growth, reviewing the evidence that inequality – including gender inequality – can affect growth.

While the potential impact of inequality on economic growth was already part of the writings of Myrdal and others, after a period of recent neglect inequality is 'back on the agenda'. A growing literature based on cross-country regressions has tried to establish links between different forms of inequality and economic growth.[54] Despite problems with these forms of analysis, there is sufficient evidence that suggests, as highlighted in *World Development Report 2006* and Nancy Birdsall's WIDER Annual Lecture of 2005, that inequalities in terms of assets are likely to reduce potential for growth (in situations of market failure), and that there need not be a trade-off between growth and equity, particularly in the long run.[55]

The literature has suggested at least seven sets of inequality–growth links. A first reason why lower inequality may be good for growth relates to demand for goods. More equal income distribution and lower poverty means a larger internal market and higher growth, which could also trigger innovation. Birdsall et al. (1999) provide a micro-model of savings, showing that lower inequality can result in higher savings, and faster growth and poverty reduction.

Second, with imperfect capital markets, high income inequality means that fewer people have access to credit, thereby possibly lowering growth. Ravallion (2003) argues that with credit market failures some people are unable to exploit growth-promoting opportunities for investment. Aggregate output – defined as the sum of the individual outputs, each depending on own capital, own wealth, and market failure – depends on the distribution of wealth. Output loss from market failure will be greater for the poor, so the higher the proportion of poor people the lower aggregate output.[56]

Third, distribution of land and other assets can have an impact on economic growth. Deininger and Squire (1998) found a weak relationship between initial income distribution and future growth, but a strong relationship between initial land distribution and growth.[57] Birdsall (2005: 13) found that inequality in the distribution of land and education were more important in affecting growth than income inequality.

Fourth, a similar argument around inequality in access to opportunities can be made for health, education and labour markets. As noted by Myrdal already, equalization in favour of low-income groups – in health, education and labour markets – is a productive investment in the quality of people and their productivity (Tzannatos, 1998).[58] Castelló and Doménech (2002), using a new measure of human capital inequality, argue that, while income inequality does not seem to have an effect on growth, inequality in human capital – which is not well correlated with income inequality – does.[59]

Fifth, the gender literature has pointed to a number of ways in which gender inequality can impact growth, for example, by reducing child mortality rates (Klasen, 2004). There is some evidence that gendered inequalities in access to productive resources reduce overall productivity (Blackden and Bhanu, 1999). Klasen (1999) used regression analysis to show how inequalities in education and employment may reduce growth and development. Gender inequality in education is found to lower the average quality of human capital, and impacts investment and population growth (possibly explaining a small part of differences in economic growth between East Asia and Africa). But not all forms of gender inequality directly impact growth, and it has been suggested, for example, that wage inequality and export-led growth have been compatible.[60]

Sixth, Ravallion (2003) noted a possible link between spatial inequalities and growth (again under conditions of market failure). With 'geographic externalities', living in a well-endowed area means that a poor household can eventually escape poverty, while an otherwise identical household living in a poor area sees stagnation or decline (if there are impediments to factor mobility, such that marginal products of capital and labour depend on location). Policies to redress spatial inequalities could compensate for the underlying factor market failures and so stimulate growth.

Seventh, and possibly most controversial, there may be a link between inequality and various social, political and institutional factors, in turn affecting growth. Birdsall (2005: 15–17), similar to *World Development Report 2006*, suggests that inequality tends to undermine good public policy, and Abu-Ghaida and Klasen (2004) suggests women's empowerment may improve governance and reduce corruption. Also, social divisions may make it more difficult to implement reforms: in India, debates about rising inequalities were key during the 2004 elections, following over a decade of economic reforms. It is often asserted that inequality leads to social unrest, and/or crime, though this link too is complex.[61] Moreover, inequality may lead to pressure to redistribute income (and hence distortionary taxes and costly transfers[62]). The 'median voter hypothesis' describes the political mechanism through which voters' behaviour would lead to pressure to redistribute income: in more unequal societies the income difference between median and mean voters is greater, therefore the median voter is expected to exert more pressure for redistributive government intervention.[63] But also, political analysis and the framework developed in *World Development Report 2006* highlight that political action and change are not independent of distribution of wealth.[64] We explore this question in a descriptive manner below.

The free lunch of the welfare state

OECD welfare states effectively redistribute income. More equal richer societies tend to have larger states, shown at least by the extremes of Sweden and the US, but not 'newcomer' Korea.[65] In the South, however, the evidence on redistributing income is less clear. Research on social spending suggests that the impact on inequality is at best very small. The 18 countries that this book looks at in some detail are plotted in Figure 3.1, and their pattern of GDP-government spending *appears* the

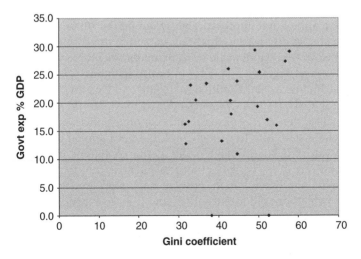

Figure 3.1   Inequality and government spending

reverse of the OECD pattern, with unequal countries having relatively large states and equal countries having smaller states. These findings themselves are no more than indicative and, for example, do not control for factors like GDP, openness, demography or relative prices. Explanation of the pattern too needs much more research. Put simply, larger states can suggest two fundamentally different patterns: they may be the result of pressure to increase redistributive spending (including, in aid dependent countries, international pressure), but also of capture by elites. Moreover current patterns need to be seen in a dynamic framework, and regressive spending itself can become subject to contestation.[66]

A growing number of incidence benefit studies have shown that the targeting of spending in the South does not tend to be progressive. Much social security expenditure, such as the pension for civil servants in Brazil (unlike newer non-contributory pensions), is highly regressive (Vélez, 2004). An overview for the Operationalizing Pro-Poor Growth research programme by Wilhelm and Fiestas (2005), drawing on work by Lionel Demery, shows that education spending tends to be more pro-poor, and health and infrastructure spending less so (the impact of social security spending is thought to be very limited). Davoodi et al. (2003) is perhaps the most extensive overview of existing benefit incidence of health and education spending: while emphasizing the limitations of existing data, they conclude that the poor have benefited less from public spending in education than the rich. Spending on primary education was slightly pro-poor, but not in sub-Saharan Africa. Its targeting improved during the 1990s. In health, even primary health care is not pro-poor, although it improved slightly during the 1990s. For the country case studies discussed in this book, data from this overview are reproduced below: Peru stands out as being exceptionally pro-poor in education spending, and Argentina pro-poor in health spending.

These findings from the South seem to find resonance in Lindert's (2004) historical analysis of OECD states referred to earlier. He highlights the potential for the synergy of social and economic policies and objectives. The welfare state is a 'free lunch', and the net national costs of social transfers are zero. But this holds under specific conditions: in democracies that show care in the design of transfers and taxes through universalistic approaches that have a more positive impact on growth than means testing (which can reduce incentives and is more expensive), and with uniform, less expensive and distorting rules.[67] While in many cases public investment in the South needs to increase, the evidence suggests that the conditions for the 'free lunch' are not met. This underlines the importance of existing work on the quality of spending, but also provides an

Table 3.2 Changes in benefit incidence of public spending in health and education

		Education				Health	
		Initial year	Latest year			Initial year	Latest year
Malawi				Argentina			
– all education	Poorest	10.0	21.0	– all health	Poorest	33.0	53.2
	Richest	38.0	19.0		Richest	6.0	3.9
– primary	Poorest	15.0	25.0	Ghana			
education	Richest	24.0	14.0	– all health	Poorest	11.6	12.5
Mexico					Richest	32.9	31.0
– all education	Poorest	14.0	17.0	– hospitals	Poorest	7.9	9.5
	Richest	27.0	22.0		Richest	32.6	30.8
Peru				Peru			
– primary	Poorest	31.4	34.2	– hospitals	Poorest	9.0	5.2
education	Richest	9.1	6.4		Richest	26.5	33.0
				– health	Poorest	13.3	23.7
				centres	Richest	15.9	10.1

Source: Davoodi et al. (2003).

important marker in the debate on expanding social spending – this needs to be embedded in analysis of both cross-sectoral analysis, and of the political economy that drives public policies.

This is by no means a comprehensive review of the rapidly growing – and contested – literature on inequality and growth, and its critiques. However, and in line with *World Development Report 2006*, it suggests that economic and social policies (in particular those that address inequalities) are not incompatible, that there can be economic gains from addressing inequalities. Often they are required for 'social peace', as China's current policy approaches suggest, for example. But the high inequalities in many countries in the South, alongside substantial public spending, indicate that the conditions for a free lunch often do not exist, and that we need better understanding of the political economy in which social policies are embedded.

3.4 Conclusion

The need to combine human resource development with economy-wide policies favourable to growth has been well recognized in discussions of policies for fighting poverty ... The key message emerging from recent research is that achieving a policy environment conducive to growth interacts multiplicatively with human resource development. By doing just economic reform or just human resource development, one may achieve very little in terms of poverty reduction, but doing both can take a nation a long way. (Datt and Ravallion, 2002)

There is much evidence, including from the gender literature, highlighting the need for a cross-sectoral view on public policies. Research in Chile suggests that economic development may follow a 'multiplicative model', in which not only the implemented policy is of relevance but also the overall policy mix (in Lopez, 2004: 20). Buvinic and Mazza (2005) emphasize the need for a cross-sectoral view, as, for example, gains in reducing inequality in education may not translate into gains in the labour market. Mehrotra (2000) stresses the need for integrated (and sequenced) approaches in health, nutrition, water and sanitation. And a recent IMF paper on public spending, too, stresses effects across sectors, for example between primary school enrollment and health care (Gupta et al., 2004).

This evidence is important in terms of the complementarity of different forms of 'resources' for development, though it does not give guidance regarding the kinds of policies needed to achieve these. Recent discussions on inequality, and evidence on the importance of social policy in 'late industrializers', clearly indicate that understanding development patterns requires an understanding of concurrent (rather than sequenced) economic and social policies. The literature indicates that neither market fundamentalism nor optimism about the benevolent developmental state are warranted, and that *specific types* of policies and institutions determine whether states are hindrances to or preconditions for growth.

Social policies play a constitutive role in creating patterns of inclusion and exclusion, and directly and indirectly shape the conditions for the functioning of markets. Successful development – particularly in economies that integrate into global markets – is contingent on state intervention, to regulate markets and to create the preconditions for populations to participate in markets. Social policies need to deal with these preconditions as much as the after-effects of economic trends and policies. They are needed to ensure social integration and provide the social investment needed for economic development, arguably particularly in a context of globalization. Moreover the discussion on social and pro-poor spending highlights that public policies need to be considered in a cross-sectoral way. Poor countries spend too little on essential provisions – but calls for increasing spending need to be seen in an integrated public policy framework.

While in theory the need for integration of social and economic policy considerations seems evident, this has important implications for development practice. It is likely that the conceptual division and disciplinary boundaries will continue. The reasons why social and economic policies are usually studied separately could be the subject of a separate study, and have deep origins in the way social sciences have evolved, in an increasingly technical and disciplinary fashion.[68] Development studies have experienced a strong dominance of development economics, in poverty and public policy analyses, and a tradition of social policy analysis similar to, for example, that of the UK has by and large not developed.[69] These divisions continue to hamper a cross-sectoral perspective.

Second, there is an important institutional challenge for development agencies, and Chapters 6 and 7 will get back to this. Coordination between social ministries, and between social and finance ministers, are important. Finance ministers may not see themselves as agents of development. International agencies, particularly in the most aid-dependent and indebted countries, have tended to strengthen the position of finance ministers, often without concomitant strengthening of line ministers. As shown by experience in Orissa, different sectoral debates – including on health, education and social protection – have operated in tight silos, inhibiting debates across sectors. The 'projectized' nature of much development experience, including targeted poverty interventions, has hindered a view of the broader set of public policies.

The review of public spending highlights the importance of these questions, through what we may call a 'double Robin Hood paradox'. On the one hand, public spending on health and education is often well below requirements for achieving the Millennium Development Goals. On the other hand, public spending in many poor countries is high relative to government resources, often with a bias towards the social sector, but with little notable progressive impact on inequality (though with exceptions).[70] We thus need a very good understanding of the conditions under which public policy is formulated, and the next chapter will try to contribute to this, through an analysis of principles of solidarity.

4
Evolving Social Policies: The Importance of National Contexts

Social policy-making is not a technocratic exercise, nor is it directly determined by levels of economic development. It is shaped by national traditions that create path dependence – of institutions, ideas and practices. It is the outcome of political settlements, and often part of political projects, related to processes of nation building and the creation of social contracts or citizenship and the rights and duties of citizens. This chapter looks at national social policies from an historical perspective, which is essential for understanding the ways in which social policies come into being. National traditions, politics and ideologies – within a dynamic international context of competition, learning and pressure – shape patterns of inclusion and exclusion. They contain solidarity principles which are expressed through specific forms of private–public mix, statutory or community-based approaches, social insurance versus national service approaches, ways in which labour markets are structured, and indeed how social objectives are matched with economic ones.

The chapter starts with a short review of debates on welfare 'regimes' in OECD contexts and explanations of national social policy approaches, primarily during the second half of the twentieth century, which show a large amount of path dependence. The question this chapter explores is whether such categorizations, or elements thereof, can be usefully applied countries in the South. Starting off from the conclusions in Chapter 3 on public spending in the South, which showed the importance of understanding how governments in the South tax its citizens, receive aid and allocate money, the following three sections describe how different approaches to social policy can be traced in the formulation of public policies in the South. We see strong elements of corporatist and productivist approaches in East and Southeast Asia, a move from corporatist to more residual approaches in Latin America, and from post-Independence universalist to residual approaches in countries in Africa and South Asia. The concluding section asks the question whether we can detect a trend towards more homogeneity in social policy-making, particularly towards a neo-liberal regime.

4.1   Are there social policy 'regimes' in the South?

In the literature of the welfare state, since the seminal work of Titmuss, many pages have been filled with typologies of national experiences. Probably the most debated contribution – and the one used in work on social policy in the South – has been Esping-Andersen's *The Three Worlds of Welfare Capitalism* (1990). This has generated an enormous amount of debate, in which Esping-Andersen has continued to engage. *Social Foundations of Postindustrial Economies* (1999) re-examines his earlier typology responding to critiques around the adequacy of criteria used, including the narrow focus on income-maintenance programmes, and the need to distinguish more than three regimes. This section highlights some of the issues in these debates, commenting on the implications of the approach proposed in this book.

Esping-Andersen differentiates welfare states from social policy. The latter is a broader concept, implying generally the 'public management of social risks' (1999: 36), while welfare states are the particular form of public policies that emerged after the Second World War, with strong political commitments related to welfare. Also, Esping-Andersen stresses, the debates on typologies occurred mainly in reflection of the golden age of the welfare state, the 'social order ... [that] succeeded in unifying social citizenship, full employment, mass education, and well-functioning industrial relations systems' (1999: 13), while the restructuring from the 1970s onwards posed new challenges to such analytical devices.

The typologies of welfare regimes focused on the 'combined, inter-dependent ways in which welfare is produced and allocated between state, market, and family' (Esping-Andersen, 1999: 34–5). To this triad, Esping-Andersen adds the voluntary or non-profit sector. Each of these has radically different ways of managing risk. The concept of decommodification is proposed to quantify the degree to which states weaken the dependence of individuals on market transactions, or the protection received by people from vulnerability and dependence on labour markets.[1] A focus on the interdependence of social policy provisions is appropriate in the context of the South too, even if the state tends to have less importance and large parts of the provisions are funded internationally. In the experience of poor and better-off people around the world it does matter – to differing degrees – what states or NGOs provide, in terms of education, health and safety nets during crises, and public provisions interact with what families themselves provide.[2]

While the basic idea of regimes revolves around the way public policy is provided, the 'models' are based on the idea that welfare state solidarity has differed systematically across OECD countries. Similar to work by Hilary Silver for the IILS that emphasizes the context-specific and historically determined nature of patterns of social integration and exclusion, and policy responses (Silver, 1994), including between France and the UK (Silver and Wilkinson, 1995), Esping-Andersen's notion of welfare state regimes focused on the 'historically dominant constellations of collective political mobilization'.[3] He distinguished three approaches to solidarity, or societal means of dealing with risks (residual, corporatist, universalistic), and three regimes on the basis of the public–private mix of provisions or entitlements (liberal, conservative, social-democratic). Regimes are characterized *predominantly* by the respective approaches, and within countries specific programmes may be based on different principles, reflecting outcomes of historical and political conjunctures. Thus, while in the UK liberal and market-oriented approaches predominate, health care is – and has remained, unlike its housing sector – strongly based on universalistic approaches. Most countries also have corporatist elements in their social policies, for example through benefits for civil service employees.

The first approach is *residualism*, which limits assistance to targeted groups, the 'bad risk' strata, of lone mothers, disabled, the 'demonstrably poor', and so on. Residual programmes are usually means-tested and not very generous, and a common explanation for their predominance is that the median voter is unlikely to support generous programmes for the poor. A residual approach divides society into 'them' and 'us' with a large group that can obtain private insurance, and a minority of people dependant on the welfare state. The corresponding welfare state regime is the liberal one, traced back to nineteenth century English political economy, and still articulated in a cluster of Anglo-Saxon countries with a strong bias towards targeting of social assistance, a narrow definition of what risks should be considered as 'social', and a strong encouragement of the market (contrasting a corporatist emphasis, as discussed next).

Second, in a *corporatist* approach risk is pooled by status membership, often on the basis of professional status. Membership is usually compulsory, ensuring corporatist solidarities. Specific histories of collective mobilization have led to different forms of occupational solidarities, for example in countries such as France and Italy with a variety of pension plans. Many of the Western European welfare states have strong corporatist and conservative characteristics, as both liberalism and socialism historically played small roles. Early social reforms, as in Imperial Germany, had a strong authoritarian character. Systems of social security – including in Japan – can be characterized as corporatist, in that status divisions permeate the system (in many countries the civil service obtained a privileged position in terms of benefits). Finally, in contrast to social democratic regimes, a male breadwinner bias in social protection and the centrality of the family as care giver are key elements of corporatist regimes.

Third, the *universalistic* approach is based on the idea of pooling all risks – whether risks are universal or the idea that risks should be shared universally – under one umbrella, and implies the solidarity of all. The roots of universalism can be diverse. They come from reformist liberals such as Beveridge (who argued that universalism reduced bureaucracy and market distortions, a theme emphasized in Lindert, 2004). Socialists and trade unionists see universalism as a means of strengthening solidarity. A social democratic welfare regime emphasizing universalism has been central to Nordic countries, particularly since the 1960s. Extensive and relatively generous systems of income transfer programmes have been combined with social services and income support for working women, based on strong egalitarian principles, but also in the promotion of productivity and full employment.

Additional regimes have been suggested (Esping-Andersen, 1999: 88–92). First, in Australia and New Zealand, while having a strong focus on residual approaches, welfare guarantees exist through the labour market and the wage arbitration system. Second, in Mediterranean countries clientism has dominated welfare programmes and bureaucracies – though Esping-Andersen does not see this as a defining feature of a welfare regime. A third category has been labelled 'corporatism without labour', and much emphasis has been placed on the 'productivist' orientation of East Asian social policies, with low government spending and carefully balanced social and economic policies.[4]

In a comparison between public policies in the US and Europe, written from a different perspective than Esping-Andersen and focusing on redistribution, Alesina and Glaeser (2004) identify two main factors to explain the substantial and continued cross-Atlantic social policy differences. First, *political institutions* – such as proportional representation, the role of the constitution in allowing changes in government policies and federalism – play a role in determining levels of redistribution. Second, *race* plays a role, in that racial divisions and racial preferences in a more heterogeneous country, like the US, where poverty is concentrated among minority groups, deter redistribution. We will come back to both these factors in the discussion of social policies in the South, but it is noteworthy that Alesina and Glaeser, like Esping-Andersen, emphasize that the 'reasons why Americans and Europeans differ on their choices of welfare state and redistribution run very deep into their different history and culture' (2004: 13). The emphasis on political institutions is re-affirmed by Taylor-Gooby's (2005) critique of Alesina and Glaeser, which highlights the importance of left-wing politics in Europe in securing a larger welfare state.[5]

What is the relevance of this notion of regimes for a development context? Contexts in the South are fundamentally different.[6] MacPherson and Midgley, for example, emphasize the need to recognize difference in terms of diversity for securing welfare, political and cultural differences, neglect of welfare in the South by governments of the North, and the importance of global political and economic forces and ways states in the South respond to this.[7] The objective in this chapter is not to contribute to the debate on concepts of welfare regimes and approaches to solidarity per se, but to highlight the elements of the debate that are useful for understanding social policy in the South. First, as mentioned, the focus here is on social policy rather than welfare state regimes, that is, a wider notion of public policies than in the welfare state context in OECD countries from the 1960s onwards.[8]

Second, and closely related, the focus of attention is the *principles* of solidarity rather than the categorization of countries. As was highlighted with the example of different approaches within the UK (liberal generally, but universalistic in health care, even though the organizational principle has been argued on grounds of efficiency), in most countries we are likely to find a combination of principles. As Barrientos (2004: 139) highlights, for example, Latin American countries have shown features of all three of Esping-Andersen's welfare regimes. The principal focus of the categorization will be those, rather than clusters of countries, though for convenience we describe these by region, alongside broad similarities in socio-economic histories.

Third, one of the main reasons for deploying the categorization is to show that, as in the North, there are patterns to social policy approaches, with degrees of path-dependence and links to political constellations. This is also where – as highlighted by Gough (2004, 2005), and Davis (2004) for Bangladesh – the international community plays an important role. Rather than seeing the international context as external to public policy formation (including in taxation), it is key to integrate this into the descriptions of the political constellations that influence social policies: from the colonial past, through the early periods of Independence, up to the period of adjustment and PRSP approaches, policies are determined in the interaction of national and international forces. From this, lessons may follow for donor agencies, for example around the impact of different aid modalities on political constellations.

Fourth, while most analyses of social policy in the South highlight labour market structures as a core difference between the North and South, I believe it to be essential to reflect on the nature of labour market regulation in the South, and how this has influenced in particular social security policies. Whereas most analysts emphasize the existence of an 'informal sector'[9] as a major obstacle to expanding social policies, the distinction between formal and informal is also the result of public policy interventions. Often under a modernization drive, and/or under international pressure, categories were created that constructed the basis for the difference between those in privileged jobs and those outside what Holmström (1984) in the Indian context called the citadel of labour (in terms of social policy regimes characterized as the corporatist element in many countries). Adjustment and reforms have tried to change this, but usually by reducing employee numbers, rather than changing the relatively privileged position. In any case, solidarities are expressed through such labour market policies.

Fifth, and perhaps least touched upon in the welfare state regime debate (though it is in US–Europe comparisons), the role of citizenship needs to be addressed, and the role of social policies in nation building. Different patterns of integration, in the sense of ethnic or racial differentiation, have led to differing norms and practices of public policies: the relatively large welfare states in Europe are partly the result of more homogeneity – France's mode of social integration and Scandinavian countries being key examples.[10] In the case of the South, where processes of nation building are more recent, the role of citizenship needs to be brought to the forefront of analysis. In Tanzania part of the *ujaama* strategy was the creation of nationalism and cultural decolonization. In Rwanda social policies became an instrument in the ethnic violence, unlike Tanzania dividing the young nation. Affirmative action played a constitutive role in India, where 'reservation' became a medium for integration of historically deprived groups, in Nigeria, where distribution of access to bureaucratic jobs and resources has played a key role in a fragile nation state (constitutionally, federal institutions must reflect its 'federal character'), and in Malaysia and South Africa, where affirmative action for the ethnic or racial majority became a key component of social and economic policies.[11]

Finally, social policies evolve and path dependence needs to be understood in its dynamic context. Again, the international context is very important in this respect – though sometimes exaggerated. There is evidence of 'learning' between nations: according to Pierson, welfare states that developed later than the classic ones in Western Europe 'have always been strongly influenced both by the example of developed welfare states elsewhere (with an evident debt to both Bismarck and Beveridge) as well as the prompting of international agencies' (ILO, UN, IMF, World Bank).[12] In many countries in the South, change and learning have taken dramatic forms, for example in Africa from a relatively brief period after Independence with a strong emphasis on inclusive policies, towards more targeted policies under adjustment, and a new emphasis under the post-Washington consensus. Finally, in Latin America a regime shift took place during the 1980s/1990s, firmly towards a liberal welfare regime.

Thus, and as a definitive history of social policies in the South still needs to be written,[13] what is proposed here is to focus on social policy regimes in the sense of the principles of solidarity that drive public policies in particular countries. Such regimes are path-dependent, and a priori one would expect colonial histories, globalization and adjustment to play an important role in influencing the spread of ideas, as well as the political constellations that lead to specific public policy interventions. The following sections describe these, suggesting that in East Asia and Latin America radical economic changes are accompanied by equally radical changes in social policy regimes, while in the African and South Asian cases dualism is a central organizing principle, but with important universalist elements.

4.2   East Asia: from developmental towards inclusive?

As discussed in Chapter 3, the East Asian experience did not conform to the free market model that had sometimes been portrayed. Much analysis now exists to show that most countries in Asia had pro-active – but selective – social policies, designed to play a key role in its pattern of economic growth. This section uses labels of productivist or developmental approaches to characterize social policy in South Korea, Malaysia, including its affirmative action, and Indonesia's strong 'pro-poor' approach under an authoritarian regime. Moreover, it suggests a move towards higher public spending and more inclusive social policies following the 1997–8 crisis.

In terms of the quantitative importance of the state, according to the simple indicator in Table 3.1 above, East Asia shows great variety. China's government expenditure forms 11 per cent of GDP according to international data, with about half of that going to social sectors. Total government expenditure has shown a continuous increase since 1980, though sharply declining till 1995 and again increasing till 2000. Expenditure on social services as a percentage of total government spending gradually increased over that period, though these data exclude spending through state enterprises and individual workers (Guan, 2005: 251–2). Korea's state spending has also remained relatively low, with relatively high shares of health and education, while Indonesia's state size is about average, with very low social spending shares. Vietnam's and, particularly, Malaysia's state are much more important, with social spending low in Vietnam (but increasing, and national level data give higher figures).

The literature on social policy in East Asia has seen rapid growth, and includes much engagement of scholars traditionally working on Europe. One of the early contributions was Hort and Kuhnle (2000), showing that countries in the region had introduced welfare policies at a lower level of development than OECD countries, and showed evidence of its expansion during the growth period, as well as after economic crises. Gough (2000) uses the welfare-state idea to analyse East and Southeast Asian social policies, though with reservations about the usefulness of the welfare regime approach – despite the early introduction of welfare measures. Using Holliday's welfare typology of 'productivist welfare capitalism', in which social policy is subordinated to economic policy, he distinguishes three aspects of the 'Bonapartist' nature of East Asian social policy: its role in nation-building, in securing the loyalty of elites, and in helping to legitimize undemocratic regimes.[14] East Asia has been labelled 'corporatist without labour', marked by egalitarian norms but authoritarian employment practices under one-party democracies,[15] and with liberal residual approaches to benefits. The 'productivist' orientation of East Asian social policies implied low government spending, and 'close and intentional congruence between economic and social policy'.[16]

In South Korea, the state has remained relatively small (measured by state expenditure as a proportion of GDP). It did introduce social welfare policies earlier than OECD countries at similar levels of development (for example, in terms of levels of urbanization), but – as in other East Asian countries – social investment was selective, often limited to workers in the formal sectors (social insurance in large firms), and with little targeting to or benefits for the poor.[17] Its social policy was very closely linked to a policy emphasis on enhancing growth and productivity, and in line with the nationalist emphasis of public policies and the strong interventionism in markets (Kwon, 2005a, b).

Indonesia's experience can possibly also be categorized as Bonapartist and productivist, though its state is larger than South Korea's.

The pro-poor performance from the late 1960s to the mid-1990s was based on a conscious strategy that combined rapid economic growth with investments and policies that insured the growth would reach the poor. This strategy integrated the macro economy with the household economy by lowering the transaction costs of operating in the markets – factor markets and product markets – which provide links between the two levels of the overall economy. This strategy was designed and implemented by highly skilled economic planners (the 'technocrats') at the direct urging of President Suharto. (Timmer, 2004)

As in South Korea, Indonesia's pattern of growth was very beneficial to the poor. It occurred under a repressive and centralized policy regime, following a violent coup, based on and actively crafting an alliance with rural inhabitants. Income inequality has been consciously kept low (Gini of 0.33). Public policies have contributed to a rapid spread of access to health and education (possibly because of a perceived preference for infrastructure with more immediate benefits), even though investments in health and education appear low. Social security spending remained very low. Indonesia's experience shows the importance of non-social sectors for poverty reduction, including rural finance, and investment in agricultural infrastructure promoting labour intensity under a low-wage regime.[18] Policies outside the agricultural sector, including minimum wage legislation and protection for specific industries, had a stronger welfarist orientation.

The crisis of 1997–8 brought very significant changes in the social policy regimes in South Korea, Thailand and Indonesia (though reform processes started earlier and ethnic tensions often played a role in policy change). Political systems came under significant pressure, including regarding levels of inequality, particularly the wealth of and corruption among the richest. Indonesia immediately expanded its social expenditure after the Asian financial crisis, building on existing programmes, with targeted subsidies in health, for schooling and rice, arguably moving a little towards a more welfarist regime alongside its process of democratization. South Korea increased its social expenditure after the 1997–8 crisis, from low levels and using its strong fiscal position, in fact continuing a trend started earlier during the 1990s (You and Lee, 2001: 306).

In terms of the organization of social policy delivery in South Korea – particularly the integration of fragmented health funds – radical reforms that had been on the political agenda for decades were implemented after the crisis (Kwon, 2005a). The reforms imply greater inclusiveness, but at the same time an emphasis on international competitiveness. Besides the strategy for technology development introduced in 1990, the Korean government put in place institutional arrangements for structural adjustment. A new developmental social policy since the mid 1990s started to provide benefits and training for people outside large companies. In 1998 the new president established a tripartite committee (employers, employees, government), which enabled the forging of a new social consensus (Kwon, 2005a: 13). Labour market policies too changed substantially, under pressure from civil society, towards greater inclusiveness from what used to be essentially a dualist system, under the banner of 'Productive Welfare' (Yi and Lee, 2005: 161).[19]

Malaysia's social policy regime fits within an 'East Asian' model where social objectives were carefully matched with economic and efficiency concerns, and managed under strong nationalist leadership. According to Kwon (2005a: 18), Malaysia's welfare state approximates the Singapore-type of exclusive welfare state. On the other hand, our simple indicator suggests it has a large state, and particularly high public spending in education. Its unique feature is no doubt the affirmative action programme introduced in 1970 under the New Economic Policy (NEP) – a year after severe ethnic riots, and introduced under emergency rule. It has been labelled one of the world's largest social engineering projects, in which education played a central role, inculcating a sense of Malaysian-ness and patriotism (Brown, 2005a). Its stated aims were to eradicate poverty independent of race or ethnicity, and to remove the identification of race or ethnicity with economic status or function. It included explicit targets for employment and capital ownership rather than income inequality. NEP's 'implementation and subsequent adjustments radically recomposed the class structure of Malaysian society, altered the balance of power between different economic and social groupings, and entrenched the role of the state in the economy' (Khoo Boo Teik, 2004: iii). NEP has been considered successful: group inequalities between *bumiputera* and non-*bumiputera* (Chinese and Indian) have been reduced, alongside economic growth.

China's communist state has had success in improving human development indicators, and the subsequent free market economy – remaining under political control – has benefited from the earlier state investments in human development (Drèze and Sen, 1989). In the pre-reform period social policy was inclusive, but had a strong dualistic character too. In particular, urban inhabitants benefited from much better provisions, and the dualism was enforced through a strict registration system, which continues to pervade public policies. The social policy reforms from the late 1970s onwards aimed to facilitate marketization and the state as regulator rather than single provider, moving towards the East Asia type of developmental welfare state, while maintaining the stability of the political order (Guan, 2004), even if the state is not a unitary actor (Howell, 2006). Its social and economic policies explicitly allowed increases in inequality, and social insurance schemes became central to its productivist welfare thinking.

Concerns about social stability led to addressing the inequalities that were felt to be increasingly unsustainable, the decline in rural health services began to be addressed after 2000 and the existence of the 'floating population' recognized in public policy. China's integration into the global economy and society, thus, is accompanied by a wide-ranging and complementary set of social policy reforms (Nielsen et al., 2005), sometimes associated with the rise of China's 'New Left' (Hook, 2007).

The opening up of the Vietnamese economy posed many questions similar to China's developments (Suwannarat, 2003: 205), as the enterprise-based system of benefits was dismantled, without signs of a weakening of the state (for example, reflected in increasing internal revenue generation, though decentralization is central to the reform strategies). Vietnam is moving to a system of contributory social insurance, addressing previous regressive benefits for politically designated groups. This is still covering only a minority, but recent legislation aims at extending provisions beyond the formal sector. World Bank data showed a decrease in government health spending from 5 to 3 per cent between 1994 and 2002, and an increase in education spending from 8 to 10 per cent; more recent trends show the share of health spending remaining about the same, and education spending going up (supported by HIPC funding – see Chapter 6). Social security spending is at about 11 per cent of government spending, and very regressive, while targeted poverty programmes take up about 3 per cent of the government budget.[20] As in China, the regional disparities brought about by a liberalized economy have been of concern to the government, and there is explicit recognition of the deprivation of, and substantial support for, ethnic minority groups through the Commission for Ethnic Minorities and Mountain Areas.

Social expenditure in Thailand is substantial as a proportion of total government spending, though this does not amount to a comprehensive system of social policy (Kwon, 2004: 19),[21] and has had less of an explicit developmental objective than some other Asian experiences. While family and community responsibility form a key part of traditions of welfare provisions, the government's role in social services started to expand during the 1970s, with emphasis on equitable access to education and health, and continued to receive priority through the crises of the early 1980s and 1997 (Tangcharoensathien et al., 2005: 258–9). Thailand has a universal health insurance system, which developed from restrictive insurance provisions for civil servants and formal sector employees, achieving universal coverage in 2002 following the East Asia crisis and the electoral success of the Thai Rak Thai Party which had universal coverage as a commitment to its voters (ibid: 259–77).

This section supports the conclusion of recent UNRISD and other research that East Asia has been far from a social-policy-free zone. If there is an East Asia model, its key characteristic would be its developmental nature, shaped to enable the entire population to participate in economic growth and mainstream development. This implies strong directions around the role of social policy vis-à-vis both economic growth and nation building – though this happened in very different ways across the region (illustrated by size of the state relative to GDP, or the differences in the extent to which specific welfare provisions had a developmental focus). Secondly, a number of the countries show the importance of – largely external – shocks for fairly drastic changes in these directions, including towards more inclusive policies, and thereby new ways of articulating links between economic and social policies. The experiences are in stark contrast with Latin America's, particularly the countries that developed relatively mature welfare provisions early on.

4.3   Latin America: corporatism to neo-liberalism

There is a much older tradition of social policy analysis in Latin America than in East Asia, and much attention has been paid to how the period of structural adjustment led to a much more neo-liberal policy regime. This section looks at how this overall trend manifested itself in a number of countries. It stresses that the move to neo-liberalism happened from an often exclusive or corporatist regime. Through crises new ('Third Way') regimes emerged, notably in Chile and Brazil, with possibly significant impacts on the very high levels of inequality.

In terms of the importance of the state and its social spending, Latin America seems to show less variation than East Asia and Africa. Argentina and Mexico's state size is close to the average of middle income countries. Social spending is substantial, in terms of proportion of GDP as well as of total government spending. Government spending in Argentina showed a substantial relative increase during the 1990s, probably partly due to the slow growth performance. According to Taylor (2001) Argentina did not cut back in social spending during liberalization. By comparison, and relative to national income, Bolivia's and Peru's state is fairly large, though shrinking a little in Peru. Bolivia spends relatively large amounts on health and education, while Peru's social spending is relatively low. Chile's aggregate and social spending expanded significantly until 1973, and has since been actively cut back.

Latin American social policies have been characterized as state corporatist, in which pressure group bargaining rather than the rights of citizens have dominated the policy-making process.[22] But there is significant diversity across the region: in South America, in the early twentieth century social security provisions were introduced around Bismarckian principles, covering specific groups, while in other parts of the region universalist-type systems were introduced, influenced by approaches like Beveridge's (Bertranou and Durán, 2005). Barrientos (2004) emphasizes that different features of Latin American countries' social policy follow different principles of 'welfare regime', as described next.

First, the aspiration of public universal provision of health and education reflects features of a social democratic welfare regime. While in principle labour, education, health and other social policies were universalist, in practice universalism – for example, in Chile, Argentina and Uruguay – was 'stratified universalism', and groups that were able to voice demands were able to have benefits extended (Palma and Urzúa, 2005: 11–12; Barrientos, 2004).

Second, low coverage of state welfare provision reflects liberal residualism. There is a general recognition that the coverage of social policies is not only low, but also often declining. Lloyd-Sherlock (2000) describes the failure of social spending in Latin America to reach the poor and vulnerable, due to uneven regional distribution, passive, fragmented and clientelist providers, and social and cultural barriers.

Third, social insurance and employment protection reflects a conservative (or corporatist) welfare regime. Like elsewhere, most workers have been excluded from access to these provisions, and from labour market protection.[23] 'Instead of developing towards universal coverage, social insurance and employment protection reinforced the segmentation in the welfare mix by excluding more vulnerable groups of workers' (Barrientos, 2005: 160) which, in combination with economic instability, crisis of the import substitution model and the related political changes paved the way for a welfare regime shift towards a (more predominantly) neo-liberal model.

Most of the features have undergone significant changes since the early 1970s, and existing welfare provisions were unable to cope with fiscal crises (Mesa-Lago, 1997). Chile played 'a paradigmatic role in Latin America's welfare regime shift' (Barrientos, 2004: 161), as its restructuring of economic and social policies happened earlier and deeper than elsewhere.[24] Changes implied increasing reliance on individuals and households for provision of welfare, targeting of safety nets, reduced labour market protection, decentralization and introduction of competition and private markets in the provision of services.

Welfare reforms in Argentina too moved from corporatist/conservative to more liberal, but were more complex than in Chile, and happened under a more open political regime. Social policy provisions expanded particularly during the Peronist period of the 1950s and 1960s, with considerable power of trade unions. Structural adjustment from 1989 onwards implied reduction of employment protection, and reforms of pension and health insurance in the mid 1990s – but with much more resistance than in Chile. Social security spending has been largely tied to the labour market. Poverty programmes have been limited, with the workfare programme TRABAJAR a fairly recent innovation. Social spending (including its financing) has been found to be progressive and has not changed over time (Gasparini, 2004: 22).

Pension reforms have been a marker of the move towards a liberal social policy regime. The World Bank – that has provided significant lending to pensions reform over recent decades – proposed a multi-pillar system, with a publicly managed unfunded plan, a mandatory privately funded plan and a voluntary privately funded plan (World Bank, 1994), and recently acknowledged that operations paid little attention to social assistance for the aged poor (Gill et al., 2005; Holzmann and Hinz, 2005). Chile introduced individual retirement plans in the early 1980s: the coverage of pensions increased while individual benefits declined, while the transfer between systems generated huge demand for additional subsidy. Bolivia was one of the countries that tried to emulate the Chilean model of pension reforms, but with unique features, including its direct link to the privatization (capitalization) of state-owned enterprises. While opposition to the plans was defused fairly quickly, the plan was unsuccessful because of financial constraints and political instability (Barrientos, 2005: 164–6). Across the region, according to Matijascic and Kay (2006), the move towards individual accounts is now being examined, problems of efficiency, financing and equity being recognized, and a wider range of options explored.

A privatization trend can be discerned elsewhere too (Barrientos, 2005). Peru implemented labour market reforms in the 1980s, and the informal sector expanded rapidly. Peru and Mexico now have significant numbers of individual retirement plans, and in both countries, social insurance coverage decreased rapidly in the two decades after 1980.[25] In Peru and Mexico, reforms in the late 1990s provided conditions for the expansion of private health insurance providers. Evaluation in Peru suggests that programmes to enhance access to health through public insurance during the 1990s have not reduced inequalities;[26] however the (real) increase in public expenditure during the 1990s may have contributed to a reduction in disparities in health (*WDR 2006*: 34). The World Bank sponsored social funds have obtained good reviews but impact upon overall levels of inequality is unclear.

Fairly recently, racial and ethnic differences have become a central part of public policies, as well as electoral politics, as highlighted by Bolivia. Affirmative action does not have a long history in Latin America, but recent political events signal the articulation of a new element of its social policies. Forms of affirmative action can be found in Colombia, Chile and Brazil, in the areas of education, integrated local development, access to land and capital markets, labour markets, and access to justice – but experience with these policies is still very limited (Buvinic and Mazza, 2005). In Brazil, severe racial inequalities, including those relating to 80 million Afro-descendants, were not officially recognized until fairly recently – a long time after independence and the abolition of slavery, and after a period in which Brazilians were made to believe there were no black or white Brazilians. But a few years back a high-level secretariat was created, which has a mandate to prepare all forms of public administration for racial equality – without programmes for economic empowerment, as in South Africa.[27]

A key question with respect to Latin America is whether we are witnessing the emergence of a new model of principles of solidarity. On the one hand, there was a common move towards liberal principles. But there have also been signs of a newly emerging social contract, manifested clearly in the case of Chile where outward economic policies are combined with increasing access to opportunities for all and specific programmes for the most marginalized, but also in the high-inequality countries such as Brazil with the expansion of new forms of social protection and affirmative action.

4.4   The poorest countries: residualism predominates?

Despite an enormous socio-political diversity across Africa and South Asia, the broad recent history of post-colonial development provides an important starting point for a discussion of social policy regimes.[28] The countries, by and large (and with the exception of South Africa), have much in common regarding a recent elite-driven attempt at nation building and explicit attempts at simultaneous economic modernization and providing redistributive justice, trying to forge a new social contract. States have taken a predominant role in changing the country's development, and this of course was challenged with the onset of structural adjustment. Social policies – often aimed at addressing historical injustices – have had a strong focus on redistribution rather than productive investment, and a key task in this section is to explore the centrality of a residual approach to social policy.

Three main factors that set these countries apart are important for the discussion here. In the first place, the large differences in levels of inequality. On the one hand, the settler economies of southern Africa show very high levels of income inequality, while, as already discussed, levels of inequality in South Asia are much lower (Ghana, which was not a settler economy, provides an intermediate case). Particularly in South Africa, social policy trends since the end of Apartheid are a direct response to inequalities, particularly the main racial divide.

Second, the size of the state or public expenditure shows large variety too, with little change during the 1990s. Unequal economies of southern Africa have large states, while those of India and, particularly, Bangladesh (but not Pakistan) are much smaller. Public spending on health and education is very low in Bangladesh, though increasing rapidly during the 1990s (Davis, 2004: 272), and in Pakistan. Spending in India was significant, increased during recent years particularly in education, and was protected during the period of adjustment (see Box 4.1). South Africa clearly suggests that state intervention historically has been related to elite

---

Box 4.1 Social spending in India

It is commonly asserted that social-sector spending in India declined during the period of liberalization. But while there is anecdotal evidence that policy makers' interest did move away from traditional social concerns, patterns of funding experienced remarkably little change. In the Indian context, it is important that there has been a continuous and very open public debate about changes in poverty, and the findings that poverty was increasing in the early 1990s in response to the crisis and adjustment probably increased spending for anti-poverty purposes (Dutt and Rao, 2001, even though according to these authors (p. 214) its political leaders neglected important opportunities to reduce inequality and improve the living standards of the poor, and failed 'to cultivate the complementarity between economic growth and social opportunity'). Research suggests that there may have been some decline in overall government spending, but not in social sectors.

The relevance of these trends is highlighted in the case of Orissa, which during the 1990s gradually became the state with the highest poverty incidence, and increasing state budget deficits. During the 9th Plan period, state social sector spending was well protected, with a high share of education and rural development falling behind. The increases in spending in Orissa were faster than elsewhere, with an

(continued)

Box 4.1 (continued)

increasing share of central government contributions, and to a large extent following hikes in civil service wages following the Fifth Pay Commission. Social sector spending was often higher than allocations, which is not unremarkable given regular reports of under-utilization of funds.

What these trends imply remains a matter of debate. On the one hand, increased social spending seems desirable given Orissa's high poverty rates. But at least three trends need to be taken into consideration. First, as elsewhere globally, increased social spending seems to have been accompanied by declines in equally important spending in rural development. Second, the increased share of social spending happens in the context of increased dependency on central (and possibly international) funding. And third, an increasing part of spending is recurrent as opposed to developmental expenditure, and teachers' salaries may be one of the main reasons for the rising shares of education, leaving little for new investment.

Sources: Shariff et al. (2001), Dev and Mooij (2002), World Bank South Asia Region (2003), de Haan (2004c), Joshi (2006).

---

capture. In Kenya public spending on education is particularly high, and public spending in Malawi and Zimbabwe are high too.

Third, the impact of structural adjustment has been significant in Ghana, Kenya and Malawi, but less so in South Africa and India. Ghana seems to have followed the path of adjustment promoted by international institutions. It reduced the size of the public sector during the early 1980s (Herbst, 1994),[29] but spending in health and education have remained substantial. Its leadership did use donor resources to build up political alliances, and with relatively good results in economic and social development. Rather than implying a particular trend in social sector spending, the most important impact of structural adjustment may well have been that it has fragmented social policy formulation and implementation, which we return to below.

Spending figures by themselves tell us little about social policy, and probably very little about poverty and human development outcomes (which are poor in interventionist states such as Zimbabwe and Pakistan) – they serve mainly as an indication of the enormous variety across the South, and a justification or urge for further investigation of the determinants of public policy in the South. The literature on social policy in the world's poorest countries is very limited, and contributions in Gough and Wood (2004) by and large deny the usefulness of using a social policy concept.[30] The contention here is that at least in a number of countries a social policy concept that focuses on principles of solidarity and its relation to economic policy can be helpful – however, the fragmentation of social policy has in many cases severely hampered the articulation of such principles.

Fragmentation of social policy formulation

Social policy formulation, particularly in Africa, has been fragmented. A group of experts that discussed the 'integration of social and economic policies' in 2001 noted that the narrow policy focus of the 1980s still existed, and highlighted an imbalance in power between finance and social ministries (De Haan, Huber and van den Heever, 2001).[31] The international community has played a key role in this, including through the strengthening of finance ministries and not social sector ministries, donors' sectoral approaches, and the unpredictability and short-term nature of aid flows.

In the case of Ghana, Aryeetey and Goldstein (2000) highlight the lack of articulated social policy. While explicit policy during the 1960s and 1970s focused on rural development and higher education, state capacity soon started to weaken, while donor influence increased. Rapid changes in government social sector spending arguably are a sign of fragmentation: while Ghana followed a path of fiscal compression early on, with state expenditure plummeting from 25 per cent of GDP in 1976 to 8 per cent in 1983 (Herbst, 1994), the social sector share of government spending increased during 1960–5, then fell, rose to 46 per cent in 1975, fell to 33 per cent in 1981, rose during the 1980s, and fell again to about 35 per cent in 1996 (Aryeetey and Goldstein, 2000: 295–301). Even in post reform Ghana expenditure patterns are driven largely by revenue flows and political expediency, and do not appear to reflect clear commitments to policies and expected outcomes (Aryeetey and McKay, 2005).[32]

Such fluctuations and lack of coordination are compounded by a disconnect with democratic processes – a problem reinforced in some cases by PRSP practices, as we discuss below. In Bangladesh, as described by Davis (2004: 269), welfare funding decisions are largely made outside the domestic political system. This in turn reduces the feedback mechanisms that followed from the political dynamic of group interests, social stratification and political mobilization described by Esping-Andersen. While such a disconnect may make budget execution more effective (that is, less contested), and as such potentially encouraged by donors, it does not promote the development of a sustained social contract, but remains caught in a charitable state–citizen relationship.

A predominant role of NGOs may reinforce fragmentation – but not necessarily, as for example North American social policy models include sustained civil society contributions to core welfare provisions. In the South, and particularly in the delivery of public provisions in the poorest countries with weak state capacity, NGOs have played a key role. They have not, however, replaced the state, for example, even in Bangladesh, where NGOs are unusually strong and 'home-grown' funding to NGOs formed only 17 per cent of total aid (Davis, 2004). Moreover, the focus of NGOs, or the principles of solidarity that they support, varies considerably: for example, many NGOs have moved away from more radical objectives like land reform, and focus on developmental objectives, now micro-finance, delivery of universal basic services such as education, rural development, or targeted programmes. This is not to underrate the importance of NGOs and civil society, but an argument to incorporate them into a broader public policy analysis. A key question in that context is how they complement government provisions, or operate under government regulation, and whether this adds up to a coherent national social policy, or – particularly in the case of external funding – primarily fuel patronage politics.

Chapter 6 discusses whether the fragmentation of social policy has been addressed, particularly in aid-dependent countries, through PRSPs and sector-wide approaches, and how this has been impacted by renewed 'vertical' initiatives, particularly in health. At this stage, we conclude that there is still substantial evidence that, despite expansion of social sector programmes, what has failed is the integration of these into a coordinated, well-articulated social policy. That context-specific social policy analysis should include a focus on the reasons for such a gap, and how this influences public policy implementation and its impacts.

Dualism and the post-colonial project

With roots in the late-colonial period, and shaped during the post-colonial period of inward-oriented economic development, social policies in many countries in South Asia and Africa obtained a strongly dualistic nature. Dualism has manifested itself along a number of axes. A first form, created under colonial rule, was between urban and rural areas.[33] In Malawi and Zambia, among others, there was a strong urban bias, for example towards higher-level, urban-based curative facilities in their health sector expenditure patterns (Tanzania avoided such a strong urban bias, see below).

Within the agricultural sector, a strong dualism manifested itself through the support to modern, often export-oriented large enterprises. For example,

Malawi's support focused on coffee and estate agriculture (disrupted by the economic shock of 1979) – even though maize production did receive support too.[34] The 2001 strategic plan for South African agriculture states that '[b]ecause of the legacy of exclusion and discrimination in South African agriculture, the challenge is now to improve participation in all facets of the sector and rid it once and for all of the many entry barriers rooted in its *historical dualism'* (South Africa, Department of Agriculture, 2001).

Within the urban sector, too, a clear dualism was created between what came to be known as the formal and informal sectors. As elsewhere, many welfare provisions became available only to employees in larger enterprises, in the public and private sectors – which in most poor countries never formed more than ten per cent of the working population.[35] Such provisions very quickly became a reason for employers to try to reduce the number of employees, often particularly women (documented for the jute industry in India; de Haan, 1994), and to my knowledge attempts to extend provisions outside the formal sector have remained very much limited. The informal–formal distinction thus is to some extent policy-induced, and there has been limited mobilization for extension of provisions outside the 'citadel of labour', including through trade unions that by and large have restricted their activities to large enterprises.

As in Latin America, the dualism has implications for the politics of reform. Liberalization – and particularly labour market reform – in India has been a fairly slow and well managed process, partly because of resistance within core sectors of nationalized industries and public sector enterprises. The form this has taken is to some extent the result of the way interest groups are structured and fragmented, and advocacy for the interests of people outside the formal sector is much more limited. The case of SEWA as described in Box 4.2 is the proverbial exception proving the rule.

The post-colonial project, with its modernist ideologies and inward-oriented development, has partly reinforced the economic and social dualism that was established under colonialism. Through this, social policies in many countries in South Asia and Africa obtained a strongly dualistic nature (despite, as in India, its rights-based approach to welfare). The advocacy activities of SEWA show the enormous barriers that this implies, practical ones but also the resistance of vested interests. With globalization, and the informalization of the labour force, an increasing number of workers fall outside the modern or organized segment of the labour force, highlighting the increasingly large need for ways of extending social policies.

Box 4.2   Dualism and advocacy: SEWA

SEWA, the Self-Employed Women's Organization, based in Ahmedabad, aims to organize women workers: to achieve full employment, with security of work, income, food, and social security (health care and child care in particular); and for women to become autonomous and self-reliant in their decision-making ability. It sees itself as an organization and a movement of self-employed workers, combining elements of the traditional labour movement, the cooperative movement and the women's movement, and is primarily a movement of self-employed workers, with about 700,000 members and aiming to expand to other states in India.

SEWA is a trade union and was registered as such in 1972. It grew out of Ahmedabad's declining trade unions in the textile sector, but was ousted from the main union in 1981. Its members are part of the unprotected or unorganized labour force (which constitutes 93 per cent of India's labour force; 94 per cent of women workers are in the unorganized sector). In Gandhian tradition, SEWA perceives their activities to be directed against the 'constraints and limitations imposed on them by society and the economy, while development activities strengthen women's bargaining power and offer them new alternatives', including new ones imposed by globalization and labour-displacing technology.

In SEWA's history, advocacy for recognition and extension of provisions that are available to the formal sector has been central. It took until 2005 before it was recognized as a central trade union, after the Delhi High Court overruled objections against the application. It has been a key advocate in debates on the extension of social security, notably in the context of the 2003 draft legislation on universal health insurance, life insurance and pensions.

Sources: www.sewa.org; www.wiego.org/news; and a SEWA/WIEGO/Cornell workshop on 'Membership based organizations of the poor' (http://www.wiego.org/ahmedabad/).

Universalism

As in Latin America, in South Asia and Africa the dualist focus on provisions for the minority of workers in the modern period has been combined with universal provisions in health and education. Most countries nominally have national health care systems and compulsory education, often constitutionally enshrined, though as discussed earlier the very high proportions of private out-of-pocket spending (particularly in health) indicate significant deficiencies.

Donor emphasis on social sectors has been strongly – and with considerable impact – on universal provision of health care and education (the debate around user fees, referred to earlier, highlighted the strength of universal approaches). This has been largely, and increasingly, on provisions at primary levels, which according to some neglects the role of higher education, including as a precondition of a developmental welfare state.[36] Recent 'vertical' donor initiatives, including by now very significant private organizations like the Gates Foundation, as we discuss in Chapter 6, are giving a renewed push to the health sector.

During the 1960s and 1970s, moves from dual to universal systems were significant. After independence, provisions for health and education expanded rapidly, often in explicit response to the stratification created under colonialism. In Zimbabwe free education was provided overnight and over 5500 schools established in six years, and massive infrastructure was put in place to enhance access to clinics. In Zambia, 880,000 new school places were created between 1964 and 1984 and the number of health centres grew by more than 160 per cent by 1988 (Osei-Hwedie and Bar-on, 1999: 93).[37] A similar move towards universalization occurred in South Africa after the end of Apartheid, under much better fiscal conditions than other African countries. Significantly, for an understanding of the evolution of social policies, the dual and racist social policies set up under the old regime provided the basis for extending provisions to the entire population.[38] In most of Africa, this progress ended abruptly with the onset of adjustment, and with the outbreak of HIV/Aids, though some countries have more recently reversed the negative trends of the 1980s.

In India, where social policies have had a strong dualistic character, the recent changes in educational provision have indicated a renewed emphasis on universalization, though with a targeting approach to reach the poorest in remote areas. Despite constitutional provisions for free and compulsory education, progress with extending education to the entire population has remained limited (with significant differences across states). Over the last decade or so, renewed attention has led to increased progress, and donors have provided strategic support to pilots and the national programme. The changes follow significant civil society pressure and a gradual change in elite perception about the desirability of universal education. The national programme Sarva Shikhsa Abhiyan focuses on ensuring that primary education reaches the children of poor families, often in remote rural communities, where community planning and management form key features. Much debate has emerged over the appointment of village teachers, and whether this would create a dual education system; but the aim remains to bring all students into the mainstream system at higher levels of education.[39]

The universalist aspirations of the post-colonial governments have been only very partially achieved, and the case of India indicates that at least in the education sector financial reasons can only partly explain the failure: in India both weak administrative capacity and lack of elite commitment played a role in the limited success in universalizing education. Current attempts have a very clear targeted approach, but arguably this is not in contradiction with, and can be seen as an important part of an overall universalist agenda, or 'targeting within universalism'.[40]

Targeted programmes

Overall, during the last two decades the most important change globally has been towards targeting of social policies, and refinement of that targeting; indeed it can be argued, as the next chapter does, that the poverty analysis that has gained popularity since the 1980s, as well as 'social funds', have played instrumental roles in this. But it is important to emphasize that the principles of targeting are by no means new, and that they fit within particular historical traditions, as much as universalist and insurance principles do.[41]

Both in Asia and Africa long traditions of targeted programmes exist, some pre-colonial. Tanzania by and large avoided the urban bias of other countries in the region, and – continuous with British colonial policy – focused on forced ujamaa villageization, which has been described as a regionally targeted anti-poverty intervention, to provide inputs, education and health to the remote rural poor. In South Asia the histories of targeted intervention – notably of public works – go back even further, and existed under both Mughal and British rule. The approach continued to be dominant in Bangladesh in a variety of food distribution and micro-credit schemes (Davis, 2004), the latter being NGO-driven, which also espouse strong targeting principles.

In India, targeting has been a common element of a wide range of social policies, carried out on the basis of a well-developed system of categorization, of social (Scheduled Caste, Scheduled Tribe, Other Backwards Caste) as well as economic ('Below the Poverty Line') categories, and on the basis of the post-colonial pact with businessmen who realized the need for anti-poverty programmes. Targeted provisions exist in the Public Distribution System, housing subsidies, pensions, and so on. One of the best known examples is the Maharashtra Employment Guarantee Scheme, which provides rural employment on the basis of 'self-targeting', in which the wages provided are low enough so that the better-off do not apply for the scheme. Similar to the public pressure for education, the role of the middle class has been extremely important in the promotion of employment schemes – in the case of Maharashtra this was partly driven by urban elites who accepted higher taxes for programme that would keep the poor in rural areas. The scheme in Maharashtra has been the example for the recent advocacy for national employment guarantee schemes in India's poorest districts, following the dramatic political reversal of the national elections of 2004.

Food distribution or subsidies have played a very important role in many countries, particularly where food security was a major concern, and because of many donors' preference for food aid (Smith and Subbarao, 2003). Food aid played a big role in the 1974 famine in Bangladesh, and while the amount of foreign aid has gradually declined food aid complemented by government resources has been used for a range of fairly successful targeted relief programmes. In India self-reliance played an important role in the development of the food distribution scheme, and both workfare and nutrition programmes have been key parts of the residual social policy approach. In the early 1990s the food distribution scheme moved from a universal to a targeted scheme. It is often assumed this was under pressure from international organizations, but the politics were complex: in any case the move towards a targeted scheme has not affected the interests of farmers as suppliers, while access to, and corruption in, delivery are central to local politics and advocacy efforts.

We return to the recent innovations in social protection instruments and the debate on targeting versus universalism in Chapter 5. The key message here is that targeting has played a key role in the history of the post-colonial project, with good economic arguments, but also because of political coalitions.

Affirmative action

Finally, though it has received little attention in the literature, the way ethnic and racial identities have been incorporated into post-colonial social policy frameworks has been central to the development of nation states, as well as the articulation of the interests of minorities or deprived groups.[42] In Latin America racial inequalities have only recently come onto the agenda. In South Africa, apartheid enshrined and codified racial differences and categories into the public policy framework. After the end of apartheid these became the subject of various forms of affirmative action, often with a productivist orientation. In Rwanda affirmative action became part of the politics leading up to the extremely violent inter-ethnic strife (Mamdani, 2001). In Nigeria 470 ethnic groups, and the long-standing inequalities between south and north, form the heart of the Federal Character Principle, the constitutional provisions for power sharing and protection of disadvantaged groups (Ibrahim, 2006). Zimbabwe's social policies of the 1990s (during growing inequality and lacking financial capacity) need to be understood in context of the 1980s which tried to reduce racial gaps in living standards, focusing on transfer of income rather than wealth.

The two prime examples in the Asian context are Malaysia, which was discussed earlier, and India (a more recent example is Nepal, documented by Bennett (2005) and Brown and Stewart (2006)). Indian public policies vis-à-vis 'historically marginalized groups' have the clearest articulation within the South Asian context. These policies too emerged out of acute political need, with the differences between Gandhi and Dr Ambedkar playing a key role in nation building in the late colonial period. While in Sri Lanka special electorates became the mode of insertion of deprived groups, in India – and against the will of Dr Ambedkar – reservation of political seats did. After Independence, a wide range of affirmative actions – reservation, promotion and protection – were put in place, initially with a short time-frame, but they continued to be part of public policy, and recently – in India's version of a new social contract – with strong advocacy efforts extended to the private sector.

4.5   Conclusion: global convergence or social policy regimes?

This chapter has explored whether a notion of social policy regime is useful for understanding public policy-making in the South. The answer is a qualified yes, with a large research agenda and more work needed to assess such regimes, including in terms of public finance. The notion emphasizes the very different institutional ways in which social policies across the North have been articulated, differences in principles of solidarity, and how these evolve in context-specific ways. Further, in the North as much as the South – despite a general trend away from universalism since the early 1980s – each country combines different forms of social policies: of universalism, occupation-based and exclusive insurance, targeting, and affirmative action. Cutting across most of these is the question of the role and importance of the state, and the way in which social policies are formulated, emphasizing welfarist or productivist objectives.

The agenda for understanding social policies in specific countries thus implies charting the different forms of solidarity, and how these combine to provide welfare for the entire population; globalization has altered but not eliminated these complexities.

Social policy-making is not a technocratic exercise, but is shaped by national traditions and the political economy of interest struggles. Understanding national traditions and politics – including the way southern trajectories have been influenced by northern patterns, through colonial links – is essential for analysing the impacts of globalization on approaches to policy-making. As with respect to labour market policies, the period of adjustment, while generally blamed for the creation of the safety net approach, has tended to reinforce more deeply rooted dualistic social policies. Choices for public–private (NGO and for-profit) mix, and processes of privatization, need to be understood in the context of interaction between national traditions and global forces. National politics have also given rise to very new social policies, in the area of cash transfers as well as affirmative action. Thus, a supposed general trend towards residual social policies does not exist, and – as Polanyi described for Europe in the nineteenth century – neo-liberal trends continue to be contested by social forces, which increasingly operate on a global scale.

The articulation of principles of solidarity through social policy is the outcome of political contestation, heavily influenced by power relations but also histories of perceived and real disadvantages. Economic structures, particularly of labour markets, play a key role in structuring interest groups, in turn determining the dynamics of, support for or resistance to social policy reforms. These dynamics are context-specific, much more so than the more defeatist analyses of globalization have predicted. However, and particularly in aid-dependent countries, donors play a key but insufficiently recognized role in the politics that drive the articulation of social policy. This question is explored further in the next two chapters, which focus on the residual poverty paradigm and recent modalities that stress national ownership and comprehensive policy formulation.

5
Structural Adjustment, Poverty Analysis and the Safety Nets Paradigm

The period after the Second World War and the end of colonialism was one of great optimism, of reconstruction in Europe, possibilities for economic independence and realization of political independence in the South, together with pro-active social policies, the rise of the welfare state in Europe and socialist policies or mixed-economy models in many post-colonial countries. The economic downturn of the 1960s and 1970s changed dominant attitudes towards state intervention and social policies, shifting the emphasis to market functioning and structural adjustment, while goals of redistribution and the instruments of an interventionist state lost popularity. Since the 1990s, following the emphasis on the 'human face of adjustment', and international civil society pressure on the international financial institutions, reducing poverty has become accepted as the central goal of international development efforts.

This chapter asks the question of whether recent trends have fundamentally altered the dominant approach to social policies, or whether this has remained 'residual'.[1] While views on the role of social policy differ between the need to correct market malfunctions and an emphasis on proactive interventions, many authors, particularly from the South, have emphasized that the period of adjustment has been characterized by a marginalization of social policy. A key question here is whether or to what extent the recent emphasis on poverty has changed this.

This chapter elaborates this theme in three sections, with a concluding section discussing whether recent changes have amended the residual approach of the period of adjustment. It starts with an exploration of the analyses that have formed the intellectual basis for approaches to social policy-making. Dominant approaches to poverty analysis, with a focus on 'outcomes', have reinforced a residual safety net approach. There is a need for analyses more strongly grounded in national politics, and paying more attention to the social and political processes responsible for deprivation. Social funds, discussed in the second section, are a prime example of a residual approach to social policy. With the rise of structural adjustment policies and the need to provide these with a 'human face', development banks have experimented with instruments to ameliorate the worst effects of crises and adjustment. Social funds have had successes and failures, but have not focused on strengthening mainstream policy-making. The third section discusses relatively new approaches to social protection and cash transfers, compares this to more traditional ideas of social security, and explores the importance of targeting versus universalism. Recent changes in the social protection debate emphasize risk management, as a cross-sectoral approach, but its practices appear to remain of a residual nature, with insufficient attention to strengthening mainstream policies.

5.1 Poverty analysis in the international development debate

With the increasing focus on poverty as overarching objective, and dating back to the 'social dimensions' focus of the World Bank, analysis of poverty has received a big push. This section reviews the history of the poverty analysis over the last two decades, and asks the question of how this has influenced policy dialogues, and in particular the conceptualization of social policy.[2] The main argument is twofold: first, measurement of poverty (and human development) has often been driven by donor rather than nationally-grown concerns, and the type of poverty analysis has tended to reinforce a residual approach to social policy.

International poverty analysis: a short genealogy

The origin of much quantitative poverty analysis, particularly in Africa, can be traced to the late 1970s/early 1980s. The *Social Dimensions of Adjustment* and the *Living Standards Measurement Studies* (LSMS) were developed to monitor progress in living standards and the consequences of government policies, and were developed first in Côte d'Ivoire, Ghana and Mauritania. They included various dimensions of household well-being, including demographic, expenditure, health and education information – though most of the attention has gone to the analysis of income and expenditure – and aimed to improve communications between survey statisticians, analysts and policy-makers.[3]

LSMS and related initiatives rapidly increased the coverage of poverty mapping: in 1980 about 10 per cent of the population in Sub-Saharan

Africa had been covered by a representative household survey; in 1993 this had increased to two-thirds of the population (Ravallion and Chen, 1997). The 1997 SPA Poverty Status Report pointed out that, since the mid 1980s, 72 national surveys of different types had been carried out in 35 African countries. The expansion has continued since, including since the start of the PRSP initiative.

But data on trends in Africa are still limited, and many of the surveys have remained one-off. Even in 2001, at the height of the PRSP debates, much poverty data on Africa was out of date (OPM 2001). Part of the reason why regular monitoring has been developed in so few countries is the technical difficulty and cost of such surveys: despite the simplicity of the results from such surveys – the number of people living in poverty – they are difficult to implement, need to be carried out over a whole year to account for seasonality, and typically take two years to complete.[4] But the lack of trend data and regular monitoring also suggests that the poverty analysis was only to a limited extent embedded in national policy-making or advocacy, as will be discussed more extensively later.

During the 1990s, quantitative poverty data collection, such as LSMS, came under criticism, for various reasons. As already mentioned, it often takes two years for the results of surveys to be available and therefore is less useful as an instrument to measure trends and impacts of policies. LSMS surveys were criticized for their strong emphasis on income or consumption poverty (the much-discussed 'money-metric' approach to poverty), neglecting the multi-dimensional nature of poverty, assets and poor people's own perceptions. With the World Development Report 2000/2001 the focus on income poverty seemed to be a thing of the past – though early reviews of poverty analysis in PRSPs suggested that income poverty remained a predominant feature. A third point of critique of LSMS-type surveys relates to quality: it has been asserted that data collection was done poorly, and that it was relatively costly.[5] Finally, there is a commonly voiced concern about the impact of these surveys, whether, for example, PRSPs reflect existing poverty analyses.

In the early 1990s, participatory approaches to poverty analysis became increasingly popular in the international debate.[6] Participatory Poverty Analyses (PPA) use a variety of methods – but generally not the fully structured interviews used in surveys. A core element is wealth (or well-being) ranking: group discussions decide about the central characteristics of poor and non-poor households, and subsequently each household is ranked in one of the wealth rank groups. They aim to describe the complexity and multi-dimensionality of deprivation, in the way this is perceived by poor people. They identify aspects of vulnerability that traditional poverty assessments do not always cover (for example, violence, powerlessness), and aim to identify processes that cause poverty, including constraints on access to services and economic opportunities. They aim to analyse the capacities of the poor, their initiatives and institutions that contribute to solving their problems. Finally, participatory assessments are meant to be not merely a research technique, but also an attempt to share the knowledge with the people involved, and make the research part of an empowerment process.

But as with quantitative poverty analysis, there are concerns about whether PPAs and similar instruments do influence policy-making. 'Second-generation' PPAs (Norton et al., 2001) – in Vietnam, Uganda and Mongolia for example – emphasized the institutionalization of the methodology and strengthening the positioning of the monitoring exercise vis-à-vis policy making. The question of whether and how participatory research influences policy was addressed by Anand et al. (2000) as part of the research *Voices of the Poor*, which found, for example, that in Vietnam it fitted in with on-going national policy discussions, and in Brazil and Bulgaria impact was achieved through close linkage to core policy-makers and proactive NGOs. Different modes of participation in macro-policy were explored as inputs to the newly emerging PRSPs (Shah and Youssef, 2002). However, over time the interest in participatory exercises seems to have waned to some extent, and there are few examples of PPAs becoming institutionalized as part of regular monitoring of well-being or poverty.[7]

Since the debate on the advantages and disadvantages of quantitative versus qualitative methods flared up in the 1990s, discussions have focused on the complementarity of different approaches – particularly household surveys and PPAs. It is now asserted that the methods are not substitutes,[8] and that there are various ways in which they can complement each other: PPAs can be used to interpret, confirm or refute quantitative data, and can help to inform the design of surveys, for example in the definition of key categories of the household. While this debate has been very influential in moving beyond the polarities of earlier debates, by and large they have remained driven by donor concerns. There is so far little evidence that the concerns have had a sustained impact on the monitoring of well-being in the South, and the debate has remained separated from wider social science debates.

There have been similarly important initiatives for measuring human development indicators. Measuring health and education progress has been supported through a range of initiatives, including Demographic and Health Surveys (DHS) and education surveys. Within the DAC/OECD context, PARIS21, the Partnership in Statistics for Development in the Twenty-First Century is to date the largest initiative in this area, aiming to promote a culture of evidence based policy-making linking statisticians and their work more closely to policy-making, and assisting countries to build up or strengthen national systems for monitoring MDG indicators (www.paris21.org). It seems of relevance for the discussion of cross-sectoral policy-making that much of the technical debate discussed in this section has focused on poverty analysis, and the measurement of human development indicators is not usually incorporated into this. Also, as income poverty monitoring, initiatives like DHS are strongly driven by donor monitoring needs rather than a concern for institutionalizing monitoring at national level.

Poverty analysis and social policy

In the context of the debate on social policy, two questions related to poverty analysis are crucial: have the analyses influenced policy-making, and does the predominant type of analysis make it possible to take social policy out of its residual corner? First, arguably, quantitative poverty surveys have served more to influence donor policy-making, and less has been achieved in terms of creating sustainable national capacity to undertake such surveys. Attempts to compare the numbers of poor people across countries (with an internationally comparable poverty line of $1 per day) illustrates an important issue: this is a useful instrument for donors to decide about allocation between countries, and has helped cross-country regressions showing links between economic growth, inequality and poverty, for example – but this international poverty line does little to inform national-level policy-making. Except for a few important and well-described cases, there is little evidence that the investment in poverty analysis – quantitative or participatory – has paid off in terms of changing development policies. No doubt we know much more about the extent, characteristics and perceptions of poverty in most countries than we did twenty years ago, but much remains to be done to link this to policy-making.

The status of poverty analyses and the potential to influence policy processes were elevated within PRSP approaches.[9] The first PRSP in Uganda (the Ugandan Poverty Eradication Action Plan) drew heavily on survey and participatory poverty assessments, addressed the task of strengthening the livelihoods of the rural poor and emphasized the significance of enhancing citizen participation, strengthening governance and dealing with livelihood and human insecurity. The poverty analysis had a strong link to the policy process and identification of priorities. But this appears an exception rather than the rule.[10] Poverty analysis in the first Tanzania PRSP, for example, was weak, limited by the non-availability of recent poverty data.[11]

Reviews of the impact of poverty analysis on PRSPs highlighted a range of problems.[12] While data and analysis produced outside the international community sphere were often ignored, conclusions from poverty analyses often were not included in the discussions on policy, and policy priorities often not derived from the analysis.[13] The experience – in poverty analysis as well as the broader PRSP process – thus pointed to tensions to create national ownership. The emphasis in many countries remained income poverty. Other dimensions of deprivation, including gender (UNIFEM 2001), ethnicity, assets, vulnerability, inequality, rights, environment – and even education and nutrition (OPM 2001) – were considered secondary. Analysis often remained descriptive, with few attempts to identify and explain the causes of poverty: they suffered from a 'missing middle' (Booth and Lucas, 2001). Most important here, poverty analysis was often badly linked to identification of policy priorities, at levels of macroeconomic, sectoral or targeted policies (OPM, 2001).

Participatory poverty assessments did no better in influencing policy-making. It was noted that it was difficult to influence even World Bank Country Assistance Strategies, which has been attributed to difficulties in assessing quality and extent of participation, lack of time and funding, and doubts about the credibility of the evidence (Robb, 1999). Creating 'ownership' by national policy-makers (as well as in-country research capacity) remained as much of a challenge as for the quantitative analysis. Review of PRSP documentation showed weak links between participatory methods and government policy-making. My own experience in Orissa indicated that the promotion of participatory methods did not square with a strong (national) tradition of quantitative poverty analysis. More recently, the interest in PPAs seems to have dwindled, confirming the limited embeddedness as highlighted earlier.

The form of poverty analysis that has been promoted, focusing on identification and categorization of the poor, has formed a very important underpinning of targeted poverty approaches. Alternative approaches to poverty analysis have found very limited entry into the debate. Not only is much of the dominant poverty analysis weak in identifying policy actions, but also in terms of 'understanding', in the sociological sense, the processes which lead to deprivation, through the conscious actions of actors, the values and norms that inform these, and how these actions are embedded in societal structures. Analysis of 'discrimination' illustra'
the point: discrimination tends to be seen as the unexplained v?

once human capital and other variables have been explored. Valuable as it is in itself, such an analysis, as Milkman and Townsley have pointed out with respect to gender analysis, 'fails to capture the depth with which gender segregation and the norms associated with it are embedded in the economic order'.[14]

Thus reviews of existing poverty analysis supported by donors suggest weak links between poverty analysis and policy priority setting, due to both a lack of identification of causal policy–poverty links, and to the practice of analysis being weakly embedded in national policy-making or advocacy structures. The fact that in many countries surveys were planned as one-offs highlights questions beyond the technical difficulties. Absence of systems that regularly monitor changes of well-being have significant implications for social policy formulation in a broad sense. Alternative approaches promoted by donors have enriched the technical poverty debate, but have not fundamentally changed the way this has been embedded in national policy-making and advocacy. Finally, poverty analysis has played an important role in the targeting of poverty programs, particularly in social funds and social protection instruments, which we discuss next.

5.2   Social funds

This section describes the instrument of social funds and tries to answer the question of whether these fit within 'residual' or more proactive social policy notions.[15] The diversity of funds is large, and this review is necessarily partial, but it will draw out common lessons regarding a poverty targeting approach, and the projectized nature of this form of social policy support.

Throughout the 1990s, social funds became an increasingly popular instrument. The first funds emerged in the late 1980s as emergency measures, to alleviate the impacts of structural adjustment and economic shocks. The Bolivia Emergency Social Fund (ESF) aimed to address the social costs of the adjustment process, particularly the unemployment of miners laid off after the collapse of tin prices and the closing of state-run mines. The Program of Action to Mitigate the Social Cost of Adjustment in Ghana and the Program to Alleviate Poverty and Social Costs of Adjustment in Uganda were set up in a similar vein. In 2000, social funds existed in over 50 countries: in Latin America and the Caribbean, in over 20 countries in Sub-Saharan Africa, several in the Middle East and North Africa (the Egypt Social Fund became the world's largest) and about a dozen in Eastern Europe and Central Asia. Social funds have been less important in Asia, but social fund support was given to the District Poverty Initiative Project in India, and agencies set up in Indonesia that share many operational characteristics with social funds. In Thailand a social fund was created with a focus on establishing a new economy after the 1997 crisis.

The World Bank and the Inter-American Development Bank (IDB) have seen its largest funders. World Bank financing was estimated at about US$ 3.5 billion during 2001–5; with government and other donor co-financing amounting to almost US$ 9 billion. Co-funding from different sources far exceeds World Bank funding in various Latin American countries, where IDB has committed US$ 1.3 billion since 1987, and for example in Egypt.[16] Funds in Chile and Mexico do not receive World Bank funding. Though social funds have remained a small part of the social protection activities in most countries (Jorgensen and van Domelen, 1999), Reddy (1998: 15) probably rightly emphasized that 'the magnitude of resources being devoted to recent social safety nets is sizeable in proportion to social expenditures in a number of countries'. One fund in Latin America, in Nicaragua, spent more than 1 per cent of GDP, though this may be reaching less than 1 per cent of the labour force (Tendler, 2000).

Modes of operation, and related impact

Social funds are extremely diverse, and various 'generations' of funds have evolved. They have been set up in the poorest countries, as well as in former communist countries marked by a crisis of social security systems. They balance multiple objectives under the umbrella of improving the living conditions of the poor: improvement in social and economic infrastructure; creation of employment (often short-term or temporary); community development, specifically to build capacity to demand and manage development resources; improvement of social service delivery; and support for decentralization and municipal strengthening. There is a wide variation in the kinds of activities that they can undertake or facilitate, and a range of different institutions.

Social funds are primarily an *intermediary that channels resources* to small-scale projects for poor and vulnerable groups, rather than a specific instrument for social protection.[17] They appraise, finance and supervise implementation of small social projects but do not implement them. They establish menus, procedures and targeting criteria to support pro-poor investments, and respond to demand from local groups, usually within a set menu of eligible and ineligible projects. Beneficiary co-financing is central, to ensure that projects are responding to demand. Social funds often have operational autonomy, enjoy exemptions from civil service and procurement rules, and staff are often employed on performance contracts, with higher salaries and performance standards.

Social funds are intended to take quick and targeted actions to reach poor and vulnerable groups. They aim to be 'demand-led', and stimulate participatory development initiatives by providing small-scale financing to local NGOs, community groups, small firms and entrepreneurs, and provide pre-investments to promote broad-based participation. They have experimented with a range of community contracting models: project funds managed entirely by communities, communities that identify contractors while resources are channeled from project to contractor, elected committees that work with intermediary organizations which manage the contract, or a combination of these approaches. Devolution of planning and executive responsibility away from capital cities to local levels has been central to social funds, in order to respond to local needs and build administrative capacity at the district and municipal levels. The Chilean fund FOSIS emphasized the integration of local interventions with regional and local government planning.[18] Other social funds, including those which focus on employment creation through labour-intensive public works, tend to work directly with local government.

Over time, the emphasis of social funds has shifted from short-term emergency relief towards more general developmental programmes.[19] In line with an evolving World Bank social protection strategy, social funds moved away from a focus on risk coping towards a more pro-active strategy dealing with risk mitigation and risk reduction, with longer-term objectives (Jorgensen and Van Domelen, 2000).[20] They extended their field of operation from publicly mandated or provided schemes like employment guarantee schemes toward supporting informal coping mechanisms. Social funds have come to pay more attention to popular participation, both to enhance sustainability and to build social capital, and have become a main instrument for facilitating community-driven development (CDD).[21]

Social funds have been praised, including in the OED evaluation (2002), for their rapid disbursement, flexibility and ability to respond to demand from poor communities. But inevitably impact and project quality have varied. Beneficiary-executed projects were found to benefit from broad participation in project definition and to meet the felt needs of the community. Private organizations and NGOs scored less well, usually because of project complexity, and lack of continuity and capacity. Interventions through line ministries tended to lack participatory practices and the resources to supervise interventions and work closely with beneficiaries (Owen and Van Domelen, 1998).[22]

Social fund modalities contain potential conflicts between efficiency goals and the need for time-consuming and costly processes of community ownership and decision-making. There are potential trade-offs between reaching the poor and demand-led approaches, the varying interests involved and the need to enhance the capacities of communities to participate.[23] Only a small proportion of the funds could be categorized as really demand-oriented (Narayan and Ebbe, 1997; Owen and Van Domelen, 1998).[24] Reviews have raised questions regarding the adequacy of the methodology to formulate community needs: for example, it has been observed that communities prioritized micro-enterprise development, yet accepted infrastructure projects because social funds asserted that they did not have the organizational resources for micro-enterprises.

Arguably, the approach tends to underestimate the importance of power relations. There is varied evidence concerning whether women and vulnerable groups and individuals *within communities* are included or supported to formulate projects. Research has emphasized the complex nature of power relations and ways in which external funding influences these: review of the District Poverty Initiatives Project in India, for example, emphasized that in funded community initiatives local governance structures (Panchayats) would cater to the interest of the powerful, and 'common interest groups' are likely to exclude the poorest (Gaiha and Kulkarni, 2006).[25] Next we discuss how poverty analysis has informed social fund approaches.

Poverty analysis in social funds

The nature of poverty analysis is inextricably linked with the nature of policy demands ... Within a residualist paradigm, in which policy intervention is aimed at mitigation, there is no in-built incentive to seek to understand the underlying causal dynamics of poverty; by definition the state of poverty is considered an unfortunate but transitional part of a longer-term process of improving socioeconomic well-being.[26]

Against the perceived need for social funds to transfer resources quickly and efficiently to mitigate effects of economic crisis and adjustment, targeting has obtained a key function in allocating project budgets. The first social fund in Bolivia, for example, was targeted at the 'urban and rural poor, suffering from income loss and unemployment resulting from the economic crisis and with poor health and nutrition' (Glaessner et al., 1994: 39). And thus poverty analyses and the identification of poor communities and people, and the question of success in targeting funds, have predominated, including in evaluations.

Not all social funds adopted a targeting methodology: sometimes objectives such as participation and decentralization have tended to supersede a targeting procedure. In Thailand poverty targeting was subsumed by a concern with restoring self-reliance and cooperation; and later generations of the Colombian *Red de Solidaridad* moved towards a model to strengthen or restore civil society. But in many social funds, commitment to reach the poorest is matched by clear instruments for poverty targeting, and allocation of project funding on the basis of easily identifiable shared characteristics. Targeting mechanisms within social funds, as among other social protection instruments, include: geographical targeting (widespread when poverty data are available, as in Latin America);[27] targeting against eligibility criteria (like poor farmers, homeless children, handicapped, and so on); prioritization of certain sub-projects like primary education or basic health care; and self-targeting through, for example, payment of wages below the market wage.

Success in targeting has been a major element in official reviews of social funds (Rawlings et al., 2004). An early World Bank Portfolio Review concluded that 'social funds have often succeeded in targeting the poor' (1997: viii).[28] The large impact assessment by the World Bank provides a comprehensive overview of targeting results – as well as providing information on impact, sustainability and cost effectiveness. Four of the five funds reached the poorest areas, with targeting being neutral in Zambia. Within districts, the funds had, with the exception of urban Zambia, reached poor households. The poor themselves did articulate demands. Different projects had different records of poverty targeting: education and health were found to be pro-poor, water provisions neutral and sewerage projects did not benefit the poor. Targeting performance had improved over time.[29]

World Bank emphasis has shifted towards dynamic approaches to poverty and 'risk management'. This builds on a dynamic notion of vulnerability, encourages a shift away from remedial crisis-response interventions for coping with risk and towards risk mitigation and reduction, broadening the scope to a more pro-active, pro-development framework. The new risk-management approach emphasized the need to move beyond descriptive poverty targeting to diagnosing the vulnerable and marginalized within broad pools of poor people. However, its influence on social funds has remained unclear. Targeting and the poverty analysis that underpins this have continued to prevail. This reinforces an approach that considers poverty as a residual issue or problem. The poverty analysis focuses on identification of the poor – but does much less in identifying causes of deprivation, relationships of power and processes of exclusion, and how these can be addressed.

Social funds: what role in social policy?

While social funds may be an appropriate mechanism for supporting community activities, it is less clear – and less attention is paid to – how the type of funding modifies existing patterns of participation and of local power relations, including with the private sector. Social fund design has not focused on long-term objectives of organizational and financial capaci-ties. Participation often focuses on the design phase and tends to ignore maintenance and other stages of implementation and monitoring. Moreover, it has been argued that design of funds tends to be insufficiently sensitive to politics, and does not incorporate lessons from wider social policies.

Social funds are usually institutionally and organizationally distinct from government sectoral policies and services.[30] Organizational set-up varies enormously, from autonomous agencies outside regular government bureaucracies to location within a ministry or office of the president, or within the finance ministry but with a substantial degree of independence. Some social funds can deal directly with donors. The central administrative entity, often a semi-autonomous unit set up for the purpose, disburses funds to intermediary organizations, including local government, private firms and NGOs. Many funds set up procedures that aim to overcome the problems of time-consuming, bureaucratic and poorly administered procedures associated with the public sector. They recruit staff at much higher rates than civil service standards, as civil service pay scales are too low to attract the best professionals. They aim to avoid complex disbursement and procurement procedures, and funds are given great control over their budgetary procedures. The funds thus create new structures rather than work to reform existing government institutions, often in reaction to the slowness of public sector reform.[31]

There is evidence of negative effects of social funds on other national and local policy and public sector institutions, though this is not an issue that has received much attention in the literature. Setting up a parallel system, particularly when conditions for fund staff are much better than in mainstream public institutions, may harm morale and efficiency outside the social fund. Establishing funds may displace other sources of funding. It may sidetrack from tackling tough issues regarding accountable government structures: donors may be paying less attention to those than they might, and social funds may deflect the attention of the users of public services. Phasing out or integration of social funds into existing structures does not seem to be a focus at the planning stage. A final question relates to fungibility, whether ministries reduce their allocations to areas that are targeted by social funds.[32]

To reiterate, there is much variety – and evolution – in the ways in which social funds are organized. Social funds have shown much adaptability and development practitioners in countries have used them to raise social and poverty issues. A demand-driven approach and pragmatic ways of combining this with supply-driven elements, so as to ensure inclusion of groups that cannot easily articulate demands have been central. Social funds have shown that they are able to target the poor, and new directions help to take funds away from a narrow understanding of poverty. Neither are the problems described unique to social funds: in a way, they illustrate dilemmas that donors are confronted with in most of their support: disputes over autonomy of funds, staff appointments, alignments with line ministries and the impact of disbursement pressures will be part of any externally funded activity.

Nevertheless, there are a number of issues that may have prevented social funds from strengthening social policy in a broad sense. To strengthen social policy-making, decisions to implement social funds should be based on a consideration of alternatives and of opportunities to reform line ministries to incorporate and implement effective community-based initiatives. Decisions regarding social funds should be part of a budget process, accountable to parliament and civil society, rather than depend on donor decision-making. Social funds should be designed to minimize negative effects on mainstream services, and enhance positive effects on the broader policy agenda, for example through the encouragement of pro-poor government budgeting through links to decentralization or strengthening local governance structures; through enhancing the effects of funds on governance and standards outside the social funds; and through mainstreaming participatory policy-making.

Thus, Cornia's conclusions (1999a) still seem valid: social funds are no panacea, they are small, and should not be seen and implemented as a substitute for national systems of social policy, or for ensuring that macro-economic and other policies take account of the effect on poor and vulnerable people. National ownership varies across funds, but social funds remain essentially a donor instrument. Therefore, the creation of parallel structures and incentives is to some extent inevitable (and is common in national policies too, as in India's primary education and basic health programmes), and social funds illustrate some crucial dilemmas of donor instruments more generally. But in the design of social funds, questions about their role in wider processes of political and administrative change, and of sustainable participation and influence on power relations and exclusion, seem to have been insufficiently considered.

5.3 Social protection and social security

As part of the renewed focus on poverty reduction in the international development debate, a concept of 'social protection' has been promoted, including by the World Bank, regional Development Banks and DFID;[33] and the concept has rapidly found entry into dialogues in and with partner countries. This section discusses the reasons behind this development, different definitions of social protection and how these relate to better-known concepts of social security and insurance, and asks the question whether these notions help to move the social policy debate out of the residual corner of the 1990s 'safety nets'.

The social protection agenda covers a wide range of policies with different elements and categorizations emphasized by different agencies, and with varying origins of the concepts (as discussed below). It contains a number of specific instruments and policies, as well as a framework for ensuring that risks and ways of managing these is ensured across all public policies. Most concepts stress the diversity of agencies responsible for social protection, the state, the private sector and civil society groups. It encompasses both social insurance and social assistance instruments.[34]

Social insurance refers to programme financing by contributions based on an insurance principle, or protection against uncertain risk by pooling resources. As emphasized by the ILO and others, coverage of social insurance is low and needs to extend from a small base in the 'formal sector' to be of relevance for poverty reduction in the South. Provisions tend to have a strong gender bias, as women are underrepresented in the formal sector, and because of a male breadwinner bias in social insurance (Razavi, 2006).[35] Biases exist through membership restrictions and procedures, and inflexible instruments of contributions and benefits. It is generally thought that it is difficult for insurers to cover workers in the informal sector and with low and irregular wages. Similarly, banks face barriers in providing savings and loan services to the poor because of high transaction costs. Health insurance is potentially of benefit, but existing statutory or private schemes are costly, and in general inadequate for major health costs, and as an instrument are thus heavily contested. Crop insurance similarly can play a function by guaranteeing a minimum income, but small farmers may be unable or unwilling to allocate a significant portion of their income to insurance premiums.

Social assistance refers to support to the poorest, forms of public action that transfer resources to groups deemed eligible due to deprivation, and has often been thought to be of little relevance for the poorest countries. It covers non-contributory, tax-financed benefits, in cash or kind. It is generally associated with some form of targeting. Subsidies and exemptions from fees can fulfill similar functions, and some forms of subsidies are used to promote other sectoral objectives, such as school meals to help get poor children into schools. A special and more widely used programme of social assistance – but in return for a contribution from labour – refers to employment programmes, in the form of public works. These can combine objectives of creation of infrastructure and the self-targeted provision of a minimum wage to poor people able to work. The approach has two key advantages: the largely self-targeting nature of employment, and the likelihood of support by elites.

Social protection in the donor literature

Apart from the renewed poverty focus of the 1990s, economic crises in Latin America and East Asia have given renewed attention to, and conceptualization of, safeguarding the interests and livelihoods of the poor and those at risk of falling into poverty. The collapse of communism and transition in Eastern Europe forced international agencies to focus on the negative consequences of reforms on well-being, and particularly the need for reform of or substitutes for the extensive welfare measures under the previous regimes. Debates on globalization gave further impetus to discussions on social protection. The crises of the 1990s were closely related to opening up, particularly of financial markets, and hence urged policy-makers to rethink policy approaches.[36] Questions have been raised about the need for broadening or expanding government intervention in response to risks associated with more open economies.

The ILO's recent thinking on social protection revolves around the observation – in the context of the 'decent work for all' strategy – that more than half of the world's population is excluded from any type of statutory social security protection. Strategies for social protection involve the strengthening of social security and social insurance, promotion of micro-insurance for rural and informal sector workers, and linking statutory social security schemes and micro-insurance schemes.[37] Whereas the World Bank's strategy focuses on a productive approach with a presumed need for justifying social protection instruments, the ILO's approach – which has had far less influence around the world, having lost ground at the time that the World Bank became more influential in this area – departs from a social democratic view, with more emphasis on redistribution, in the context of improving conditions of labour. There is a strong emphasis on universalism, for example in advocacy for provision of basic income security (Standing, 2003), and the 'social floor of the global economy', a term used at the 1995 Social Summit to include entitlements relating to social protection (van Ginneken, 2000).

The Asian and Latin American Development Banks have been proactive in promoting notions of social protection, often with a very broad range. Within the Asian Development Bank, five sets of activities or policies are brought under a social protection banner (Ortiz, 2000): labour market policies designed to facilitate labour adjustments and promote operation of labour markets; social insurance programmes to cushion the risks associated with unemployment, disability, work injury and old age; social assistance and welfare service programmes for those without means of adequate support; agricultural insurance to cushion the risk of crop failures; and community-based social funds and temporary employment generation programmes. The Ford Foundation's interest in the subject resulted in a review of the role of social protection and safety nets in the context of transition from planned economies, and impacts of crises and declines in public service provisions (Cook et al., 2003).

The beginning of recent interest in social protection is often associated with *World Development Report 1990*, which defined 'safety nets' as the third leg of the three-prong strategy of economic growth, human development and safety nets.[38] This has often been characterized as merely a two-and-a-half leg strategy, but this did not hamper the rapid growth of the social protection portfolio within the World Bank. Alongside this growth, there has been a renewal of the conceptualization of what around 1990 was captured under the term safety nets, perceived largely as a residual approach to the negative effects of adjustment. By 2000, the theorization had fundamentally changed towards a 'risk management framework'.

As described earlier, while pension reforms in Chile played a pivotal role in the radical changes in social policies, the 1994 World Bank report *Averting the Old Age Crisis* – and support for pension reforms around the world – was very important in the international debate on social protection. The report argued for a three-pillar system, but non-contributory pensions featured little. They were perceived as a safety net against gaps in the second pillar of pension plans. Commonly voiced concerns included the fiscal pressures they would create, and the risk they would reduce incentives to save and crowd out intergenerational support (James, 1999). Many of these arguments have been heavily contested, notably by HelpAge International (2003, 2004), and the critiques have recently been acknowledged by the World Bank (Gill et al., 2005; Holzmann and Hinz, 2005).

In the words of the people who conceptualized the idea of 'social risk management' (Holzmann and Jorgensen, 2000), while individual social protection programmes do have a role in improving poor people's welfare, a 'holistic' approach would be required to make significant advances in poverty reduction. A social risk management concept asserts that all individuals, households and communities are vulnerable to multiple risks, natural and man-made, from different sources. But poor people face more risks, and have fewer options for effective risk management – and as a result tend to be risk averse. Their mechanisms for self-protection – savings, diversification or risk pooling – tend to be expensive and inefficient, and coping strategies after shocks can lead to reducing 'human capital', for example through taking children out of school. This reasoning forms the basis for the call for public intervention, in the form of specific instruments and through other sectors to improve effects on risk management.[39]

One of the critiques of *World Development Report 2000* was that it entailed little or no discussion of redistribution and emphasized the instrumental rather than intrinsic reasons for redistribution (Maxwell, 2001; White, 2001), and hence the social protection agenda arguably was largely incomplete. *World Development Report 2006* seems to address this, with its focus on equity. However, analysis of social protection is not radically different from earlier work. Its emphasis is on 'equity', focusing on the sphere of opportunities rather than outcomes, including how inequality matters for economic growth. A group of researchers at ODI emphasized that, despite increased attention to social protection (for example, early childhood development programmes), 'these do not constitute more than a slight change of emphasis' (Anderson and O'Neil, 2006: 22), Cling et al. (2006) also note that the policy implications in the report, for example in health, education and infrastructure, do not depart from accepted approaches within the World Bank.

Direct transfers to the poor: new debates on conditionalities and targeting

Partly spurred by debt relief initiatives and commitments to scale up aid, and partly as a reaction to a strong emphasis on adjustment and budget aid, during the last few years increased attention has been paid to direct transfers to poor people. For example, DFID, building on, *inter alia*, the Commission for Africa's recommendations, in a paper in 2005 highlighted that 'social transfers', regular and predictable grants provided to vulnerable households 'may offer an important option to tackle inequality and ensure that the benefits of growth reach those living in chronic poverty' (p. 1).[40]

Most of the recent experience in conditional cash transfers has been gathered in Latin America. This recent history is usually traced back to the start of the programme *Bolsa Escola* in Brasil in the mid-1990s. This started with pioneer activity in the city of Campinas, was later extended to several other localities, and made uniform through legislation in 2001. It is funded at the federal level, though monitoring is left to municipal governments. According to an IADB note for a high-level panel on cash transfer programmes,[41] by 2006 twelve countries in the region had introduced such programmes, with the largest being *Plan Familias* in Argentina, *Bolsa Familia* in Brazil and *Oportunidades* in Mexico.

A large number of recent programmes – such as *Food for Education* in Bangladesh, *Bolsa Escola* in Brazil and *Progresa* in Mexico – are means-tested and/or conditional, with simple rules. The means test typically is defined in terms of a maximum household income level. The conditionality implies a requirement that applicant households have members undertaking a specific action, such as young children to be enrolled and attending school, or – as in Mexico's *Progresa* – pre- and post-natal visits for pregnant women or lactating mothers. Empirical evidence has found positive impacts, particularly on school attendance, though less on income distribution (in the case of *Bolsa Escola* (Bourguignon et al., 2003)).[42]

A key question has been whether these instruments are suitable for the poorest countries, with weakest administrative capacity. Most of the recent experience is not from the poorest countries, though large-scale targeted programmes have long and not unsuccessful histories in South Asia. The case has recently been made that in Sub-Saharan Africa there is much more scope – and of course need – for extending systems of direct transfers. Pilots such as in Zambia to provide cash transfers to the poorest ten per cent have generated some positive interest, targeted but without conditions (Schubert, 2005), and work on financing has made the argument that such systems on a national scale may be affordable (Cichon et al., 2004).

The recent literature on cash transfers, conditional or unconditional, is explicit about the range of implementation challenges (Smith and Subbarao, 2003). This usually includes a need to 'build political support', which arguably does not do sufficient justice to the deeply political nature of such direct transfers to the poor. For example, the recent IADB publication quoted above includes in a 'what next' section to 'solve political and fiscal dilemmas associated with targeting versus universal provisions'.

Indeed many analyses of new instruments are largely silent about their politics, though these were clearly brought out in the June 2006 Mexican elections, for example, the question of political support also brings us back to the old question of universalism versus targeting, which we turn to next.

Targeting and universalism

As discussed in Chapter 4, targeting has played, and continues to play, a central role in the mix of social policies of low-income countries, and as part of the post-colonial social contract, which we illustrated with particular reference to India. While on the one hand, targeting is key to recent social protection programmes around the world, the social policy literature, including that generated by UNRISD, has been extremely critical of principles of targeting, Mkandawire (2005) argues that policy advice has not learnt from the historical experience with targeting, and that more equal societies have tended to lean towards universalism.[43] Four issues in the debate on targeting are important for the discussion here.

First, there is the cost dilemma. On the one hand, targeting is seen, and became increasingly popular during the 1970s and 1980s, as a mechanism for reducing expenditure. On the other hand, it is generally recognized that the cost of targeting can be high: 'leakage' is common, and the administration of targeting expensive. Moreover, the required administrative apparatus may not be available in the poorest countries (where they are most necessary from a financing point of view). Costs and leakage tend to vary greatly according to types of targeting: targeting on income criteria is likely to be very difficult, while self-targeting as in employment schemes, or targeting on the basis of group characteristics (for example, pregnant women) less expensive and less likely to lead to leakage.

A second argument revolves around the impact of targeting on its beneficiaries. Targeted benefits can stigmatize groups of beneficiaries, as they single out a group of people as 'poor' and as 'beneficiaries' rather than 'participants', may lower their self-esteem (for example, Galanter, 1984: 551, with respect to affirmative action in India), and might divide them according to specific programmes. Because benefits are targeted, they provide little incentive for beneficiaries to 'graduate' out of the programme (as they would lose the benefit), a problem that universal benefits would avoid. Again, these issues are very context-specific and to a great extent a question of design. Targeted benefits can be a 'right', as in the Maharashtra Employment Guarantee Scheme, thus achieving a great deal of inclusion in terms of access to state provisions. Targeted schemes can encourage participation and can lead to political mobilization. The incentive issue too has been incorporated into programme design: for example, if wages are provided below market level, and schemes only operate during times when no employment is available, it is unlikely that beneficiaries would become dependent on the scheme.

The third issue is whether targeting of benefits leads to reduced political support. There is a common assertion (for example, in Mkandawire, 2005, quoting Amartya Sen) – though not to my knowledge sufficiently tested, and evidence produced to the contrary – that programmes for the poor tend to be poor programmes. Also, universal programmes would engender political support from the middle classes, unlike targeted programmes, which imply the better-off have to pay for a programme from which they derive no benefits.[44] While this certainly contains some truth, it is definitely possible for targeted programmes to be supported by a progressive middle class, and it may be equally true that support for benefits depends on the assurance that they do reach the 'deserving poor' (particularly if the delivery comes with conditions, such as sending children to school). For example, India's Integrated Child Development Programme and many other primary health, nutrition and school programmes are seldom openly opposed by the powerful. In any case, it is important to retain a notion of political agency in the analysis of social policy, and the historical lessons that much social policy is driven by the (enlightened) self-interest of elites or middle classes.

Finally, Tendler (2004) in particular has argued that targeting tends to contribute to a 'parcelization' and 'projectization' of social policy, including because of the 'partnerships' that these approaches tend to encourage. While it is certainly true that much international support has been of a projectized nature, including the substantial funding for social funds, targeting is not responsible for such projectization. The key question is about where the targeted programmes fit, and as we concluded in Chapter 4, 'targeting within universalism'[45] is likely to continue to play an important and potential progressive role – and thus 'projects within policy' will remain important within broad social policy frameworks.

5.4   Conclusion: Beyond residualism?

The kinds of programmes and projects discussed in terms of social protection, security and transfers are by no means new. What is new is that the thinking on such issues has received priority on the agendas of major international agencies, while it was always a core part of work by the ILO. A second new feature, compared to the 1980s/1990s conceptualization of safety nets, is the emphasis on 'mainstreaming' thinking on social protection, and regarding risk and vulnerability. It acknowledges that all policies have or can have a social protection element, and all policies can be improved by incorporating understanding of the risks to which particular groups are exposed, and the dynamic nature of poverty and well-being.

The key question in this chapter has been whether the renewed emphasis on poverty reduction, and new approaches to social protection in particular, have taken social policy out of its residual corner. New social protection approaches have taken the thinking a long way away from the 1980s safety net paradigm and dominant focus on effects after crises, and social funds have undergone a great deal of evolution. But there are a number of reasons why this move is only a partial one, even if it is accepted that the practices of donor agencies usually are quite a way behind new conceptualization.[46]

The social protection agenda seems to be formulated largely in isolation from other social sectors, particularly health and education and often not seen as a form of productive investment. There is considerable emphasis on inter-linkages between sectors at programme level – such as the beneficial impact of nutrition programmes on education – but much less at the levels of integrated policy formulation, reform and implementation. The move has been towards preparedness for crisis and shocks, but much less in terms of overall social policy planning. This gap is driven by organizational divides within donor agencies, and may be particularly large at the level of donors' budget support to governments, where social sectors – and particularly social security – tend to be seen primarily as consumptive expend-iture, and not as investment in more productive and cohesive societies.

Furthermore, the focus of the social protection discussion has remained on the level of projects and programmes. It is not usually linked to the strengthening of national policy-making, social policy concerns across public policies, or efforts to strengthen national ownership of an agenda around social protection, building on specific priorities and national traditions of social policy.[47] This has been partly the unintended result of focusing on impacts of a wide range of policies on vulnerability and risks, without engaging agencies within and outside government that are responsible for small but often highly relevant public policies. The poverty analysis that lies at the basis of many of those programmes similarly has undergone much evolution, but remains largely restricted to the identification of the poor, to be targeted by specific programmes, with too little attention to analyses of causes of poverty, and the underlying structures and beliefs that keep groups of people deprived.

Finally, the longish lists of instruments suggest that the emphasis in the debate is on the technical aspects of the social protection agenda. There is much less attention to political-economy aspects, the creation of political support for programmes, the need to strengthen 'social contracts' or national policies to promote social integration, and public finance considerations for social protection from such a perspective beyond a dominant focus on affordability and targeting.[48] Analyses and policy advice on social protection have remained largely technical and by and large have failed to incorporate an understanding of the political economy of such policies.

Social policies, including social protection, are central to political contestation, elections and the building up of national unity and social contracts. In turn, programmes can become areas of contestation around extension of rights: non-contributory pension schemes in Brazil and South Africa, now thought to play an important redistributive and anti-poverty role, originated under autocratic rule and included motivations to stem migration to urban areas. Also, and with great potential for supporting participation, anti-poverty schemes can themselves contribute to enhancing voice and empowerment, as has been argued, for example, for the Maharashtra Employment Guarantee Scheme. The interaction of delivery and politics of social policy will be part of the discussion in the next chapter, which highlights the dilemmas regarding donor-driven approaches and national ownership, in PRSP and sectorwide approaches.

6
New Poverty Reduction Strategies and the Missing Middle

Since the period of adjustment, international development practices have evolved rapidly. A new generation of poverty reduction strategies has been developed, and new approaches to public policies, in particular governance. This chapter explores the implications of these recent trends for the formulation and implementation of social policy in the South. The chapter first describes the theoretical approach of the post-Washington consensus, and the progress this entails in terms of broad-based and comprehensive approaches to development and poverty reduction. It discusses the increased attention to institutions in the reform debates, and reviews critiques of recent approaches. This section includes a discussion of the implications of the Monterey consensus, and of scaling-up aid and what this implies for public policy-making. The second section focuses on sector-wide approaches, which have recently not received as much attention as, for example, PRSPs, but which are crucial in a discussion that focuses on public policy capacity. Key questions in this section are whether these are compatible with a perspective that focuses on inter-sectoral public policy-making, and what the influence has been of recent 'vertical' initiatives, for example, in the case of HIV/Aids. Section 3 looks at Poverty Reduction Strategies as one of the major instruments put forward under the process of debt relief for heavily indebted countries. In particular, in the context of the argument in this book, we are interested in the experiences with participatory and comprehensive policy planning that were among the central tenets of the PRSP initiative. The fourth section concludes, looking at the recent debates on the scaling-up of aid, and the new challenges this poses for the main theme of this book.

6.1 Washington, post-Washington and the Monterey consensus – what role for politics?

Recent writings on the 'post-Washington Consensus' suggest new approaches to economic policies have emerged, with a wider role for public policies. The term 'Washington Consensus' appears to have been coined by John Williamson. This emphasized the now familiar policy preferences around fiscal discipline, market-determined exchange and interest rates, protection of property rights, liberalization, privatization, and openness to trade, as well as (but less commonly debated) redirection of public expenditure toward education, health, and public infrastructure (Stern, 2002: 9). These directions were by and large a global phenomenon, and in aid-dependent countries heavily imposed, introduced with a large amount of pressure from the lending organizations.

While many observers have proclaimed the failure of the Washington Consensus, it is probably fair to say that the evidence is mixed. On the one hand, for example, in a large number of countries fiscal and monetary stability was achieved during the 1990s. Moreover, the recent growth performance of countries that have adjusted is fairly positive, and countries that have grown, by and large, have reduced poverty and improved human development indicators. On the other hand, the growth performance has not been uniformly favourable, and it has been acknowledged that the 'supply response' to adjustment measures has been weak.[1] Killick (1999) concludes that the evidence on the impact on poverty is really not strong enough to show that adjustment has either failed or succeeded, or even that the kinds of policy prescription would allow for reasonable expectations in terms of poverty reduction.

The 'Post-Washington Consensus' takes into account many of these critiques, essentially concluding that the policy prescriptions were not wrong, but insufficient. It stresses, as before, the complementary role of the state vis-à-vis the market, the importance of economic growth for poverty reduction, and the role of the private sector and trade. But it also recognizes, from the perspective of international organizations, that national ownership of the development agenda is crucial (the PRSP initiative as described below is a clear illustration). Empowerment of people, and basic health and education are seen as essential ingredients for development and poverty reduction. Whereas, according to Stern (2002), there was nothing wrong with the principles of the Washington Consensus, it

said nothing about governance and institutions, the role of empowerment and democratic representation, the importance of country ownership, or the social costs and the pace of transformation. The development community has learned the hard way, through the setbacks of the structural adjustment programs in developing countries of the 1980s, and the transition of the 1990s in eastern Europe and the former Soviet Union, that these elements are at the heart of the development challenge.

The post-Washington consensus thus pays much more attention to the interaction between states and markets, and is, for example, hopeful that processes of democratization will support a vibrant market economy. In a critical review of the potentials for African states in the context of globalization, Eyoh and Sandbrook (2003: 228) label the new approach a 'pragmatic neo-liberal development model', and highlight the similarities with the 'Third Way' promoted by Tony Blair and Bill Clinton, and how the approach found expression in the Comprehensive Development Framework promoted by former World Bank President James Wolfensohn. A key component is the emphasis on 'institutions' and 'good governance', and the coming decade will show whether the international community will be able to provide the right kind of support under these banners.

Apart from new approaches to economic policies, and following a period of aid fatigue, the early twenty-first century has witnessed renewed optimism about the role of international development.[2] Well-organized civil society pressure and reform attempts within international organizations led to significant initiatives around debt relief and more recently to commitments for increased aid, highlighted in the Monterey Consensus and the agreements at Gleneagles.

For the purpose of the discussion here, it is not just the ideas of increased aid commitments that matter, but also the fact that the Monterey Consensus put politics – domestic and international – at the heart of development, including for work on governance. It stresses that governments in developed and developing countries alike must build public support to translate development aspiration into action. It notes the need for political leadership, in the South for undertaking institutional and policy reform and in the North to strengthen solidarity with poverty reduction efforts in the South. It highlights thus the need for strong political will – but admitted it was not clear where the 'political will' would come from.[3]

Good governance

The 1990s witnessed increasing emphasis on the importance of governance for development outcomes and the provision of services (as in *World*

Development Report 2004).[4] Initially, aid practices sought governance 'quick fix technical solutions', following blueprint approaches with little attention to local conditions and questions of legitimacy. The list of necessary reforms grew exponentially, from 'rule of law' to 'capacity building'.[5] While there has been considerable success in governance reforms,[6] soon it became clear that 'supply-driven' and generic governance solutions were not working. The optimism of the early 1990s concerning the implementation of 'good governance' gave way to an understanding of the influences of local context on how reforms were implemented (Fanelli, 2004), and more focused and realistic ideas around 'good enough governance' (the term was coined by Grindle, 2002) that tried to target fewer but more prioritized and feasible interventions.

Governance was conceptualized primarily as a technocratic phenomenon rather than as a political process. Governance indicators have become a key component of aid delivery, including for the Millennium Challenge Corporation and World Bank allocations. They produce assessments and scores on a fairly large number of indicators, but they remain narrow against the wide array of existing governance or political dimensions, such as informal political 'voice' or influence, and inequality. Moreover, questions remain about how the indicators are constructed, what they really measure ('rule of law'), hidden assumptions (for example, rules associated with liberal-democratic societies), and how they are being used.

These changes in approach soon led to calls for better understanding of local politics. Forms of political analysis have been introduced in a number of agencies, for example SIDA's 'power analysis', the World Bank's Institutional and Governance Reviews, and DFID's Drivers of Change analysis and, more recently, governance assessments. The term 'political economy' is now widely used by donors and the World Bank, recognizing that politics and power cannot be separated from economic policy or asset distribution. But the term is often used in a deterministic way, asserting that political power and the policies and institutions of states reflect economic structures and the interests of the dominant economic interests, rather than in a way that provides insight into the complex and context-specific linkages. The political role of donors themselves is often not part of the framework of analysis.

Perhaps surprisingly, these forms of analysis typically do not incorporate social policies, often because they are deemed unimportant within the larger sphere of public policy-making. As discussed earlier, their quantitative importance should in fact not be underestimated. But Chapter 4 also highlights how important they are as part of the broader political economy and complexity of state–citizen relations or the social contract, and the impact of aid, particularly in aid-dependent countries.

With 'governance', aid practices have come a long way from the Washington Consensus. But it is also clear that this has come with as many challenges as solutions. In particular, and this will also be taken up as one of the central questions in the following sections, even – or perhaps especially – a move to work on governance appears to have difficulty conceptualizing the politics of public policy-making and how the international community relates to them. The Monterey consensus rightly acknowledges the political nature of development, but entails more questions than answers. And debates on scaling-up of aid indicate that even if the analysis is restricted to fairly narrow questions around economic growth, many questions remain, and these questions are likely to be even more difficult if the analysis includes the kinds of questions around the role of public policy in political contestation and social contracts.

6.2   Sector-wide approaches, scaling up aid, and cross-sectoral planning

The 1990s saw the emergence (or return) of emphasis within the donor community on the importance of country ownership, leading to the development of sector programmes, direct budget support and partnership – followed more recently by much work, particularly in the OECD context, on donor coordination and harmonization. The next section will discuss approaches to Poverty Reduction Strategies, which emphasize integrated and cross-sectoral policy formulation; this section focuses on donor initiatives at the sectoral level, particularly sector-wide approaches, followed by a discussion of the implications of 'vertical initiatives'.

Sector-wide approaches

Sector-wide approaches have been defined as an aid modality in which 'all significant funding for the sector supports a single sector policy and expenditure programme, under government leadership, adopting common approaches across the sector and progressing towards relying on Government procedures for all funds (Foster, 2000: 9).[7] In 2000, around 80 sector programmes were thought to be in existence, mostly in Sub Saharan Africa, and mostly in health and education (less so in agriculture, and apparently no cases in social protection). Successes have supposedly been achieved, for example, in Uganda, reflecting the general agreements between government and donors, and where sectoral approaches have been behind the government programme for Universal

Primary Education. In less aid-dependent countries, such as India, the principles of sectoral support have been applied in multi-donor support for the national primary education and health programmes.

This aid modality emerged as a response to three issues: ownership, policy environment and expenditure frameworks (Foster, 2000: 7–8). First, donors found that conditionality – in general – did not work. Sectoral approaches became a way of providing support against government commitment and track record in providing services for poverty reduction: a shift from 'conditionality' to 'ownership'. The emphasis has been on working within government management structures and responsibilities, though cases where project units were used have been recorded too.[8] It has remained focused on donor dialogue with governments; civil society engagement, while important, has not been as central as in the PRSP approach (as we see below), though there has been much flexibility in involving non-governmental actors in delivery of services (World Bank, 2002a).

Second, the emergence of sectoral approaches was an attempt to focus support on creating a sound policy environment. Rather than donors directly funding services in a project mode, sectoral approaches imply a mode of funding towards changes in policies and institutions (at macro and sectoral level, and with respect to budgeting), which in turn are seen as essential for nationwide services. This is thought to be particularly important in sectors where public funding is a substantial part of overall spending, hence the predominance of programmes in education and health.

The third set of issues discussed by Foster is around public expenditure frameworks and management, in which much experience has been gained by donors and increasing recognition of its importance for improvements in well-being. Sectoral approaches were thought to help provide a solution to the fragmentation in the budgeting process, with many – and in some cases most – spending being outside the government budget, and with reliance on donor rather than government financial management. In this sense, the rationale of sectoral approaches was: 'Government and donors should work together to implement a single, coherent expenditure programme which prioritises the use of all sources of public funding' (Foster, 2000: 8).

There is evidence of success of donor sector support, for example in the health sector in Ghana (Cheru, 2006: 362). Sector support may have helped to enhance political commitment, efficiency in resource use, and capacity for sectoral and inter-sectoral policy formulation and implementation (World Bank, 2002a). For donors, sector-wide approaches are an important vehicle for aid harmonization and alignment on the ground across a wide range of different participants. On the down-side, it has been noted that the processes of establishing joint-donor support are time consuming, monitoring frameworks tend to be costly, and a joint-donor response at times has also been considered a disadvantage by recipient governments if this involved the risk of a complete halt to support.

Scaling up of aid and 'vertical initiatives'

Under the Monterey Consensus, the international development community expects a radical increase in aid flows. One mechanism for this has been through budget support and PRSPs, as we discuss below. Another possibility is increased funding for sector initiatives, particularly in health and education, and possibly in social protection. This is closely linked to the sectoral approaches discussed above, but whereas the sector approaches resulted from the urge to improve aid delivery, new 'vertical' initiatives follow urges to scale up aid and significant private donor funding.

Vertical initiatives often focus on individual (or groups of) diseases, and there are now dozens of health funds and partnerships, with the Global Fund for Aids, Tuberculosis and Malaria and the Global Alliance for Vaccines and Immunisation among the largest so far (US$8.7 billion and US$1.7 billion), and the International Finance Facility for Immunisation expected to raise a further US$4 billion (UK Government, 2006). Pharmaceutical companies have donated particular drugs to eliminate a particular disease, like the well-known Mectizan Donation Programme, within the framework of which Merck have donated Ivermectin for as long as necessary to rid African countries of river blindness. The last decade has also seen the rise of 'new philanthropists' who donate large sums of money for specific health-related projects: the Melinda and Bill Gates Foundation donations in particular are enormous, with resources far outstripping the annual budget of WHO.

It is as yet unclear what the impact of these vertical initiatives will be. It is difficult to criticize the enhanced aid flows, and private donors like the Gates Foundation have established good track records (even getting other philanthropists to let them manage their donations). And Jeffrey Sachs of course has a point when he expresses doubt about the focus on improvement in public institutions, when the per capita spending on health is less than $10 per head, which it is in many poor countries – even the hugely increased resources for HIV/AIDS are still only a proportion of what is required. In the context of this book, however, it is important to reflect on the impact of public policy-making more generally.

Commitments for increasing aid are made in the face of clearly documented doubts about 'capacity for aid absorption', and increased scrutiny of the 'outcomes' of aid under new public sector management in the North. On the one hand, the Millennium Project (UN, 2005), the Commission for Africa (2005) and Jeffrey Sachs (2005) have put much stress on the need for increasing aid. Sachs has been a fervent supporter of increased aid to Kenya or Ethiopia, for example, opposing ideas that increased aid should be subject to improvements in governance, arguing that it is impossible to run a health system on current per capita allocations. Howard White in an IDS Bulletin on 'Increased Aid: Minimising Problems, Maximising Gains' (September 2005) also concludes there is a serious shortfall in aid disbursements. On the other hand, Tony Killick in the same IDS Bulletin, with many others, argues that additional aid will divert attention from quality and effectiveness of aid. Easterly (2006) suspects that the increased commitments will be subject to the dominance of 'planners', including those who think they can plan a market, and suffer from the failure to learn from past mistakes. As summarized by Manor (2005), views continue to differ around questions of absorptive capacity, possibilities for governance reform, the likelihood that aid will be delivered in a coordinated manner, donors' 'unhelpful habits' and continued questions about aid dependency.

The particular aid modality potentially has enormous implications for the balance of power within public policy-making. This relates to the availability of resources in particular sectors, and for particular agencies within that, vis-à-vis other sectors. The medium-term perspective will be important: it is likely that international support will remain volatile, and there are questions about the sustainability of many well-funded initiatives. The recent vertical initiatives may imply, in the view of Poku and Whiteside (2002: 192) a (further) move away from the state as central actor in providing legislative frameworks and standards, towards 'a multiplicity of new – and largely unaccountable – actors in the health arena', with public–private partnerships 'as potentially radical new systems of global governance'.

A number of agencies have now argued for a dramatic increase in aid efforts in social protection (discussed in Chapter 5) though this has not as yet resulted in initiatives on the scale of health and education sectors. The social protection literature by and large has remained disconnected from the debate on absorption capacity and scaling-up aid. Recent increased international commitments to social or pro-poor sectors, however, suggest that it will be increasingly important to link the two sets of debates, and to pay more attention to the reform of social sectors (in particular social protection), and to be clearer about the capacity for cross-sectoral policy-making, as well as the politics of social policies under increased aid flows. Also, aid dependency is important at the sectoral level, including its impact on existing or emerging social contracts, and accountability in terms of service provision.

6.3   Poverty reduction strategies: aid modality or development model?

There have been rapid and radical changes in the development approaches of donor agencies in the last ten years. A first indication was the development of the Comprehensive Development Framework (CDF) by the World Bank, piloted in a small number of countries, which aimed to encourage partnership and ownership. In 1999, the World Bank and IMF endorsed the framework of Poverty Reduction Strategy Papers (PRSPs). This was an instrument for borrower countries seeking to benefit from the Highly Indebted Poor Countries programme (HIPC),[9] to strengthen links between debt relief and poverty reduction by making debt relief integral to broader efforts to implement broad poverty reduction strategies (Gupta et al., 2001). The 'model' was broadened to policy dialogue in all countries receiving concessional funding from the IFIs, with significant implications for national poverty strategy formulation, and for the way donors engage with this. By 2005, about forty countries had a poverty

---

Box 6.1   Qualifying for HIPC and lending instruments

Countries qualified for HIPC assistance if they faced an unsustainable debt burden, established a track record of reform and sound policies through IFI -supported programmes, and produced a full or interim Poverty Reduction Strategy Paper. Qualifying for debt relief involved two stages. First, the debtor country needed to demonstrate a capacity to use 'prudently' the assistance granted, by demonstrating a strong commitment to reduce macroeconomic imbalances and sustain growth-oriented policies. At 'decision point' IFIs decided on a country's eligibility based on a debt sustainability analysis. If the external debt situation of the country was found to be unsustainable, it qualified for HIPC assistance, and the international community committed itself to provide sufficient assistance for the country to achieve debt sustainability. In the second stage the country had to establish a further track record of good performance, of key structural policy reforms agreed at the decision point, the maintenance of macroeconomic stability, and adoption and implementation of the PRSP. During this stage, bilateral and commercial creditors were expected to reschedule obligations. At the end of this stage, the country reached a 'floating' completion point and the remaining amount of debt relief committed became irrevocable. In 2003 the ambition for debt rescheduling was made less ambitious with respect to debt sustainability.

Financial support for PRSP implementation was to be provided through the World Bank's Poverty Reduction Support Credit (PRSC) and the IMF Poverty Reduction Growth Facility (PRGF), the successor of the Extended Structural Adjustment Facility (ESAF). In 2001, 77 low-income countries were eligible for IMF PRGF assistance. The targets and policies embodied in PRGF programmes were thought to emerge directly from PRSP or similar frameworks. It integrated poverty reduction with macroeconomic policies, and discussions of the macroeconomic framework were made subjects for public consultation. Key social and sectoral programmes and structural reforms for poverty reduction and growth were to be identified and prioritized in the PRSP (the IMF emphasized that health and education spending had shown a rising trend in PRGF countries and during adjustment), and their budgetary impact costed. PRGF-supported programmes were said to have a focus on governance (management of public resources, transparency and accountability, public scrutiny), underpinning macroeconomic stability, growth and poverty reduction.

By 2001, 24 countries reached decision point – when debt relief was approved and interim relief begins – and they would over time receive $36 billion in relief through HIPC, which would reduce present value of debt by half. Debt relief equals almost 2% of the first HIPC countries' GDP, or 50 per cent of their health and education spending. In 2006, the initiative had reduced $19 billion of debt in 18 countries, and net transfers to HIPC countries had doubled from $8.8 billion in 1999 to $17.5 billion in 2004. Over time, the pressure of HIPC has become less, and other initiatives – such as the MDG review – have become bigger donor preoccupations.

Sources: Adam and Bevan (2001), review of about 10 PRGFs; Ter-Minnasian et al. (2001), World Bank DEC (March 2002); World Bank, IEG (2006), www.imf.org/external/np/exr/facts/hipc.htm

reduction strategy, and a few had gone on to a second-generation strategy (Driscoll, with Evans, 2005).

Why the PRSP emerged

To understand the direction of change in the new aid architecture, some of the factors that led to the emergence of PRSPs are worth emphasizing. First, the PRSP came about partly as a result of the successful NGO pressure on the IFIs, particularly through Jubilee 2000 (Whaites, 2002), and helped by the changes in European governments in the late 1990s. This broad movement argued for increasing debt relief, particularly but not only by the IFIs.[10] It also increased pressure to make this debt relief pro-poor, and to address the negative consequences of structural adjustment. The international financial crisis in East Asia also increased the pressure on the IFIs to review their policies and the effects on poverty. There has been a general agreement that the IFIs did become more responsive to a broad range of international actors, and that a much more open debate emerged, as highlighted by the increased number of IFI documents published, and the wide range and regularity of NGO publications. The pressure also contributed to considerable time pressure, with some undesirable results.

Second, the changes happened against the background of an intensive debate about the effectiveness of aid. The World Bank in 1998 produced the influential Assessing Aid report, which emphasized the need for good economic management for aid to be effective.[11] The report also acknowledged problems with traditional lending conditionalities, the need for (recipient) government ownership and problems of fungibility. Changes in the IMF included a response to the critique of the inflexibility of its macroeconomic and fiscal options (Adam and Bevan, 2001), and of the way conditionality had evolved over time and the need for better prioritization of policy measures (as well as division of labour between international institutions).[12] With respect to social policy, the changes implemented by the IMF seemed more far-reaching than those by the World Bank: while it used to restrict its mandate to monitoring expenditure ceilings, in the new IMF approach started to look at the quality of budgets and sectoral spending (Toye, 2000), including how additional funding through debt relief is to be used for, among other things, spending in health and education. After a number of years, and following evaluations stressing relatively large increases in shares of social expenditure and the need for balance between growth-enhancing and social expenditures (World Bank, IEG, 2006: 3), the IMF emphasized its lack of capacity to engage in dialogue about the composition of public spending (Heller et al. 2006).

Elements of the PRS(P) approach

The PRSP approach has been based on the following (interrelated) principles: an emphasis on country ownership and partnership between donors and recipients, formulation of a PRSP through broad national-level participation, a results-oriented approach, including establishing a link between debt relief and impact on poverty, and comprehensive and long-term planning. Much empirical material has been generated reviewing the experience, and there are few doubts that at least the debate has brought a much stronger focus on poverty reduction. It was acknowledged that time pressure greatly influenced early experiences, that the design of the approach had focused too much on the strategy *paper* (and hence it became common to refer to PRS), and reviews indicated much diversity of country experiences (World Bank and IMF, 2005). The following is a very selective review of existing evidence, with a focus on our questions regarding social policy.[13]

First, perhaps most discussion has focused on the question of whether the PRS approach has made the aid relationship more country-owned. On the one hand, there has been a common acknowledgement that the PRS approach – with related emphases on harmonization – has made a large difference to the way donors approach the aid relationship. There is no space here to review the wide range of experience on harmonization and alignment, but it seems fair to say that the challenges in leaving countries in the 'driving seat' remain substantial, and that experiences have varied substantially. For the purpose of the discussion in this book it is relevant that early experiences indicated a strong tendency to apply the approach in a fairly bureaucratic manner, in a way as a solution to the aid relationship – subsequent emphasis that the PRS approach 'is no panacea' highlights how high expectations were that the approach would resolve problems in the aid relationship. More recent reviews, for example by Booth et al. (2006) on countries in Latin America, indicate that donors tend to get closely tied to paths set out through the PRS process, and that a disarray sets in when the partner government's policies do not follow the plans set out earlier, and do not (continue to) show commitment to the PRSP. Donors in many cases are not well equipped to deal with the politics of public policy-making.

Second, the PRSP approach was radical in the promotion of participation in the formulation of national plans for poverty reduction. A great amount of technical work emerged to support this, building on, for example, poverty assessments and community participation, trying to move this 'up-stream' to influence the macro-policy discussions.[14] In many countries a wide range of civil society organizations engaged in the donor dialogue, and saw the process as an opportunity to open up the space for political engagement.

There has been considerable critique of practices in participation. First, it has been argued that participation has remained ritualistic, and that the macroeconomic framework has not changed following even good processes of participation. NGOs have often felt the economic model was a 'given'. The term participation – in the context of PRSPs, as elsewhere – has been used to mean different things. Secondly, in some cases the process of participation remained outside the area of mainstream politics, for example ignoring parliaments. Other groups that have frequently been excluded include trade unions, the private sector, women and marginalized groups.[15] In any case, there are many questions about the institutionalization of participation (Cheru, 2006: 364 ff). Thirdly, in cases where the policy dialogue did heavily engage with political leaders, as in Bolivia, subsequent political dynamics imposed great difficulties for the donors to 'implement the PRS' (Booth et al., 2006).

The third element of the approach consisted of the emphasis on a results orientation, including the link between debt relief and poverty reduction. This emphasis was part of a broader process forcing international development to show clearer results (for donor country tax money spent), and linked to the increased emphasis on poverty reduction, as discussed below. It involved an emphasis on clear costing of PRSPs and linking them to Medium Term Expenditure Frameworks, the key instrument for policy dialogue between borrowers and lenders. The strengthened emphasis on poverty monitoring, as discussed earlier, was also part of the efforts to be more precise about achievements.

The general evaluation was fairly optimistic that the PRS approach has to a great extent strengthened the focus on poverty reduction. Preparation of PRSPs led to discussion of poverty issues across government ministries. It enhanced the position of poverty analyses that had developed during the 1990s, and the pressure on IFIs and other donors has forced them to review the impact of aid on poverty much more carefully – the institution of the Poverty and Social Impact Analysis was a clear example of how under civil society pressure innovative new instruments were introduced.

However, while most reviews highlight that progress has been made in this area, the challenges are as large as the progress. While partner country governments have often stressed the importance of economic growth and modernization, many observers, such as Stewart and Wang (2003: 19), have emphasized that 'there is no fundamental departure from the kind of policy advice provided under earlier structural adjustment programmes', for example related to the role of the market, fiscal and monetary matters, inflation and privatization.[16] There have been concerns about the links between PRS and lending instruments, whether donor lending sufficiently follows the PRS priorities (no doubt hindered by a common lack of prioritization and clear budgeting in PRSs). Gaps between poverty profiles and proposed policies remain, even in poverty analysis itself. It has been noted that the poverty analysis in some cases has insufficiently informed the development strategy – even if incorporated in the same document.[17] In terms of costing of PRSPs, it is often noted that these lack detail, that they seem unrelated to budgets, financial management is poor in many cases, and that in the context of limited national capacity the proposals amount to wish lists (Cheru, 2006: 361ff).[18] Pro-poor expenditure was highlighted in a small though increasing number of PRSPs.

The fourth aspect of the PRSP approach discussed here is the emphasis on a comprehensive plan for development and poverty reduction. PRSPs cover most relevant areas of development, though there are regular reviews of whether sectoral (for example, agriculture) or cross-cutting (for example, gender) are sufficiently covered; in fact most international agencies, bilateral and specialized UN, have weighed into the debate and reviewed particular concerns. There is evidence that the PRSP modality has extended the policy dialogue beyond finance ministries and specific sectors. Line ministries have played a role in the formulations of PRSPs, and this has often brought weak (despite considerable financial support) social ministries to the table of important policy discussions from which they are usually absent. The IMF and World Bank review of PRSP progress highlighted that 'comprehensiveness is important in order to capture the complementary nature of public actions across sectors', and quote evidence from a review in Tanzania that 'a comprehensive strategy does not mean sacrificing priority setting. In fact, the more comprehensive the strategy, the more important it is to identify its main priorities' (IMF and World Bank, 2005: 16).

There are many questions regarding whether this has contributed to comprehensive and cross-sectoral policy-making, and potential trade-offs which the earlier writings on PRSPs tended to gloss over. The question of emphasis on growth versus social sectors has also come up frequently in this respect. Driscoll and Evans (2005: 12) note a lack of integration or match of strategies for the social sectors and the productive sectors (they see donors as responsible for a social sector bias). Ownership of line ministries (and sub-national governments) of the plans has remained limited. Cheru (2006: 367) with others emphasizes the weak state capacity in Africa – particularly but not only in post-conflict countries – as a hindrance for poverty analysis, implementation of programmes, monitoring; 'co-ordination of economic policy formulation and implementation has been hampered by constant inter-ministerial infighting, as well as by the disconnect between key sector ministries and ministries of finance' (Cheru, 2006: 369).

While one side of the critique has stressed the gaps in comprehensiveness in the development plans, and the limited capacity for comprehensive planning, another – partly contradictory – critique emphasizes that donors' insistence on comprehensive plans may be counter-productive. Booth et al. (2006) in the context of Latin American countries that have developed a PRSP (Bolivia, Honduras and Nicaragua) conclude that the comprehensiveness of the plans causes fundamental difficulties in terms of ownership: none of the leaders feel, or can reasonably be expected to be, committed to such PRSPs. In their view, rather than continuing to work with the PRSPs, donors should be pragmatic and flexible in supporting initiatives that arise from the leaders of the day, and be more strongly committed to the PRS *approach* than the output in papers. Because of political imperatives, such initiatives are likely to be specific, with space for political rhetoric, rather than comprehensive.[19]

PRSP and social policy

Many of the priorities put forward by a broad social policy agenda, as presented in this book, are mirrored in the PRSP approach, and so are its challenges for international development. Two of the four elements discussed above appear uncontroversial. First, the emphasis on – and challenges regarding – country ownership is clearly in line with the idea of *reclaiming* social policy, particularly in the context of most aid-dependent countries, where global social and economic policy debates have had the most unmitigated influence. There is a need for more long-term support for the capacity for national policy-making, across sectors and in a way that facilitates collaboration between government and non-governmental providers. Second, the emphasis on a results-oriented approach also appears by and large uncontroversial, and much work has been undertaken to improve links between policy formulation and outputs. The, partly unintentional, focus on social sectors remains subject to debate, but it is important to retain a notion of social policy as a central rather than residual element of public policy formulation, which recognizes the impact of social development on growth, and the fact that non-social sectors have equally important poverty implications – the focus on social sectors as uniquely 'pro-poor' too may be based in a welfarist or residual notion of social policy.

The two other elements may be more controversial. First, the emphasis on broad national-level participation in the formulation of PRSPs. Neither official nor external documentation shows much awareness of the kinds of social policy processes described in Chapter 4. The in-country processes promoted in the new approach are far removed from – and potentially cut across – the long-term articulation of class and other interests, and how these relate to public policy formulation and implementation, and the need for developing a social contract. The official donor analysis, as Booth et al. (2006) emphasize, is not a good substitute for political analysis, including relating to the way international pressure affects budgeting, and how patronage politics locally influence these.

Finally, and perhaps most surprising, the PRSP emphasis on comprehensive and long-term policies for poverty reduction does not square very well with the social policy approach put forward here. On the one hand, the emphasis in Chapter 3 on cross-sectoral policies and impacts, and concerns about fragmentation of social policy formulation discussed in Chapter 4, fit well with the attempt to go beyond sectoral and project approaches. But on the other hand, and to a large extent driven by time pressure, public policy-making has been conceptualized largely in a technocratic fashion. This includes the participatory approach, as mentioned above, but also the promotion of 'pro-poor' public policy, without paying much attention to the constituencies that are essential for progressive policies, and limited reflection on whether and how international support can galvanize these.

It has often been argued that the time pressure underneath PRSPs has been responsible for many of its shortcomings, and the challenges indeed have been openly articulated.[20] Also, many have argued the need to get away from the blueprint approach that marked some of the experiences (in a way inevitable in the bureaucratic set-up of donor organizations). The key question will be whether the support will, against inevitable disappointments, continue to focus on and provide support to long-term objectives, and adapt and develop flexible responses to these challenges.

6.4 Conclusion: is there still a missing middle? Does it matter?

New approaches to international development have emerged rapidly over the last ten or twenty years. From periods of adjustment and aid fatigue, the early twenty-first century is a period of renewed and broader approaches to development, with a much stronger focus on poverty reduction, highlighting the importance of national ownership of development and poverty agendas and commitments for substantially increased aid. With the prioritization of poverty elimination as the major concern of international development, the objectives of policies are hardly a matter of dispute. But the ways to achieve these, and the role of social policy, is less clear.

Progress has been made towards more integrated strategies for poverty reduction. But evidence suggests that development practices still fall short in strengthening national processes for social policy-making and analysis, similar to the strengthening of finance ministries or departments that dominated during the period of adjustment. They need to focus more strongly on cross-sectoral dialogue while recognizing the long-term challenges this may involve, as reflected in 'Christmas tree' PRSPs, and of particular importance for large-scale vertical initiatives. International agencies, often unintentionally, have marginalized social ministries and integrated planning, reinforced by a conceptualization of social expenditure as consumptive and not productive expenditure.

Moreover, while poverty reduction strategies have managed to bring deprivation to the core of the international development agenda, international development perspectives need to be broadened beyond the confines of addressing 'poverty', and incorporate a better understanding of the political economy that underlies policy-making for the poor and the non-poor. This implies positioning itself more strategically in terms of inclusive social policies: in many cases reform of existing policies is as important as expansion. The politics of these policies are paramount, and not well reflected in more technocratic governance analysis, and donors are often a central part of the politics.

7
Conclusion: A Framework for Social Policy

As stated in this book's introduction, 'reclaiming social policy' is an ambitious project. It draws on different academic disciplines and takes sides in theoretical debates, particularly around the separation of economic from social-policy analysis. The project implies a call for development agencies to come out of their silos of sectoral policy, and for social development to have a stronger focus on policy reform, also because social policy can be as regressive as other forms of public policies. Finally, the book emphasizes improved understanding of the deeply political nature of development. But its ambitious nature also leads to practical suggestions.

This last chapter provides proposals on how a notion of social policy as used in this book can make a difference for the poverty and development agenda in the early twenty-first century. It provides a framework for supporting social policy-making from an international development perspective. This has both a normative and a rights-based element, emphasizing the context and path-dependent character of social policy, and a practical perspective, focusing on entry points into the strengthening of integrated policy-making for development and poverty reduction – which we discuss first.

Practical entry point

First, and perhaps least controversial, we can list entry points for social policy analysis and advice, directed primarily at international development agencies.[1] Such a social policy framework emphasizes the interrelated nature of public (including social) policies, the need for strengthening capacity for policy-making at macro-level, and to embed this in an understanding of the political economy of social policy. Despite its origins in northern debates, this book has argued, a social policy framework can be of value for international development practices. This includes the following practical entry points.

First, the emphasis is on social *policy* rather than social development. This implies a need for social development advice to move 'upstream', to engage at the level of macroeconomic policy debate and public expenditure, and to encourage dialogue and coordination between ministries. It should focus on the capacity of institutions, as in many cases, as the African Union (2006: 7) highlights 'public institutions for social development are inadequately governed'. It implies critical assessment of project and targeted approaches – which are particularly dominant in social sectors, and are particularly likely to be provided on a charitable basis. Engagement at the policy level should and can be based in a rights approach (discussed below) and focus on the strengthening of social contracts between the state and citizens. This implies an assessment of both the responsiveness of state institutions and citizens' voice and advocacy, based in an understanding of national principles of solidarity, of institutions, of financing needs and possibilities, and modes of delivery of services – as highlighted under the notion of social policy regimes.

Second, the proposed approach to integrated public policy-making has implications for the frameworks used by development agencies. As highlighted in work on nutrition and education, the long-term impact of investment calls for cost-benefit analysis over decades, not years. The potential beneficial impact of reducing inequality on economic growth similarly has important implications for the way economic investment is considered: what appears as a trade-off, in the long run, under specific conditions, may well constitute a win–win situation. In any case, as it is important for donors to work better across sectors, specific forms of analysis should take better account of cross-sectoral impacts, including how these play out in the longer run.

Third, a social policy framework should adopt a wide view on the *agencies* involved – often seen as fundamentally different from a welfare state context, but relevant there too. It should take account of the limited role played by the state in many contexts, and the significant role of private efforts, for example, in health or elderly care. Social policy should try to crowd-in such efforts, and ensure incentives are compatible, and avoid stigma and dependency. The framework should thus also include an understanding of the role of NGOs, very important in Bangladesh for example, and in the context of international charity, as well as private sector agencies in delivering services: these form central parts of social policy regimes, articulating specific principles of solidarity. It needs to engage with debates and policies on devolution, while continuing to emphasize the importance of national policy in shaping local processes. In the context of a diversity of providers, the role of the state as regulator and its capacity for often very complicated functions become even more important.

Fourth, social policy should be *responsive* to the needs of poor people. This implies, first, that social policy and advice need to be context specific, to region, but also groups of people, as the poor do not form a homogeneous group. Timing of social policy delivery can be critical with respect to work requirements during agricultural seasons, or for migrant groups – much experience exists to show that specific needs can be taken into account. Moreover, forms of delivery inevitably interact with social norms and often shape them, particularly but not only in education. Social policy should be flexible, able to respond to new challenges and prepared for emergencies. This once again highlights the importance of a multi-sectoral approach: for poor people and their often complex lives the compartmentalization of policies is likely to restrict the extent to which they can respond to particular needs. Also, although overall universal provisions have proven to be more efficient, responsiveness to particular groups may assign an important role to targeted policies. Finally, and challenging in many countries, is the management of diversity within delivery and policy formulation to ensure that the interests of different racial and ethnic groups are sufficiently incorporated.

Fifth, social policy can be assessed on the question of *access* by its users and citizens. This refers to access to services, which implies a range of mechanisms for accountability, feedback and participation, and to quality and relevance. But it also refers to access to policy-making processes, for which there are important lessons in recent initiatives in participation in budget formulation, and indeed, though not always successfully, through PRSPs. A key challenge in this respect, too, is the institutionalization of such mechanisms for feedback and participation, including in cross-sectoral budget decision-making and sustained reform of top-down policy processes.

Sixth, and following from the previous point, a social policy framework should be based on a good understanding of *politics*, in many cases calling for much more and more frequent political analysis by donor agencies, including how international debates and norms interact with local ones. While aiming to enhance social integration and reduce conflict, analysis should assess the various interests and politics in providing social services, and how such services in turn shape state–citizen relations, create expectations and public responses, and often are part of nation-building projects. It should assess the public support for programmes to assist the poorest, and consider these against universal provisions which can generate broader public support. Crucially, an understanding of politics should form the basis for programmes that simultaneously enhance access to services and citizens' voice.

On globalization and the primacy of national policies

Globalization has been shown to contain as many risks as potentials. While there may not be a simple trend towards increased global inequality, it is clear that parts of the world and large numbers of people are rapidly falling behind, and that public policy in many cases has failed. Perceptions about globalization itself are important, as they inform global politics as much as 'reality'. The reasons for global trends in well-being and inequalities, of course, are complex, but one of the key ones relates to public policy capacity and the conditions under which globalization can be managed or negotiated. Histories of East Asia and India show very clearly the central role of public policies in managing globalization, and here lies the key question, as many countries, particularly in Africa, are likely to benefit from current globalization 'only if they possess what most of them manifestly lack – sound institutions' (Eyoh and Sandbrook, 2003: 244–5).

Social policy has a key role to play in the way countries negotiate globalization. There is no evidence of a general demise of the state – though its role has changed during two decades of neo-liberal ideology and policies. Human development is central in integration into global markets, and while the links between inequality and growth are disputed, more equal countries do not necessarily perform worse in international markets. When countries' economies have opened up, social protection often comes to play a more important role (even if with some delay). And as argued in Chapter 4, while there may not be clearly articulated welfare regimes in the South, particularly where social policy-making has been fragmented, social policy and its reform do depend on national traditions and the socio-political dynamics in which they are embedded, thus calling for good understanding of local politics and dynamics to inform development approaches.

National social policy-making does not happen in isolation. Countries learn from each other, and regional economic integration does influence – as social policy does not operate independently of economic policy and trends – national social policy. The crisis in East Asia impacted upon social policy dynamics, partly making them more inclusive, partly more welfarist. In the case of countries subject to adjustment, ideas put forward – and imposed – by international organizations have played a key role.

The debate on social spending shows that the directions these interactions have taken are by no means straightforward. Social policy advice needs to be based on a good understanding of the interaction between international aid efforts, and national politics and vested interests.

The hypothesis put forward is that the agenda in a globalizing world should be about reform of international institutions, northern protectionist policies, and so on, but also to reaffirm the primacy of national politics. Nation states remain the principal political institutions. An effective global social policy needs stronger policies that allow countries to integrate in global markets on a more equitable basis, and political and cultural capital that allows countries to engage in debates about global architecture. With the emergence of an emphasis on national ownership, for example through the PRSP approach, national capacities are – once again – being taken more seriously; but the lessons from PRSPs indicate that much still needs to be done to support the strengthening of national capacity in a way that integrates an understanding of local politics and aims to embed national public policy capacity in progressive social policy traditions.

A cross-sectoral view of social policy

> In developmental contexts, social policy has typically had a multiplicity of objectives that have included equity, social inclusion, nation-building, conflict-management, human capital formation [and] social transformation.
>
> (Mkandawire, 2005: 15)

The analysis in this book concurs strongly with Mkandawire's assessment – who emphasized the role of social policy, for example, in the context of the 'late industrializers' that successfully caught up with the global economy – that social policy is about development, not just poverty eradication. There has been much criticism of the residual or safety net approach to social policy – as articulated, for example, in *World Development Report 1990* – approaches to social funds, and even much poverty analysis. Available evidence suggests that a range of social policies play key roles in overall development paths: policies that are harmful in the long run, but equally the central role of social policies in economic growth. The well-documented inter-linkages of economic and social policies call for a much stronger cross-sectoral focus on public policy-making. Donor practices have limited such a cross-sectoral focus, not only through the marginalization of social protection, but also through the vertical approaches – firmly based in institutional divisions, possibly reinforced through private international efforts – to health and education.

Specific policies and programmes, themselves perhaps rightly categorized as residual, can have enormously important functions for specific vulnerable groups. Much evidence on the reasons for success is now available. The Maharashtra Employment Guarantee Scheme, for example, has been a successful solution to specific problems, social funds experience contains interesting lessons about what can and cannot work, and the new generation of cash transfers in Latin America shows important successes. Such 'residual' schemes may even influence more mainstream policy-making and public sector provisions, by empowering people, or by setting standards which can contribute to increasing accountability. Targeted programmes can have important functions within overall universalist regimes. The key point is not that these programmes are important or not – they clearly can be from both pro-poor and political perspectives – or that one approach is better than the other. The main message is that the policy dialogue needs to pay more attention to the wide range and interaction of public policies, which jointly determine and are embedded in the social contract between states and their citizens.

Social spending matters

A fourth proposal refers to making social policy more central to public finance and management approaches. From a simple quantitative point of view state expenditure in the South is of great importance, and thus a key consideration within economic growth policies. State revenue and expenditure form a significant part of GDP, and social spending is often a substantial component, with much spending off-budget. Public spending should be higher, for example to achieve the MDGs, and the quality of such spending in many cases needs to be much improved. But the literature and policy dialogue pay too little attention to social spending, highlighted, for example, in the lack of cross-sectoral data that are internationally comparable, and the often conflicting message about the role of the state.

Patterns of public expenditure are important in a cross-sectoral focus on public policies and reforms. Calls for enhancing spending on education, for example, can be justified only in a cross-sectoral public policy perspective, that is, one that identifies the needs and political and financial margins to allocate public finance across a range of sectors, on the basis of needs for investment in rural areas, social protection and health. Again, the way governments and, not least, donor agencies are structured has undermined the capacity to systematically develop such a public policy perspective.

Apart from the simple quantitative importance, social spending matters because of what Chapter 3 called the double Robin Hood paradox, extending the conclusion put forward by Peter Lindert. There is less social spending where it is most needed, both because of limited state resources in poor countries and because of limited advocacy by poor people for spending that would benefit them. Moreover, existing public spending can be regressive, as benefit incidence studies as well as an overall picture of state spending in unequal countries suggest. This is not meant as a generalized conclusion – indeed much more research is necessary – but as a hypothesis to explore in particular contexts, particularly where aid flows are increasing.

Social spending is not simply a cost. Much evidence exists about the positive impact of health, nutrition and education on economic growth, thus requiring substantial investments, often public. The study by Peter Lindert shows that social spending can be a 'free lunch', that the returns are positive. But this happens under specific conditions only, of accountability and political processes. For international development practices this implies the need to strengthen mechanisms of accountability – primarily to citizens, not the aid agencies – as well as improving the understanding of the politics of public policies, with social policies as a core component and international agencies as an important link in the chains of accountability.

Social development, too, is political

While internationally development practice increasingly recognizes governance, institutions and politics (or 'political governance') as core to the agenda, the fifth key point here is that social policies too need to be seen as intensely political. Debates about social policy tend to have a technocratic character. They tend to be about practical solutions to problems and needs, without much attention to the political nature of such solutions. But social policies are outcomes of historical processes of political, power and ideological struggles, in which elite interests, the agency of professionals and concerns for nation building can be as import-ant as the struggle of deprived groups and altruism (Hill, 1996). In aid dependent countries these politics play out very differently, but are as important as the much-better documented processes in OECD countries. The huge difference between OECD welfare states and policies in the South should not prevent us from seeing social policies as historically specific and politically determined outcomes.

As Mackintosh and Tibandebaga (2004: 156–7) stress with respect to health, the 'redistributive commitment within a health care system ... is deeply influenced by the general patterns of social class and inequality in a society, and ... the particular institutions of the system and the norms of behaviour established within them'. Education is central to the construction of citizenship, a theme taken up in a recent paper by the Inter-American Development Bank (Cox et al., 2005). Social programmes – even small ones – are important elements in political and electoral contestation, and of political patronage (often severely regressive). International social sectoral funding adds a particular and insufficiently studied dimension to these politics, of altruism, self-interest, patronage and corruption.

A useful starting point, linking to the rights approach discussed below, is to think of social policies as embedded in a social contract. Graham (2002) notes that extension of social protection and the establishment of permanent systems 'ultimately requires the development of a politically sustainable social contract'. Countries that have expanded publicly financed social protection in the last two decades, such as Brazil, have achieved this on the basis of a renewal of the social contract. As we saw in Chapter 4, new social policies – like extension of health insurance in Thailand, reforms in Korea – followed crises and a perceived need by leaders to respond to public and political pressure. Developing countries often finance temporary programmes with international support, thus avoiding difficult political economy choices that are necessary for longer term programmes (Graham, 2002). But these difficult choices will need to be made in the longer run. This involves preparedness for crises (rather than one-off responses), but also enhancing accountability of services and citizens' feedback, and progressive expansion of taxation as the core of social contracts to be developed in the long run, and of course to reduce aid dependency.

A rights approach to social policy

Besides the quantitative targets of Millennium Development Goals, the ultimate aim of development efforts is the realization of human rights: civil, political, economic and social. The Universal Declaration of Human Rights, reaffirmed globally at the Copenhagen and Copenhagen+10 summits, forms the basis of the framework proposed here, and as we have mentioned, linking this to the idea of a social contract seems a fruitful starting point.

As in the work of Marshall, the idea of social policies, and welfare states in particular, is intimately linked to an idea of citizens' rights. Assessing social policy needs to start from the recognition that provision of social services structures citizenship, which in practice often implies reinforcements of patterns of inequality on the basis of gender, race, and so on. These services in turn provide the grounds for contestation over particular services and policies, often implying struggles over rights and what it means to be a citizen. Recent examples captured under the title 'new democratic spaces' highlight a global movement towards strengthened accountability, and it may be no coincidence that many of the examples have originated in countries with high inequality, like Brazil and South Africa.

Social provisions and rights and citizenship can be mutually reinforcing. *Chile Solidario* aims to

> move from a formal to a more real, active citizenship, capable of defending its rights and complying with its corresponding duties. The most important of these duties is the 'family contract', which commits the State to deliver the goods and services to which the participant family is entitled, and commits the family to carrying out the tasks assigned by the family support monitor in order to meet the minimum conditions.
> (Palma and Urzúa, 2005: 33)

There are many other examples of programmes that strengthen the rights of citizens and their contract with the state: it is essential that the perspectives of social policy provisions and a rights agenda are combined within policy design.

International development practices need to incorporate a better understanding of a rights perspective on social policy, and, vice versa, a social policy perspective on rights approaches. First, this regards social policy essentially as a right for its citizen, or progressive realization towards such rights (based on international frameworks, translated into national frameworks). Second, a rights framework incorporates a notion of duties as well, and particularly taxation plays a critical but under-valued role in the development of social contracts. Third, a rights agenda does not assume a state role just as provider of services, but is equally important for its role as regulator and as such as final guarantor of citizens' rights. Fourth, particular modes of funding in social sectors – project mode, vertical initiatives – can be and have been of an altruistic and voluntary nature, possibly improving outcome indicators, but not necessarily strengthening the state–citizen relationship. It is essential to ensure that the interaction of voluntarism (global and national) and state action is taken into account in the analysis. Finally, as in the analysis of OECD welfare states, social policy analysis in the South should focus squarely on the linkages between social policy formation and implementation, and forms of political representation, voice, and the strengthening of public institutions.

References

Abedian, I., and M. Biggs (eds) (1998) *Economic Globalization and Fiscal Policy*, Oxford University Press.

Abu Ghaida, D., and S. Klasen (2004) The Costs of Missing the Millennium Development Goal on Gender Equity, *World Development*, Vol. 32, No. 7: 1075–107.

ACC/SCN (various years) *Reports on The World Nutrition Situation*, Geneva.

ACC/SCN (2002) *Nutrition: A Foundation for Development*, Geneva.

Acemoglu, D., and J.A. Robinson (2001) 'Inefficient Redistribution', Mimeo, MIT, Cambridge, MA, MIT website (accessed August 2004).

Acemoglu, D., S. Johnson and J. Robinson (2004) Institutions as the Fundamental Cause of Long-Run Growth, Mimeo, prepared for Handbook of Economic Growth, MIT website (accessed August 2004).

Adam, C.S., and D.L. Bevan (2001) PRGF Stocktaking Exercise on behalf of DFID, mimeo, Oxford University.

Addison, T. (2003) Do Donors Matter for Institutional Reform in Africa?, in Kayizzi-Mugerwa, (2003), pp. 54–76.

Addison, T., A. Roe and M. Smith (2006) Fiscal Policy for Poverty Reduction, Reconstruction and Growth, Policy Brief, No. 5, Helsinki: UNU-WIDER (www.wider.unu.edu).

Adelman, I. (2000) Introduction to Redrafting the Architecture of the Global Financial System, *World Development*, Vol. 28, No. 6 (June).

Adesina, J. (2006) In Search of Inclusive Development: Social Policy in the Sub-Saharan African Context, Presentation at UNRISD-Sida/SAREC Workshop on Social Policy and Equality, Buenos Aires, 21–22 February.

African Union (2006a) Meeting Social Development Challenges. Social Policy Framework in Africa, Addis Ababa.

African Union (2006b) Report of the Experts' Meeting, Fourth Ordinary Session of the Labour and Social Affairs Commission, Cairo, Egypt, 22–27 April.

Ahmed, E., J. Drèze, J. Hills and A. Sen (eds) (1991) *Social Security in Developing Countries*, UNU/Oxford University Press.

Ahmed, M., T. Lane and M. Schulze-Ghattas (2001) Refocusing IMF Conditionality, *Finance and Development* (December): 40–43.

Ahuja, V. et al. (1997) *Everyone's Miracle? Revisiting Poverty and Inequality in East Asia*, Washington DC: World Bank.

Aina, T.A. (1999) West and Central Africa: Social Policy for Reconstruction and Development, in Morales-Gómez (1999), pp. 69–87.

Aizenman, J., and Y. Jinjarak (2006) Globalization and Developing Countries – A Shrinking Tax Base?, http://econ.ucsc.edu/faculty/jaizen/pubs/Glob_dev_countries.pdf

Alemayehu, G. (2002) Debt Issues: Africa. Thinking beyond the HPIC Initiative to Solving Structural Problems, UNU-WIDER Discussion Paper No. 2002/35, Helsinki.

Alesina, A., and E.L Glaeser (2004) *Fighting Poverty in the US and Europe. A World of Difference*, Oxford University Press.

Anand, A., K. Brock, P. Kabakcheiva, A. Kidanu, M. Melo, C. Turk and H Yusuf (2000) Who Is Listening: The Impact of Participatory Poverty Research on Policy, mimeo, Brighton: IDS.

Anand, S., and M. Ravallion (1993) Human Development in Poor Countries: On the Role of Private Incomes and Public Services, *Journal of Economic Perspectives*, Vol. 7, No. 1: 133–50.

Andalón, M., and L.F. Lopez-Calva (2002) The Many Mexicos: Income Inequality and Polarization in Urban Mexico During the 90s, paper presented at Cornell-LSE-WIDER Conference on Spatial Inequality, London, June, www.wider.unu.edu/conference/conference-2002-2/papers/luis-f-lopes-calva.pdf, accessed April 2006.

Anderson, E., and A. McKay (2004) Why Is Inequality So High, But Also So Variable, in Sub-Saharan Africa?, mimeo, London: ODI.

Anderson, E., and T. O'Neil (2006) A New Equity Agenda? Reflections on the 2006 World Development Report, the 2005 Human Development Report, and the 2005 Report on the World Social Situation, Working Paper 265, London: Overseas Development Institute, www.odi.org.uk/pppg/activities/country_level/inequality/index.html

Andersson, M., and C. Gunnarsson (2004) Egalitarianism and the Process of Modern Economic Growth: The Case of Sweden, background paper for *World Development Report 2006*, www.worldbank.org/socialpolicy.

Appleton, S. (2001) User Fees Expenditure Rationalisation and Voucher Systems in Education, in G. Murasu, C. Ugaz and G. White (eds), *Social Provision in Low-Income Countries*, Oxford University Press, pp. 157–85.

Aryeetey, E., and M. Goldstein (2000) The Evolution of Social Policy, in E. Aryeetey, J. Harrigan and M. Nissanke (eds), *Economic Reforms in Ghana. The Miracle and the Mirage*, Trenton, NJ: Africa World Press, pp. 284–303.

Aryeetey E., and A. McKay (2004) Operationalizing Pro-Poor Growth. A Case Study on Ghana, paper for the multi-donor research programme Operationalizing Pro-Poor Growth, London: DFID.

Asian Development Bank (2002) *Defining an Agenda for Poverty Reduction*, Manilla.

Atkinson, A.B., and J. Hills (1991) Social Security in Developed Countries: Are There Lessons for Developing Countries?, in Ahmad et al. (1991).

Atkinson, A.B. (1999) Is Rising Income Inequality Inevitable? A Critique of the Transatlantic Consensus, WIDER Annual Lecture 3, Helsinki.

Baldacci, E., B. Clements, S. Gupta and Q. Cui (2004) Social Spending, Human Capital and Growth in Developing Countries: Implications for Achieving the MDGs. www.imf.org/external/pubs/ft/wp/2004/wp0417.pdf

Balioumune-Lutz, M., and S. Lutz (2004) Rural–Urban Inequality in Africa: A Panel Study of the Effects of Trade Liberalization and Financial Deepening, ZEI Working Paper B06-2004, Bonn (www.zei.de).

Balisacan, A.M., and G.M. Ducanes (2006) *Inequality in Asia: A Synthesis of Recent Research on the Levels, Trends, Effects and Determinants of Inequality in Its Different Dimensions*, Inter-Regional Inequality Facility, London: ODI.

Baltodano, A.P. (1999) Social Policy and Social Order in Transnational Societies, in Morales-Gómez (1999), pp. 19–42.

Bangura, Y. (2005), Ethnicity, Inequality, and the Public Sector: A Comparative Study, Manuscript, UNRISD, http://hdr.undp.org/events/forum2005/papers.cfm.

Barrientos, A. (2004) Latin America: Towards a Liberal-Informal Welfare Regime, in Gough and Wood, (2004a), pp. 121–68.

Barrientos, A. (2004a) Financing Social Protection, mimeo, Manchester, paper commissioned by DFID, UK.

Barrientos, A. (2006) Protecting Capability, Eradicating Extreme Poverty: The Failure of Social Protection?, IDS Sussex, work in progress.

Barrientos, A., and P. Sherlock-Lloyd (2001) Can Social Protection Policies Reduce Poverty in Developing Countries? DFID Seminar Series, London.

Barro, R.J. (1997) Determinants of Economic Growth. A Cross-country Empirical Study, Development Discussion Paper No. 579, Cambridge, MA Harvard Institute for International Development.

Barro, R.J., and J.W. Lee (2000) International Data on Educational Attainment. Updates and Implications, Harvard, Mimeo, http://post.economics.harvard.edu/faculty/barro/papers/p_jwha.pdf.

Basu, K. (2001) Marginalization in a Globalizing World. Some Plausible Scenarios and Suggestions, paper for the Asia and Pacific Forum on Poverty: Reforming Policies and Institutions for Poverty Reduction, Asian Development Bank, Manila, 5–9 February.

Bennett, L. (2005) Gender, Caste and Ethnic Exclusion in Nepal: Following the Policy Process from Analysis to Action, paper for Arusha Conference New Frontiers of Social Policy, December, www.worldbank.org/socialpolicy.

Berg. J., and L. Taylor (2001) External Liberalization, Economic Performance, and Social Policy, in Taylor, (2001), pp. 11–55.

Berger, M.T., and H. Weber (2006) Beyond State-Building: Global Governance and the Crisis of the Nation-state System in the 21st Century, *Third World Quarterly*, Vol. 27, No. 1: 201–8.

Berry, A. (2006) A Review of Literature and Evidence on the Economic and Social Effects of Economic Integration in Latin America: Some Policy Implications, paper presented at the conference Lives and Livelihoods, University of Guelph, May (www.livesandlivelihoods.org).

Bertranou, F.M., and O.J. Durán (2005) Social Protection in Latin America: The Challenges of Heterogeneity and Inequity, *International Social Security Review*, Vol. 58 (July): 3–13.

Bertranou, F.M., and O.J. Durán (2005) Introduction, *International Social Security Review*, Vol. 58, No. 2–3: 3–13.

Besançon, M.L. (2005) Relative Resources: Inequality in Ethnic Wars, Revolutions, and Genocides, mimeo, Harvard University, forthcoming in *The Journal of Peace Research*.

Besley, T., R. Burgess, and B. Esteve-Volart (2004) Operationalizing Pro-Poor Growth. A Case Study on India, paper for the multi-donor research programme Operationalizing Pro-Poor Growth, London: DFID.

Besley, T., R. Burgess, and I. Rasul (2003) Benchmarking Government Provision of Social Safety Nets, Social Protection Discussion Paper No. 0315, Washington, DC: The World Bank.

Bevan, P. (2004) The Dynamics of Africa's In/security Regimes, in Gough and Wood (2004), pp. 202–52.

Bigio, A.G. (ed.) (1998) *Social Funds and Reaching the Poor. Experiences and Future Directions*, EDI Learning Resources Series, Washington DC: World Bank.

Bigsten, A., and D. Durevall (2006) Openness and Wage Inequality: Kenya, 1964–2000, World Development, Vol. 34, No. 3: 465–80.

Birdsall, N. (2005) *The World Is Not Flat: Inequality and Injustice in our Global Economy*, WIDER Annual Lecture 9, Helsinki: UNU-WIDER.

Birdsall, N., T. Pinckney and R.H. Sabot (1999) Equity, Savings, and Growth, mimeo, Carnegie Endowment.

Birdsall, N., D. Ross and R. Sabot (1995), Inequality and Growth Reconsidered: Lessons from East Asia, *World Bank Economic Review*, Vol. 9, No. 3: 477–508.

Blackden, M., and C. Bhanu (1999) Gender, Growth and Poverty Reduction, World Bank Technical Paper No. 429, Washington DC: World Bank.

Boix, C. (2003) *Democracy and Redistribution*, New York: Cambridge University Press.

Boix, C. (2004) Spain: Development, Democracy and Equity, Background Paper for World Development Report 2006, www.worldbank.org/socialpolicy.

Bonilla Garcia, A., and J.V. Gruat (2003) Social Protection: A Life Cycle Continuum Investment for Social Justice, Poverty Reduction and Sustainable Development, ILO, Social Protection Sector, Geneva.

Booth, D. (2005) Politics: The Missing Link in the G8 Africa Debate, Presentation at ODI, 23 June.

Booth, D. (2005b) Missing Links in the Politics of Experiment, ODI Working Paper 256, London: ODI, www.odi.org.uk/publications/working_papers/wp256.pdf

Booth, D., A. Grigsby and C. Toranzo (2006) Politics and Poverty Reduction Strategies: Lessons from Latin American HIPCs, ODI, Working Paper 262, London.

Booth, D., J. Holland, J. Hentschel, P. Lanjouw and A. Herbert (1998) *Participation and Combined Methods in African Poverty Assessment: Renewing the Agenda*. UK Department for International Development, London.

Booth, D., and H. Lucas (2001) Initial Review of PRSP Documentation, Report commissioned by DFID for the Strategic Partnership with Africa, ODI, London.

Booth, D., and H. Lucas (2001) Desk Study of Good Practice in the Development of PRSP Indicators and Monitoring Systems, Report commissioned by DFID for the Strategic Partnership with Africa, London and Sussex.

Borraz, F., and E. López-Córdova (2004) Has Globalization Deepened Income Inequality in Mexico?, GTAP Resource 1455, www.gtap.agecon.purdue.edu/resources/download/1707.pdf, accessed April 2006.

Bourguignon, F. (2003) The Poverty-Growth-Inequality Triangle, paper prepared for Conference on Poverty, Inequality and Growth, Paris (November).

Bourguignon, F., F.H.G. Ferreira and P.G. Leite (2003) Conditional Cash Transfers, Schooling and Child Labor: Micro-Simulating Bolsa Escola, mimeo (www.eldis.org)

Bourguignon, F., and C. Morrisson (2002) Inequality among World Citizens: 1820–1992, *American Economic Review*, Vol. 92, No. 4: 727–44.

Bowles, S.S. (2000) Globalization and Economic Justice, Benjamin H. Hibbard Memorial Lecture, University of Wisconsin-Madison.

Bratton, M., and N. van de Walle (1992) Popular Protest and Political Reform in Africa, *Comparative Politics*, Vol. 24 (July).

Brawley, M.R. (2003) *The Politics of Globalization. Gaining Perspective, Assessing Consequences*, Peterborough: Broadview Press.

Breman, J.C. (1980) 'The Informal Sector' in Research: Theory and Practice, CASP 3, Rotterdam: Erasmus University.

Breman, A., and C. Shelton (2001) Structural Adjustment and Health: A Literature Review of the Debate, Its Role Players and Presented Empirical Evidence, Commission on Macroeconomics and Health Working Paper Series, No. WG6:6, WHO (June).

Brett, E.A. (2003) Participation and Accountability in Development Management, *Journal of Development Studies*, Vol. 40, No. 2: 1–29.

Brown, A., M. Foster, A. Norton and F. Naschold (2001) The Status of Sector Wide Approaches, Working Paper 142, London: ODI.

Brown, G. (2005) The Formation and Management of Political Identities: Indonesia and Malaysia Compared, Working Paper 10, Oxford: Centre for Research on Inequality, Human Security and Ethnicity (www.crise.ox.ac.uk/pubs/workingpaper10.pdf).

Brown, G. (2005a) Making Ethnic Citizens. The Politics and Practice of Education in Malaysia, Working Paper 23, Oxford: Centre for Research on Inequality, Human Security and Ethnicity, www.crise.ox.ac.uk/pubs/workingpaper23.pdf.

Brown, G., and F. Stewart (2006) The Implications of Horizontal Inequality for Aid, paper presented at UNU-WIDER Conference on Aid: Principles, Policies and Performance, Helsinki, 16–17 June, http://www.wider.unu.edu/conference/conference-2006-1.

Bruno, M., M. Ravallion and L. Squire (1996) Equity and Growth in Developing Countries. Old and New Perspectives on the Policy Issues, Policy Research Working Paper 1563, Washington DC: World Bank.

Budd, E. (2004) *Democratization, Development, and the Patrimonial State in the Age of Globalization*, Maryland: Lexington.

Budlender, D. (2000) The Political Economy of Women's Budgets in the South, *World Development*, Vol. 28, No. 7.

Budlender, D. (2003) Gender Budgets and Beyond: Feminist Fiscal Policy in the Context of Globalisation, *Gender and Development*, Vol. 11, No. 1 (May): 15–24.

Burgoon, B. (2001) Globalization and Welfare Compensation: Disentangling the Ties that Bind, *International Organisation*, Vol. 55, No. 3 (Summer): 509–52.

Bussolo, M., and H.-B. Sollignac Lecomte (1999) Trade Liberalization and Poverty, ODI Poverty Briefing No. 6, London: ODI.

Buvinic, M., and J. Mazza (2005) Gender and Social Inclusion: Social Policy Perspectives from Latin America and the Caribbean, paper for Arusha Conference New Frontiers of Social Policy, December, www.worldbank.org/socialpolicy.

Carter, M. (2004) Land Ownership Inequality and the Income Distribution Consequences of Economic Growth, in Cornia (2004) pp. 57–80.

Carvalho, S., and H. White (1997) Combining the Quantitative and Qualitative Approaches to Poverty Measurement and Analysis. The Practice and the Potential, World Bank Technical Paper No. 366, Washington, DC.

Castelló, A., and R. Doménech (2002) Human Capital Inequality and Economic Growth, *The Economic Journal*, Vol. 112 (March): C187–200.

Chang, H.-J. (2003) *Globalisation, Economic Development and the Role of the State*, London: Zed Books.

Chang, H.-J. (2004) The Role of Social Policy in Economic Development: Some Theoretical Reflections and Lessons from East Asia, in Mkandawire, (2004) pp. 246–61.

Chapman, K. (2006) Using Social Transfers to Scale Up Equitable Access to Education and Health Services, background paper, London: DFID.

Chen, S., G. Datt and M. Ravallion (1993) Is Poverty Increasing in the Developing World?, WPS No. 1146, Policy Research Department, Washington D.C.: World Bank.

Cheru, F. (2006) Building and Supporting PRSPs in Africa: What Has Worked Well So Far? What Needs Changing?, *Third World Quarterly*, Vol. 27, No. 2: 355–76.

Chopra, M. Sanders, R. Shimpton and A. Tomkins (2002) Making Nutrition a Part of Social Sector Reform: Challenges and Opportunities, Draft Background paper for the 5th Report on the World Nutrition Situation, presented in Berlin.

Christiansen, C., B.C. Yamba and S.R. Whyte (2004) Arenas of Child Support. Interfaces of Family, State and NGO Provisions of Social Security, paper for Arusha Conference New Frontiers of Social Policy (December), www.worldbank.org/socialpolicy.

Christiaensen, L., J. Hoddinott and G. Bergeron (2001) Comparing Village Characteristics Derived from Rapid Appraisals and Household Surveys: A Tale from Northern Mali, *Journal of Development Studies*, Vol. 37, No. 3: 1–20.

Christiaensen, L., L. Demery and S. Paternostro (2002) Growth, Distribution and Poverty in Africa. Messages from the 1990s, mimeo, Washington DC: World Bank.

Chu, Ke-young, H. Davoodi and S. Gupta (2000) Income Distribution and Tax and Government Social Spending Policies in Developing Countries, IMF Working Paper WP/00/62, Washington DC.

Cichon, M., W. Scholz, A. van de Meerendonk, K. Hagemejer, F. Bertranou and P. Plamondon (2004) *Financing Social Protection*, Geneva: International Labour Office and International Social Security Association.

Cigno, A., F.C. Rosati and L. Guarcello (2002) Does Globalisation Increase Child Labour?, *World Development*, Vol. 30, No. 9: 1579–90.

Clements, B., S. Gupta and G. Inchauste (2004) Fiscal Policy for Economic Development: An Overview, in Gupta et al. (2004) pp. 1–22, www.imf.org/external/pubs/nft/2004/hcd/ch01.pdf, accessed April 2006.

Cling, J.-P., D. Cogneau, J. Loup, J.-D. Naudet, M. Razafindrakoto and F. Roubaud (2006) Development, a Question of Opportunity? A Critique of the 2006 World Development Report: Equity and Development, *Development Policy Review*, Vol. 24, No. 4: 455–76.

Commission for Africa (2005) *Our Common Interest*, www.commissionforafrica.org

Commonwealth Secretariat (1999) *Gender Budget Initiative*, Commonwealth Secretariat, London.

Conway, T., A. de Haan, and A. Norton (eds) (2000) *Social Protection: New Directions of Donor Agencies*, DFID, London.

Cook, S., and G. White (2001) Alternative Approaches to Welfare Policy Analysis: New Institutional Economics, Politics, and Political Economy, in Mwabu et al. (2001) pp. 26–52.

Cook, S., N. Kabeer and G. Suwannarat (2003) *Social Protection in Asia*, Ford Foundation, New Delhi: Har-Anand Publications.

Corbridge, S., and G. Jones (2005) The Continuing Debate on Urban Bias, www.lse.ac.uk/collections/geographyAndEnvironment/research/Researchpapers/99%20corbridge%20jones.pdf

Cornia, G.A. (1999a) Social Funds in Stabilization and Adjustment Programmes, UNU/WIDER, Research for Action 48, Helsinki.

Cornia, G.A. (1999b) Liberalisation, Globalisation and Income Distribution, WIDER Working Paper No. 157.

Cornia, G.A. (ed.) (2004) *Inequality, Growth, and Poverty in an Era of Liberalization and Globalization*, UNU/WIDER, Oxford University Press.

Cornia, G.A., R. Jolly and F. Stewart (1987) *Adjustment with a Human Face*, Oxford: Clarendon Press.

Cornia, G.A., and L. Menchini (2005) The Pace and Distribution of Health Improvements During the Last 40 Years: Some Preliminary Results, UNDP–French Government Sponsored 'Forum on Human Development' Paris, 17–19 January.

Cornwall, A. (2004) New Democratic Spaces? The Politics and Dynamics of Institutionalised Participation, *IDS Bulletin*, Vol. 35, No. 2: 1–10.

Cornwall, A., and J. Gaventa (2000) From Users and Choosers to Makers and Shapers. Repositioning Participation in Social Policy, *IDS Bulletin*, Vol. 31, No. 4 (October): 50–62.

Coudouel, A., A. Dani and S. Paternostro (2006), *Poverty and Social Impact Analysis of Reforms. Lessons and Examples from Implementation*, Washington DC: World Bank.

Covey, J., and T. Abbot (1998) Social Funds: An Expanded NGO Critique in Bigio (1998), pp. 167–78.

Cox, R.H. (1998) 'The Consequences of Welfare Reform: How Conceptions of Social Rights are Changing, *Journal of Social Policy*, Vol. 27, No: 1: 1–16.

Cox, C., R. Jaramillo and F. Reimers (2005) *Educar Para la Ciudadanía y la Democracia en las Américas: Una Agenda para la Acción*, Washington DC: Inter-American Development Bank.

Craig, D., and D. Porter (2003) Poverty Reduction Strategy Papers: A New Convergence, *World Development*, Vol. 31, No. 1: 53–69.

Cramer, C. (2003) Does Inequality Cause Conflict?, *Journal of International Development*, Vol. 15: 397–412.

Datt, G., and M. Ravallion (2002) Is India's Economic Growth Leaving the Poor Behind, World Bank, Policy Research Working Paper.

Davies, R., and J. Rattsø (2001b) Zimbabwe: Economic Adjustment, Income Distribution and Trade Liberalization, in Taylor (2001), pp. 365–86.

Davis, P. (2004) Rethinking the Welfare Regimes Approach in the Context of Bangladesh, in Gough and Wood (2004) pp. 255–86.

Davoodi, H.R., E.R. Tiongson and S.S. Asawanuchit (2003) How Useful Are Benefit Incidence Analyses of Public Education and Health Spending, IMF Working Paper WP/03/227, Washington DC: IMF.

Deacon, B. (1997) *Global Social Policy: International Organisations and the Future of Welfare*, Sage.

Deacon, B. (1999) Social Policy in a Global Context, in A. Hurrell and N. Woods (eds), *Inequality, Globalization and World Politics*, Oxford University Press.

Deacon, B. (2000) Globalization and Social Policy, UNRISD Occasional Paper 5, Geneva.

Deacon, B. (2001) The Social Dimension of Regionalism. A Constructive Alternative to Neo-Liberal Globalisation?, GASPP Occasional Papers, No.8/2001.

Deacon, B. (2003) Prospects for Equitable Social Provision in a Globalising World, in P. Mosley and E. Dowler (eds), *Poverty and Social Exclusion in North and South. Essays on Social Policy and Global Poverty Reduction*, London and New York: Routledge, pp. 17–33.

Deacon, B. (2004) Globalization of the Welfare State? World Society, Transnational Social Policy and 'New Welfare State', paper for international conference at the Hanse Institute for Advanced Studies, Delmenhorst, Germany.

Deaton, A., and J. Drèze (2002) Poverty and Inequality in India. A Re-examination, *Economic and Political Weekly* (7 September): 3729–48.

De Ferranti, D., G.E. Perry, I. Gill and L. Servén (2000) *Securing Our Future in a Global Economy*, Washington DC: World Bank.

De Grauwe, P., and M. Polan (2003) Globalisation and Social Spending, Working Paper No. 885, http://www.econ.kuleuven.be/ew/academic/intecon/Degrauwe/PDG-Publications_recent.htm#discussion papers.

De Haan, A. (1994) Towards a Single Male Earner: Decline of Child and Female Employment in an Indian Industry, *Economic and Social History in the Netherlands*, Vol. 6.

De Haan, A. (1998) Social Exclusion: an Alternative Concept for the Study of Deprivation?, *IDS Bulletin*, Vol. 29, No. 1 (January).

De Haan, A. (1998a) Liberalisation, Employment and Changing Contours of the Informal Sector: A Note, *Manpower Journal*, Vol. 34, No. 3: 1–9.

De Haan, A. (2000) Components of Good Social Policy: Lessons Emerging from Social Policy Research, DFID Presentation, London (September).

De Haan, A. (2002) Nutrition in Poverty Reduction Strategy Papers, Background Paper for the 5th Report on the World Nutrition Situation.

De Haan, A. (2003) Globalisation and Social Policy – Thoughts for International Development Cooperation, in E. Dowler and P. Mosley (eds), *Poverty and Social Exclusion in North and South*, Routledge.

De Haan, A. (2004a) Conceptualising Social Exclusion in the Context of India's Poorest Regions: A Contribution to the Quantitative-Qualitative Debate, presented at conference 'Q-squared in Practice: Experiences of Combining Qualitative and Quantitative Methods in Poverty Appraisal', Toronto.

De Haan, A. (2004b) Globalisation, Exclusion and Social Policy, *Indian Journal of Labour Economics*.

De Haan, A. (2004c) Social Protection in the DFID India Programme, mimeo, Delhi: DFID.

De Haan. A. (2004d) Disparities within India's Poorest Region: Why Do the Same Institutions Work Differently in Different Places, Background Paper for World Development Report 2006, presented at World Bank, Washington DC, www.worldbank.org/socialpolicy.

De Haan, A. (2006) Migration in the Development Studies Literature: Has It Come Out of Marginality?, UNU-WIDER Research Paper RP/2006/19, Helsinki: WIDER, www.wider.unu.edu/publications/publications.htm.

De Haan, A., and A. Dubey (2003) Extreme Deprivation in Remote Areas in India: Social Exclusion as Explanatory Concept, paper for Manchester Conference on Chronic Poverty.

De Haan, A., and M. Everest-Phillips (2006) Can New Aid Modalities Handle Politics?, paper presented at Wider Annual Conference, Helsinki, June 2006.

De Haan, A., J. Holland and N. Kanji (2002) Social Funds: An Effective Instrument to Support Local Action for Poverty Reduction?, *Journal of International Development*, 14: 643–52.

De Haan, A.B. Huber and A. van den Heever (2001) Report of a Workshop on Integrating Social and Economic Policies, DFID and UNDESA, mimeo.

De Haan, A., with J Koch Laier (1997) Employment and Poverty Monitoring, Issues in Development Discussion Paper No. 19, Geneva: ILO.

De Haan, A., and M. Lipton, (1998) Poverty in Emerging Asia: Progress, Setbacks and Log-jams, *Asian Development Review*, Vol. 16, No. 2: 1–42.

De Haan, A., and M. Lipton (1998a) Anti-poverty Projects in Developing Countries: Towards Evaluating Success, paper commissioned by World Bank, Operations Evaluation Department, mimeo, Brighton: University of Sussex.

De Haan, A., M. Lipton, et al. (1999) Poverty Monitoring in Sub-Sahara Africa, Background Paper for the 1999 World Bank SPA Status Report on Poverty, mimeo, University of Sussex.

De Mello, L. (2002) Public Policies and the Millennium Development Goals, *IMF Research Bulletin*, Vol. 3, No. 4: 1–7.

De Mello, L.R., and E.R. Tiongson (2003) Income Inequality and Redistributive Government Spending, IMF Working Paper No. 03/14, Washington DC: IMF.

Degnbol-Martinussen, J., and P. Engberg-Pedersen (2003) *Aid: Understanding International Development Cooperation*, London: Zed Books.

Deininger, K., and L. Squire (1996) A New Data Set Measuring Income Inequality, *The World Bank Economic Review*, Vol. 10, No. 3: 565–91.

Deininger, K., and L. Squire (1998) New Ways of Looking at Old Issues: Inequality and Growth, *Journal of Development Economics*, Vol. 57: 259–87.

Deininger, K., and P. Olinto (2000) Asset Distribution, Inequality and Growth, Policy Research Working Paper 2375, Washington DC: World Bank.

Demery, L., M. Ferroni, C. Grootaert and J. Whong-Halle (1993) *Understanding the Social Effects of Policy Reform*, Washington DC: World Bank.

Dev, S.M., and J. Mooij (2002) Social Sector Expenditures and Budgeting. An Analysis of Patterns and the Budget-Making Process in India in the 1990s, Working Paper 43, Hyderabad: CESS.

Devereux, S., and S. Cook (2000) Does Social Policy Meet Social Needs?, *IDS Bulletin*, Vol. 31, No. 4 (October): 63–73.

DFID, Social Development Department (2001) Integrating Social and Economic Policies: A Contribution to the Debate, mimeo, London.

DFID (2005) Social Transfers and Chronic Poverty: Emerging Evidence and the Challenge Ahead. A DFID Practice Paper, DFID, London.

Dijkstra, G. (2005) The PRSP Approach and the Illusion of Improved Aid Effectiveness: Lessons from Bolivia, Honduras and Nicaragua, *Development Policy Review*, Vol. 23, No. 5.

Dijkstra, G. (2006) Rejoinder, *Development Policy Review*, Vol. 24, No. 4: 481–2.

Dijkstra, G., and J.K. van Donge (2001) What Does the Show Case Show? Evidence of and Lessons from Adjustment in Uganda, *World Development*, Vol. 29, No. 5: 841–63.

Dollar, D., and A. Kraey (2002) Growth is Good for the Poor, *Journal of Economic Growth*, Vol. 7, No. 3: 195–225.

Dow, J. (2003) The Social Inclusion/Exclusion Dichotomy in Guyana and the Caribbean, paper presented at seminar 'Good Practices in Social Inclusion: A Dialogue between Europe and Latin America and the Caribbean', 21 and 22 March, Milan.

Dreher, A. (2006) The Influence of Globalization on Taxes and Social Policy: An Empirical Analysis for OECD Countries, *European Journal of Political Economy*, Vol. 22: 179–201.

Drèze, J., and A. Sen (1989) *Hunger and Public Action*, Oxford: Clarendon Press.

Drèze, J., and A. Sen (2002) *India. Development and Participation*, New Delhi: Oxford University Press.

Drèze, J., and P.V. Srinivasan (1996) Poverty in India: Regional Estimates, DEP No. 70, Development Economics Research Programme, London: London School of Economics.

Drèze, J., and A. Sen (1991) Public Action for Social Security: Foundations and Strategy, in Ahmad et al. (1991), pp. 3–40.

Driscoll, R., with A. Evans (2005) Second-Generation Poverty Reduction Strategies: New Opportunities and Emerging Issues, *Development Policy Review*, Vol. 23, No. 1: 5–25.

Durevall, D., and F. Munshi (2006) Trade Liberalization and Wage Inequality: Empirical Evidence from Bangladesh, mimeo, Department of Economics, School of Business, Economics and Law, Göteborg University.

Dutt, A.K., and J.M. Rao (2001) India: Globalization and its Social Discontents, in Taylor (2001), pp. 179–216.

Easterly, W.R. (2006) *The White Man's Burden: Why the West's Efforts to Aid the Rest Have Done So Much Ill and So Little Good*, New York: Penguin Press.

Eastwood, R., and M. Lipton (2004) Rural and Urban Income Inequality and Poverty: Does Convergence between Sector Offset Divergence within Them?, in Cornia (2003) pp. 112–41.

Echeverri-Gent, J. (1993) *The State and the Poor. Public Policy and Political Development in India and the United States*, Berkeley: University of California Press.

Elson, D. (2004), Social Policy and Macroeconomic Performance: Integrating 'the Economic' and 'the Social', in Mkandawire (2004), 63–79.

Elson, D., and N. Çagatay (2000) The Social Content of Macro-economic Policies, *World Development*, Vol. 28, No. 7: 1347–64.

Elson, D., and N. Çagatay (2003) Introduction, *World Development*, Vol. 28, No. 7: 1145–56.

Esping-Andersen, G. (1990) *The Three Worlds of Welfare Capitalism*. Cambridge: Polity.

Esping-Andersen, G. (1999) *Social Foundations of Postindustrial Economies*, Oxford University Press.

Eyben, R. (2005) World Development Report 2006: Equity and Development. Response, http://www.ids.ac.uk/ids/news/EybenWDRresponse.pdf.

Eyoh, D., and R. Sandbrook (2003) Pragmatic Neo-liberalism and Just Development in Africa, in Kohli et al. (2003) pp. 227–57.

Falkinger, J., and V. Grossmann (2005) Institutions and Development: The Interaction between Trade Regime and Political System, *Journal of Economic Growth*, Vol. 10: 231–72.

Fan, S., and N. Rao (2003) Public Spending in Developing Countries: Trend, Determination and Impact, Discussion Paper, International Food Policy Research Institute . Washington DC.

Fanelli, J.M. (2004) Understanding Reform. A Global GDN Research Project, overview paper presented at the 5th Annual Global Development Conference 'Understanding Reform', New Delhi, 28–30 January.

Ferguson, C. (1999) Global Social Policy Principles: Human Rights and Social Justice, DFID, Social Development Department, London.

Ferreira, F., G. Prennushi and M. Ravallion (n.d.) Protecting the Poor from Macro-economic Shocks: An Agenda for Action in a Crisis and Beyond, World Bank (http://econ.worldbank.org/docs/791.pdf)

Ferreira, F.H.G., J. A. Litchfield and P.G. Leite (2006) The Rise and Fall of Brazilian Inequality, 1981–2004, World Bank Policy Research Working Paper 3867, Washington DC: World Bank.

Figueroa, A., and M. Barrón (2005) Inequality, Ethnicity, and Social Disorder in Peru, CRISE Working Paper No. 8, Oxford: Centre for Research on Inequality, Human Security and Ethnicity (www.crise.ox.ac.uk/pubs).

Fontana, M., and A. Wood (2001) Modelling the Impact of Trade Liberalisation on Women at Work and at Home, ESCOR Report, London: DFID.

Forbes, K. (2000) A Re-assessment of the Relationship between Inequality and Growth, *American Economic Review*, Vol. 90: 869–87.

Foreign Policy (2004) Measuring Globalization. Economic Reversals, Forward Momentum, *Foreign Policy* (March/April): 54–69.

Foster, M. (2000) New Approaches to Development Co-operation: What Can We Learn from Experiences with Implementing Sector Wide Approaches?, Working Paper 140, London: ODI.

Frankenberger, T., R. Caldwell and J. Mazzeo (2002) Empowerment and Governance: Basic Elements for Improving Nutritional Outcomes, background paper for the ACC/SCN 5th Report on the World Nutrition Situation.

Fumo, C., A. de Haan, J. Holland and N. Kanji (2000) *Social Fund: An Effective Way to Support Local Action for Poverty Reduction?*, London: DFID.

Gaiha, R., and V.S. Kulkarni (2006) Common Interest Groups, Village Institutions and Rural Poor in India – A Review of the District Poverty Initiatives Project, mimeo, to appear in *Contemporary South Asia*, New Delhi.

Galanter, M. (1984) *Competing Equalities. Law and the Backward Classes in India*, Berkeley and Los Angeles: University of California Press.

Gasparini, L. (2004) Poverty and Inequality in Argentina: Methodological Issues and a Literature Review, Centro de Estudios Distributivos, Laborales y Sociales, Universidad Nacional de La Plata.

Gasparini, L., and F.M. Bertranou (2005) Social Protection and the Labour Market in Latin America. What Can Be Learned from Household Surveys, *International Social Security Review*, Vol. 58, No. 2–3: 15–42.

Gaspart, F., and J.-P. Platteau (2006) The Perverse Effect of Cheap Aid Money, paper presented at UNU-WIDER Conference on Aid: Principles, Policies and Performance, Helsinki, 16–17 June, http://www.wider.unu.edu/conference/conference-2006-1.

Gayi, S. (1995) Adjusting to the Social Costs of Adjustment in Ghana: Problems and Prospects, *European Journal of Development Research*, Vol. 7 (June): 77–100.

Gelb, S. (2003) *Inequality in South Africa: Nature, Causes and Responses for DFID Policy Initiative on Addressing Inequality in Middle-income Countries*, Johannesburg; The Edge Institute (www.the-edge.org.za/publications.htm).

Gelbach, J.B., and L.H. Pritchet (1997) More for the Poor Is Less for the Poor, Policy Research Working Paper 1799, Washington DC: World Bank.

Ghosh, D.N. (1999) Globalization and National Policies, *Economic and Political Weekly* (25 September).

Gibbon, P. (1996) Structural Adjustment and Structural Change in Sub-Saharan Africa: Some Provisional Conclusions, *Development and Change*, Vol. 27: 751–84.

Gill, I., T. Packard and J. Yermo (2005) *Keeping the Promise of Social Security in Latin America*, Washington DC: World Bank; Palo Alto, CA: Stanford University Press.

Gillespie, S., and L. Haddad (2001) Attacking the Double Burden of Malnutrition in Asia and the Pacific, Asian Development Bank, Manila, Nutrition and Development Series No. 4, and IFPRI, Washington.

Gilson, L., and D. McIntyre (2005) Removing User Fees for Primary Care in Africa: The Need for Careful Action, *British Medical Journal*, Vol. 331: 762–5.

Glaessner, P. et al. (1994) Poverty Alleviation and Social Investment Funds: the Latin American Experience, Discussion Paper No. 261, Washington, DC: World Bank.

Glewwe, P., M. Gragrolati and M. Zaman (2000) Who Gained from Vietnam's Boom in 1990s? An Analysis of Poverty and Inequality Trends, World Bank Policy Research, Working Paper No. 2275, Washington DC: World Bank.

Glewwe P., S. Koch and Buihing Nguyer (2002) Child Nutrition, Economic Growth and the Provision of Health Care Services in Vietnam in the 1990s, Policy Research Working Paper Series 2776, Washington DC: World Bank.

Global Social Policy (2006) Forum on the World Bank and Social Development Policy, Vol. 6, No. 3: 259–87.

Gottschalk, R. (2005) The Macro Content of PRSPs: Assessing the Need for a More Flexible Macroeconomic Policy Framework, *Development Policy Review*, Vol. 23, No. 4: 419–42.

Gough, I. (2000) Welfare Regimes: On Adapting the Framework to Developing Countries, Global Social Policy Working Paper No.1, IFIPA, University of Bath.

Gough, I. (2004) Welfare Regimes in Development Contexts: A Global and Regional Analysis, in Gough and Wood (2004) pp. 15–48.

Gough, I. (2004a) East Asia: The Limits of Productivist Regimes, in Gough and Wood, (2004) pp. 169–201.

Gough, I. (2005) European Welfare States: Explanations and Lessons for Developing Countries, paper for Arusha Conference New Frontiers of Social Policy (December) www.worldbank.org/socialpolicy.

Gough, I., and G. Wood (2004) *Insecurity and Welfare Regimes in Asia, Africa and Latin America*, Cambridge University Press.

Government of Malawi (2002) Malawi Poverty Reduction Strategy Paper. Final Draft, http://povlibrary.worldbank.org/files/Malawi_PRSP.pdf.

Government of Malawi, Ministry of Economic Planning and Development (2006) Malawi Poverty Reduction Strategy: 2004/2005 Annual Review Report, http://siteresources.worldbank.org/INTPRS1/Resources/Malawi_APR2_Jan2006_.pdf.

Graham, C. (2002) Crafting Sustainable Social Contracts in Latin America: Political Economy, Public Attitudes, and Social Policy, The Brookings Institute, Working Paper, http://www.brookings.edu/es/dynamics/papers/socialcontracts/socialcontracts.pdf

Graham, C. (2002a) Public Attitudes Matter: A Conceptual Frame for Accounting for Political Economy in Safety Nets and Social Assistance Policies, Social Protection Discussion Paper Series, No. 0233, Washington DC: World Bank.

Grindle, M.S. (2002) Good Enough Governance: Poverty Reduction and Reform in Developing Countries, Harvard University, Mimeo.

Grootaert, C., and T. Marchant (1991) The Social Dimensions of Adjustment Priority Survey. An Instrument for the Rapid Identification and Monitoring of Policy Target Groups, SDA Working Paper Series No. 12, Washington DC: World Bank.

Grosh, M.E., and P. Glewwe (1995) A Guide to Living Standard Measurement Study Surveys and Their Data Sets, LSMS Working Paper No.120, Washington DC: World Bank.

Grown, C., D. Elson and N. Cagatay (2000) Introduction, *World Development*, Vol. 28, No. 7: 1145–56.

Guan, X. (2005) China's Social Policy Reform and Development in the Context of Marketization and Globalization, in Kwon (2005) pp. 231–56.

Gupta, S., M. Verhoeven and E.R. Tiongson (2004) Public Spending on Health Care and the Poor, in Gupta et al. (2004) pp. 213–32.

Gupta, S., B. Clements and G. Inchauste (eds) (2004) *Helping Countries Develop. The Role of Fiscal Policy*, Washington DC: International Monetary Fund.

Gupta, S., B. Clements, M. Teresa Guin-Siu and L. Leruth (2001) Debt Relief and Public Health Spending in Heavily Indebted Poor Countries, *Finance and Development*, vol. 38, no. 3.

Hall, A., and J. Midgley (2004) *Social Policy for Development*, London: Sage.

Harriss, E., and C. Kende-Robb (2005) Integrating Macroeconomic Policies and Social Objectives: Choosing the Right Policy Mix for Poverty Reduction, paper for Arusha Conference New Frontiers of Social Policy, December, www.worldbank.org/socialpolicy.

Harriss, J. (2001) Globalisation and the World's Poor: Institutions, Inequality and Justice, *Economic and Political Weekly* (9 June).

Heller, P., et al. (2006) Managing Fiscal Policy in Low Income Countries: How to Reconcile a Scaling Up of Aid Flows and Debt Relief with Macroeconomic Stability, paper presented at UNU-WIDER Conference on Aid: Principles, Policies and Performance, Helsinki, 16–17 June, www.wider.unu.edu/conference/conference-2006-1.

HelpAge International (2003) *Non-contributory Pensions and Poverty Prevention. A Comparative Study of Brazil and South Africa*, London.

HelpAge International (2004) *Age and Security. Summary Report. How Social Pensions Can Deliver Effective Aid to Poor Older People and Their Families*, London, www.helpage.org.

Herbst, J. (1994) The Dilemmas of Explaining Political Upheaval: Ghana in Comparative Perspective, in Widner (1994), pp. 182–98.

Herbst, J. (2000) *States and Power in Africa. Comparative Lessons in Authority and Control*. Princeton University Press.

Hermes, N., and R. Lensink (2001) Changing the Conditions for Development Aid. A New Paradigm?, *Journal of Development Studies*, Vol. 37, No. 6.

Heslop, A. (1999) Ageing and Development, Social Development Department Working Paper No. 3, London: DFID.

Hickey, S. (2005) The Politics of Staying Poor: Exploring the Political Space for Poverty Reduction in Uganda, *World Development*, Vol. 33, No. 6: 995–1009.

Hill, M. (1996) *Social Policy: A Comparative Analysis*, London: Prentice Hall.

Hillman, A., and E. Jenker (2004) User Payment for Basic Education in Low-Income Countries, in Gupta et al. (2004) pp. 213–64.

Hirst, P., and G. Thompson (1996) *Globalisation in Question: the International Economy and the Possibilities of Governance*, Cambridge: Polity.

Hoekman, B., and A.L. Winters (2005) Trade and Employment. Stylized Facts and Research Findings, Policy Research Working Paper 3676, Washington DC: World Bank.

Holland, Jeremy (1999) The Role and Process of Poverty Analysis in Social Funds: Implications for the Egypt Social Fund for Development, mimeo, Swansea.

Holmström, M. (1984) *Industry and Inequality. The Social Anthropology of Indian Labour*, Cambridge University Press.

Holmqvist, G., and K. Metell Cueva (2006) If the PRSP Experiment in Latin America Is a Disappointment, What Is the Alternative?, *Development Policy Review*, Vol. 24, No. 4: 477–80.

Holtz, S. (1998) Integrating Environmental, Social and Economic Policies, Chapter 12, *The Cornerstone of Development. Integrating Environmental, Social and Economic Policies*, http://www.idrc.ca/en/ev-64483-201-1-DO_TOPIC.html (accessed February 2006).

Holzmann, R. (2003) Risk and Vulnerability: The Forward-Looking Role of Social Protection in a Globalizing World, in P. Mosley and E. Dowler (eds), *Poverty and Social Exclusion in North and South. Essays on Social Policy and Global Poverty Reduction*, London and New York: Routledge: pp.47–79.

Holzmann, R., and R. Hinz (2005) *Old Age Income Support in the 21st Century. An International Perspective on Pension Systems and Reform*, Washington DC: World Bank.

Holzmann, R., and S. Jorgensen (2000) Social Risk Management: A New Conceptual Framework for Social Protection and Beyond. Social Protection Discussion Paper 0006, Washington DC World Bank.

Hook, L. (2006) The Rise of China's New Left, *Far Eastern Economic Review*, Vol. 170, No. 3: 8–14.

Hort, S. (2005) The Geography of Comparative Welfare State Research. A Comment, *Global Social Policy*, Vol. 5, No. 1: 14–17.

Hort, S.E.O., and S. Kuhnle (2000) The Coming of East and South-East Asian Welfare States, *Journal of European Social Policy*, Vol. 10, No. 2: 162–84.

Howell, J. (2006) Reflections on the Chinese State, *Development and Change*, Vol. 37, No. 2: 273.

Ibrahim, J. (2006) Affirmative Action. Nigeria, Inter-Regional Inequality Facility, Policy Brief 15, http://www.odi.org.uk/inter-regional_inequality/papers/Policy%20Brief%2015%20-%20Nigeria.pdf

IMF (2000) Globalization: Threat or Opportunity? An IMF Issues Brief, April, www.imf.org/external/np/exr/ib/2000/041200.htm.

IMF and World Bank (2005) PRS Review: Balancing Accountabilities and Scaling Up Results, Washington DC: World Bank, http://siteresources.worldbank.org/INTPRS1/Resources/PRSP-Review/2005_Review_Final.pdf.

James, E. (1999) Old Age Protection for the Uninsured – What are the Issues?, mimeo, Washington DC: World Bank.

Jamison, D.T., and S. Radelet (2005) Making Aid Smarter, *Finance and Development*, Vol. 42, No. 2; www.imf.org/external/pubs/ft/fandd/2005/06/jamison.htm.

Jenkins, C., and L. Thomas (2004) The Changing Nature of Inequality in South Africa, in Cornia (2004) pp. 376–404.

Jenkins, R. (2003) Globalisation and Employment: Working for the Poor?, *Insights*, June, www.id21.org.

Jha, R. (2004) Reducing Poverty and Inequality in India: Has Liberalization Helped, in: Cornia (2003) pp. 297–326.

Johannsen, L. (2005) The Responsive State: Openness and Inclusion in the Policy Process, paper for Arusha Conference New Frontiers of Social Policy, December, www.worldbank.org/socialpolicy.

Jonsson, U. (1997) Malnutrition in South Asia, paper at the ACC/SCN 24th Session Symposium, Kathmandu, Nutrition Policy Paper No. 6.

Jorgensen, S.L., and J. Van Domelen (1999) Helping the Poor Manage Risk Better: the Role of Social Funds, Paper presented at the IADB Conference on Social Protection and Poverty, February 1999.

Joshi, A. (2005) Do Rights Work? Law, Activism and the Employment Guarantee Scheme, IDS Sussex, http://www.ids.ac.uk/gdr/cfs/drc-pubs/summaries/summary%2013%20-Joshi-EGS-DoRightsWork.pdf

Joshi, S. (2006) Impact of Economic Reforms on Social Sector Expenditure in India, *Economic and Political Weekly*, Vol. XLI, No. 4 (28 January): 358–65.

Kabeer, N. (2004) Imagining 'the Social': Social Policy Analysis for the Poor in Poor Countries, IDS Working Paper 191, Brighton: IDS.

Kabeer, N. (2004) Gender Equality, Economic Growth, Poverty Reduction: Maximizing Synergies, Minimizing Trade-offs, presentation at DFID, London.

Kabeer, N., and S. Cook (2000) Editorial Introduction: Revisioning Social Policy in the South: Challenges and Concepts, *IDS Bulletin*, Vol. 31, No. 4: 1–10.

Kabeer, N., S. Mahmud and Tran Thi Van Anh (2003) The Poverty Impacts of Female Employment, *Insights*, June, www.id21.org.

Kaiser, P.K. (1996) Structural Adjustment and the Fragile Nation: the Demise of Social Unity in Tanzania, *The Journal of Modern African Studies*, Vol. 34, No. 2: 227–37.

Kakwani, N., H.H. Son and R. Hinz (2006) Poverty, Old-Age and Social Pensions in Kenya, Working Paper 26, International Poverty Centre, Brasilia, www.undp.org/povertycentre.

Kanbur, R. (2001) Economic Policy, Distribution and Poverty: The Nature of Disagreements, www.people.cornell.edu/pages/sk145/papers.htm.

Kanbur, R. (ed.) (2003) *Q-Squared. Qualitative and Quantitative Methods of Poverty Appraisal*, Delhi: Permanent Black.

Kanbur, R. (2005) What's Social Policy Got to Do with Economic Growth?, Arusha Conference New Frontiers of Social Policy, December, www.worldbank.org/socialpolicy.

Kanbur, R. and A.J. Venables, Spatial Inequality and Development', introduction to edited volume of conference papers, http://people.cornell.edu/pages/sk145/papers.htm.

Kanbur, R., and X. Zhang (2004) Fifty Years of Regional Inequality in China. A Journey Through Central Planning, Reform and Openness, WIDER Discussion Paper, 2004/50, http://www.wider.unu.edu/publications/rps/rps2004/rp2004-050.pdf

Kaul, I., and P. Conceição (eds) (2006) *The New Public Finance. Responding to Global Challenges*, published for UNDP, Oxford University Press.

Kayizzi-Mugerwa, S. (ed.) (2003), *Reforming Africa's Institutions. Ownership, Incentives, and Capabilities*, UNU/WIDER, United Nations University Press, Japan.

Kearny, A.T. and Foreign Policy (2004) 'Measuring Globalization', *Foreign Policy*, March/April, pp. 54–69.

Kerr, J., and C. Sweetman (2003) Editorial, *Gender and Development*, Vol. 11, No. 1: 3–12.

Khoo Boo Teik (2004) Managing Ethnic Relations in Post-Crisis Malaysia and Indonesia. Lessons from the New Economic Policy?, Identities, Conflict and Cohesion Programme Paper No. 6, Geneva: UNRISD.

Killick, T. (1999) Making Adjustment Work For the Poor, ODI Poverty Briefing No. 5, London: Overseas Development Institute.

Killick, T. (2005) Policy Autonomy and the History of British Aid to Africa, *Development Policy Review*, Vol. 23, No. 6: 665–81.

Klasen, S. (1999) Does Gender Inequality Reduce Growth and Development? Evidence from Cross-Country Regressions, World Bank Policy Research Report Working Paper No. 7, Washington DC: World Bank.

Klasen, S. (2005) Pro-Poor Growth and Gender. What Can We Learn from the Literature and the OPPG Case Studies?, unpublished paper for the multi-donor Operationalizing Pro-Poor Growth research program.

Klump, R., and T. Bonschab (2005) Operationalizing Pro-Poor Growth: A Case Study on Vietnam, paper for joint-donor Operationalizing Pro-Poor Growth research programme.

Kohli, A., C. Moon and G. Sörensen (eds) (2003) *States, Markets, and Just Growth, Development in the Twenty-first Century*, Tokyo: United Nations University Press.

Kraay, A. (2004) When Is Growth Pro-Poor? Cross Country Evidence, IMF Working Paper No. 04/47, Washington DC: IMF.

Kuhnle, S., and S.E.O. Hort (2004) The Developmental Welfare State in Scandinavia. Lessons for the Developing World, Social Policy and Development – Paper No. 17, UNRISD, Geneva.

Kulundu Manda, D. (2003) Incentive Structure and Efficiency in the Kenyan Civil Service, in Kayizzi-Mugerwa (2003) pp. 149–69.

Kumar, S. (2001) Study of Political Systems and Voting Behaviour of the Poor in Orissa, Report for DFID-India, Delhi.

Kwon, Huck-Ju (ed) (2005) *Transforming the Developmental Welfare State in East Asia*, UNRISD, Palgrave Macmillan.

Kwon, Huck-Ju (2005a) An Overview of the Study: The Developmental Welfare State and Policy Reforms in East Asia, in Kwon (2005) pp. 1–23.

Kwon, Huck-Ju (2005b) Reform of the Developmental Welfare State in Korea: Advocacy Coalitions and Health Politics, in Kwon (2005) pp. 27–49.

Lavalette, M., and A. Pratt (eds) (1997) *Social Policy: A Conceptual and Theoretical Introduction*, London: Sage Publications.

Lavergne, R., and A. Alba (2003) *CIDA Primer on Program-based Approaches*. Gatineau, Quebec: CIDA Policy Branch, http://www.acdi-cida.gc.ca/INET/IMAGES.NSF/vLUImages/CapacityDevelopment2/$file/Program%20Based%20Approaches-E.pdf (accessed February 2006).

Lecours, A. (2005) New Institutionalism: Issues and Questions, in A. Lecours (ed), *New Institutionalism: Theory and Analysis*, University of Toronto Press, pp. 3–25.

Lewis, P. M. (1996) Economic Reform and Political Transition in Africa, *World Politics*, Vol. 49, No. 1: 92–129.

Lindert, P.H. (2004) *Growing Public: Social Spending and Economic Growth since the Eighteenth Century*, 2 vols, Cambridge University Press.

Lipton, M. (1998) *Successes in Anti-poverty*, Geneva: International Labour Organisation.

Lipumba, N.H.I. (2006) Aid, Growth and Achieving Millennium Development Goals in Tanzania, paper presented at UNU-WIDER Conference on Aid: Principles, Policies and Performance, Helsinki, 16–17 June, http://www.wider.unu.edu/conference/conference-2006-1.

Lister, R. (1997) *Citizenship: Feminist Perspectives*, Basingstoke: Palgrave Macmillan.

Lloyd-Sherlock, P. (2000) Failing the Needy: Public Social Spending in Latin America, *Journal of International Development*, 12: 101–19.

Lofgren, H., and S. Robinson (2004) Public Spending, Growth, and Poverty Alleviation in Sub-Saharan Africa: A Dynamic General Equilibrium Analysis, paper prepared for presentation at the conference 'Growth, poverty reduction and human development in Africa', Centre for the Study of African Economies, University of Oxford, 21–22 March, revised 21 May.

Lopez, H. (2004) Pro Growth, Pro Poor. Is There a Trade Off?, paper for the PREM Pro Poor Growth Program, Washington DC: The World Bank.

Lundberg, M., and L. Squire (1999) The Simultaneous Evolution of Growth and Inequality, Mimeo, Washington DC: World Bank.

Mackintosh, M., and P. Tibandebaga (2004) Inequality and Redistribution in Health Care: Analytical Issues for Developmental Social Policy, in Mkandawire (2004) pp. 143–74.

Mamdani, M. (2001) *When Victims Become Killers. Colonialism, Nativism, and the Genocide in Rwanda*, Princeton University Press.

Mamdani, M. (2005) Political Violence and the Dilemma of Citizenship in Post Colonial Africa, paper for the Conference New Frontiers of Social Policy, Arusha, www.worldbank.org/socialpolicy.

Mander, H. (2004) *The Ripped Chest. Public Policy and Poor People in India*, Bangalore: Books for Change.

Manji, F. (2000) Social Policy and Rights in Africa: From Social Contract to Loss of Self-determination, *IDS Bulletin*, Vol. 31, No. 4.

Manov, J. (2005) Introduction, *IDS Bulletin* on Increased Aid: Minimising Problems, Maximising Gains, Vol. 36, No. 3: 1–7.

Marphatia, A.A., and D. Archer (2005) *Monetary Policies of IMF Reduce Country Spending on MDGs*, ActionAid International.

Marshall, T.H. (1950) *Citizenship and Social Class*, Cambridge University Press.

Marshall, K., and O. Butzbach (eds) (2003) *New Social Policy Agendas for Europe and Asia. Challenges, Experiences and Lessons*, Washington D.C.: World Bank.

Mason, M. (1997) *Development and Disorder. A History of the Third World since 1945*, Hanover and London: University Press of New England.

Mason, J., J. Hunt, D. Parker and U. Jonsson (2001) *Improving Child Nutrition in Asia*, Asian Development Bank. Nutrition and Development Series No. 3, Manila and UNICEF, New York.

Matijascic, M., and S.J. Kay (2006) Social Security at the Crossroads: Towards Effective Pension Reform in Latin America, *International Social Security Review*, Vol. 59, No. 1: 3–26.

Maxwell, S. (2001) Innovative and Important, Yes, But Also Instrumental and Incomplete: The Treatment of Redistribution in the New 'New Poverty Agenda', *Journal of International Development*, Vol. 13, No. XX: 331–41.

Maxwell, S. (2006) What's Next in International Development? Perspectives from the 20% Club and the 0.2% Club, Working Paper 270, London: ODI.

Mayer, D. (2001) The Long-Term Impact of Health on Economic Growth, *World Development*, Vol. 29, No. 6, 1025–33.

Mcleod D., and P. Dudzik (2000) Including the Most Vulnerable: Social Funds and People with Disabilities, World Bank: HDNSP, mimeo.

Medrano, P., C. Sanhueza and D. Contreras (2006) *Inequality in Latin America: A Synthesis of Recent Research on the Levels, Trends, Effects and Determinants of Inequality in its Different Dimensions,* Inter-Regional Inequality Facility, London.

Mehrotra, S. (2000) Integrating Economic and Social Policy: Good Practices from High-Achieving Countries, Innocenti Working Papers No. 80, Florence, http://www.unicef-icdc.org/publications/.

Mekong Economics Ltd (2005) Vietnam Inequality Report 2005: Assessment and Policy Choices, Paper for DFID Vietnam.

Mesa-Lago, C. (1997) Social Welfare Reform in the Context of Political-Economic Liberalization: Latin American Cases, *World Development,* Vol. 25, No. 4: 497–517.

Mesa-Lago, C., with A. Arenas de Mesa, I. Brenes, V. Montecions and M. Samara (2000) *Market, Socialist, and Mixed Economies. Comparative Policy and Performance. Chile, Cuba, and Costa Rica,* Baltimore: Johns Hopkins University Press.

Milanovic, B. (1999) Do More Unequal Countries Redistribute More? Does the Median Voter Hypothesis Hold?, Washington DC: World Bank.

Milanovic, B. (2003) The Two Faces of Globalization: Against Globalization as We Know It, *World Development,* Vol. 31, No. 4: 667–83.

Milanovic, B. (2003b) Is Inequality in Africa Really Different?, Mimeo, World Bank.

Milly, D.J. (1999) *Poverty, Equality, and Growth. The Politics of Economic Need in Postwar Japan,* Cambridge, MA: Harvard University Press.

Mishra, R. (1998) Beyond the Nation State: Social Policy in an Age of Globalization, *Social Policy and Administration,* Vol. 32, No. 5: 481–500.

Mishra, R. (1999) *Globalization and the Welfare State,* Cheltenham: Edward Elgar.

Mkandawire, T. (2000) *Social Policy in a Development Context,* Geneva: UNRISD.

Mkandawire, T. (ed.) (2004) *Social Policy in a Development Context,* UNRISD, Palgrave Macmillan.

Mkandawire, T. (2005) Targeting and Universalism in Poverty Reduction, Social Policy and Development Programme Paper No. 23, Geneva: UNRISD.

Moncrieffe, J. (2004) Beyond Categories: Power, Recognition and the Conditions for Equity, Background Paper for WDR 2006, www.worldbank.org/socialpolicy.

Moncrieffe, J., and R. Eyben (eds) (Forthcoming) *The Power of Labelling. How People Are Categorized and Why It Matters.* London: Earthscan.

Moore, M. (1994) Support for Good Government: Strategies for Donors, mimeo, Brighton: Institute of Development Studies.

Moore, M. (2000) States, Social Policies and Globalisations: Arguing on the Right Terrain?, *IDS Bulletin,* Vol. 31, No. 4, (October): 21–31.

Morales-Gómez, D. (ed.) (1999) *Transnational Social Policies. The New Challenges of Globalization,* London: Earthscan.

Morgan, R. (1991) Social Security in the SADCC States of South Africa: Social Welfare Programmes and the Reduction of Household Vulnerability, in Ahmad et al. (1991), pp. 415–66.

Moser, C. (1992) From Residual Welfare to Compensatory Measures: The Changing Agenda of Social Policy in Developing Countries, Silver Jubilee Paper 6, Brighton: IDS Sussex.

Motonishi, T. (2003) Why Has Income Inequality in Thailand Increased? An Analysis Using 1975–1998 Surveys, ADB ERD Working Paper No. 43, Manila: Asian Development Bank, www.adb.org/Economics.

Munck, R. (2005) *Globalization and Social Exclusion. A Transformationalist Perspective*, Bloomfield: Kumarian Press.

Musgrove, P., R. Zeramdini and G. Carrin (2002) Basic Patterns in National Health Expenditure, *Bulletin of the World Health Organization*, Vol. 80, No. 2: 134–46.

Mwabu, G., C. Ugaz and G. White (eds) (2001) *Social Provision in Low-Income Countries. New Patterns and Emerging Trends*, Oxford: UNU/WIDER and Oxford University Press.

Narayan, D., et al. (2000) *Voices of the Poor: Can Anyone Hear Us?*, New York: Oxford University Press for the World Bank.

Narayan, D., and K. Ebbe (1997) Design of Social Funds. Participation, Demand Orientation and Local Organizational Capacity. Discussion Paper No. 375 Washington DC: World Bank.

Nayyar, D. (ed.) (2002) *Governing Globalization. Issues and Institutions*, Delhi: Oxford University Press.

Nel, P. (2003) Income Inequality, Economic Growth, and Political Instability in Sub-Saharan Africa, *Journal of Modern African Studies*, Vol. 41, No. 4: 611–39.

Nel, P. (2006) The Return of Inequality. Review Article, *Third World Quarterly*, Vol. 27, No. 4: 689–706.

Nemer, L., H. Gelband and P. Jha (2001) The Evidence Base for Interventions to Reduce Malnutrition in Children under Five and School-age Children in Low and Middle-Income Countries, WHO, CMH Working Paper Series, No. WG5: 11, www3.who.int/whosis/cmh/cmh_papers.

Nielsen, I., C. Nyland, R. Smyth and C. Zhu (2005) Marketization and Perceptions of Social Protection in China's Cities, *World Development*, Vol. 33, No. 11: 1759–81.

Nissanke, M., and E. Thorbecke (2005) Channels and Policy Debate in the Globalization-Inequality-Poverty Nexus, WIDER Discussion Paper No.2005/08.

Nyamu-Musembi, C., and A. Cornwall (2004) What Is the Rights-based Approach All About? Perspectives from International Development Agencies, IDS Working Paper 234, Sussex, UK.

Norton, A., and B. Bird (1998) *Social Development Issues in Sector Wide Approaches*, London: DFID.

Norton, A. et al. (2000) Social Protection Concepts and Approaches: Implications for Policy and Practice. An Issues Paper for DFID in Conway et al. (2000).

Norton, A. et al. (ed.) (2001) *A Rough Guide to PPAs – Participatory Poverty Assessments 2001. An Introduction to Theory and Practice*, London: ODI.

Norton, A., and S. Conlin (2000) Globalisation Processes and the Implications for the Development of Global Responses in the Field of Social Policy, DFID, SDD, Background Paper for White Paper 2.

Norton, A., and D. Elson (2002) *What's Behind the Budget? Politics, Rights and Accountability in the Budget Process*, London: ODI.

Ohno, K. (2003) The Role of Government in Promoting Industrialization under Globalization: The East Asian Experience, paper based on presentation at Work shop on Capacity Enhancement, Yangon, http://www.markets4poor.org/.

Okidi, J.A., S. Ssewanyana, L. Bategeka and F. Muhumuza (2005) Operationalizing Pro-Poor Growth: A Case Study on Uganda, paper for joint-donor Operationalizing Pro-Poor Growth Research programme, www.dfid.gov.uk.

Okojie, C., and A. Shimeles (2006) Inequality in Africa: A Synthesis of Recent Research on the Levels, Trends, Effects and Determinants of Inequality in its Different Dimensions, Inter-Regional Inequality Facility, London: ODI.

Önis, X. (2006) Varieties and Crisis of Neoliberal Globalisation: Argentine, Turkey and the IMF, *Third World Quarterly*, Vol. 27, No. 2: 239–63.

OPM, Oxford Policy Management (N. Thin, M. Underwood and J. Gilling) (2001) Sub-Saharan Africa's Poverty Reduction Strategy Papers: Social Policy and Sustainable Livelihoods Perspectives, Report for DFID, Oxford.

Ortiz, I. (2000) ADB's Social Protection Framework, in Conway et al. (2000).

Osei-Hwedie, K., and Arnon Bar-on (1999) Sub-Saharan Africa. Community-Driven Social Policies, in Morales-Gómez (1999) pp. 89–115.

Osmani, S.R. (1997) Poverty and Nutrition in South Asia, paper at the ACC/SCN 24th Session Symposium, Kathmandu. Nutrition Policy Paper No. 6.

Osmani, S.R. (2002) *Exploring the Employment Nexus: Topics in Employment and Poverty*, report prepared for the Task Force on the Joint ILO-UNDP Programme on Employment and Poverty, UNDP/ILO.

Owen, D., and J. Van Domelen (1998) Getting an Earful: A Review of Beneficiary Assessments of Social Funds, World Bank, Social Protection Discussion Paper 9816.

Owens, T., and A. Wood (1997) Export-Oriented Industrialization through Primary Processing?, *World Development*, Vol. 25, No. 9: 1453–70.

Owusu, F. (2003) Pragmatism and the Gradual Shift from Dependency to Neoliberalism: The World Bank, African Leaders and Development Policy in Africa, *World Development*, Vol. 31, No. 10: 1655–72.

Palma, J., and R. Urzúa (2005) Anti-poverty Policies and Citizenry: the Chile Solidario Experience, UNESCO, MOST Policy Papers 12, www.unesco.org/shs/most.

Parker, A., and R. Serrano (2000) Promoting Good Local Governance through Social Funds and Decentralization, paper presented at World Bank 2nd International Conference on Social Funds, Washington DC.

Paternostro, S., E.R. Tiongson and A. Rajaram (2005) How Does the Composition of Public Spending Matter?, Policy Research Working Paper 3555, Washington DC: World Bank.

Pattillo, C., S. Gupta and K. Carey (2005) Sustaining Growth Accelerations and Pro-Poor Growth in Africa, IMF Working Paper WP/05/195, www.imf.org.

Peden, G.C. (1991) *British Economic and Social Policy. Lloyd George and Margaret Thatcher*, New York: Philip Allan, 2nd ed.

Peng, I. (2005) The New Politics of the Welfare State in a Developmental Context: Explaining the 1990s Social Care Expansion in Japan, in Kwon, pp. 73–97.

Pierson, C. (2004) Late Industrializers and the Development of the Welfare State, UNRISD Social Policy and Development Paper No. 16, Geneva, www.unrisd.org.

Poku, N.K. (2002) Poverty, Debt, and Africa's HIV/AIDS Crisis, *International Affairs*, Vol. 78, No. 3: 531–46.

Poku, N.K., and A. Whiteside (2002) Global Health and the Politics of Governance: An Introduction, *Third World Quarterly*, Vol. 23, No. 2: 191–5.

Polanyi, K. (1968 [1944]) *The Great Transformation*, Boston: Beacon Press 9th ed.

Pritchett, L. (1995) Divergence, Big Time, Policy Research Working Paper, Washington DC: World Bank.

Pritchett, L. (2004) Reform Is Like a Box of Chocolates. Understanding the Growth Disappointments and Surprises, http://lpritchett.org/reform_chocolates_v1.doc

Purfield, C. (2006) Mind the Gap – Is Economic Growth in India Leaving Some States Behind?, IMF Working Paper WP/06/103, Washington DC: IMF.

Raczynski, D. (2001) Provision of Social Services in Chile: A Search for a New Model, in Mwabu et al. (2001) pp. 211–27.

Ravallion, M. (1996) How Well Can Method Substitute for Data? Five Experiments in Poverty Analysis, *The World Bank Research Observer*, Vol. 11, No. 2.

Ravallion, M. (2000) Growth and Poverty: Making Sense of the Current Debate, mimeo (July).

Ravallion, M. (2001) Growth, Inequality and Poverty: Looking Beyond Averages, *World Development*, Vol. 29, No. 11: 1803–15.

Ravallion, M. (2003a) Targeted Transfers in Poor Countries: Revisiting the Tradeoffs and Policy Options, Social Protection Discussion Paper No. 0314, Washington DC: World Bank.

Ravallion, M. (2003b) The Debate on Globalization, Poverty and Inequality: Why Measurement Matters, World Bank Policy Research Working Paper 3038.

Ravallion, M. (2004a) Pro-Poor Growth: A Primer, World Bank Policy Research Working Paper 3242, March 2004.

Ravallion M. (2004b) Competing Concepts of Inequality in the Globalization Debate, World Bank Policy Research Working Paper 3243, March 2004.

Ravallion, M., and S. Chen (1997) What Can New Survey Data Tell Us about Recent Changes in Distribution and Poverty? *World Bank Economic Review*, Vol. 11, No. 2: 35–82.

Ravallion, M., and G. Datt (1999) *When Is Growth Pro-poor? Evidence from the Diverse Experiences of India's States*, Washington DC: World Bank.

Ravallion, M., and S. Chen (2004) China's (Uneven) Progress Against Poverty, World Bank Research Working Paper 3408, Washington DC.

Rawlings, L.B. (2004) A New Approach to Social Assistance: Latin America's Experience with Conditional Cash Transfer Programs, Social Protection Discussion Paper Series, No.0416, Washington DC: World Bank.

Rawlings, L.B., L. Sherburne-Benz and J.Van Domelen (2004) Evaluating Social Funds. A Cross-Country Analysis of Community Investments, Regional and Sectoral Studies, Washington DC: World Bank.

Razavi, S. (2006) Gender and Social Policy in a Global Context: Uncovering the Gendered Structure of 'the Social', presentation at the UNRISD – Sida/SARES Workshop on 'Social Policy and Equality', February, Buenos Aires.

Reddy, S. (1998) Social Funds in Developing Countries: Recent Experiences and Lessons, Staff Working Papers, EPP-EVL-98-002, New York: UNICEF.

Reddy, S. (2001) Strategies of Social Provision: Key Design Issues, in Mwabu et al. (2001) pp. 101–22.

Republic of Kenya (2004) Investment Programme for the Economic Recovery Strategy for Wealth and Employment Creation 2003–2007, Revised, 12 March, posted at www.worldbank.org/prsp

Resnick, D., and R. Birner (2006) Does Good Governance Contribute to Pro-Poor Growth?: A Review of the Evidence from Cross-Country Studies, IFPRI, DSGD Discussion Paper No. 30, http://www.ifpri.org/DIVS/DSGD/dp/dsgdp30.asp

Reddy, S. (1998) Social Funds in Developing Countries: Recent Experiences and Lesson, UNICEF Staff Working Papers, EPP-EVL-98-002, New York.

Richter, K. (2006) Thailand's Growth Path: From Recovery to Prosperity, World Bank Policy Research Working Paper 3912, Washington DC: World Bank.

Robb, C. (1999) Can the Poor Influence Policy? Participatory Poverty Assessments in the Developing World, Washington DC: World Bank.

Robb, C. (2000) How the Poor Can Have a Voice in Government Policy, *Finance and Development*, Vol. 37. No. 4: www.imf.org/external/pubs/ft/fandd/12/robb.htm.

Robb, C. (2001) Linking Participatory Poverty Assessments to Poverty Reduction Strategy Papers, Washington, mimeo.

Robb, C. (2003) Poverty and Social Impact Analysis – Linking Macroeconomic Policies to Poverty Outcomes: Summary of Early Experiences, Working Paper 03/43, Washington DC: IMF.

Roberts, J. (2003) Poverty Reduction Outcomes in Education and Health, Public Expenditure and Aid, ODI Working Paper 210, London.

Roberts, J. (2003a) ODI Workshop 2003, http://www.thenewpublicfinance.org/overview/english.pdf.

Rocha Menocal, A. (2004) And If There Was No State? Critical Reflections on Bates, Polanyi and Evans on the Role of the State in Promoting Development, *Third World Quarterly*, Vol. 25, No. 4: 765–77.

Rodrik, D. (1998) Why Do Open Economies Have Bigger Governments?, *Journal of Political Economy* / Abstract SSRN Journal (November).

Rodrik, D. (2000) Institutions for High-Quality Growth: What They Are and How to Acquire Them, NBER Working Paper W7540, February.

Rodrik, D. (ed.) (2003) *In Search of Prosperity: Analytical Narratives on Economic Growth*, Princeton University Press.

Rodrik, D., and A. Subramanian (2004) From 'Hindu Growth' to Productivity Surge: The Mystery of the Indian Growth Transition, draft (March).

Rondinelli, D.A., and G. Shabbir Cheema (eds) (2003) *Reinventing Government for the Twenty-First Century. State Capacity in a Globalizing Society*, Bloomfield: Kumarian Press.

Ros, J., and N. Lustig (2001) Mexico: Trade and Financial Liberalization with Volatile Capital Inflows: Macroeconomic Consequences and Social Impacts during the 1990s, in Taylor (2001), pp. 217–50.

Rothgang, H., H. Obinger and S. Leibfried (2006) The State and Its Welfare State: How Do Welfare State Changes Affect the Make-up of the Nation State?, *Social Policy and Administration*, Vol. 40, No. 3: 250–66.

Saavedra, J., M Torero and H. Ñopo (2002) Social Exclusion in Peru: An Invisible Wall, mimeo, GRADE, Lima, Peru.

Sabates-Wheeler, R. (2004) Asset Inequality and Agricultural Growth. How Are Patterns of Asset Inequality Established and Reproduced?, Back-ground Paper for *World Development Report 2006*, www.worldbank.org/socialpolicy.

Sachs, J. (2005) *The End of Poverty. How We Can Make It Happen in Our Lifetime*, London: Penguin Books.

Sala-I-Martin, X. (2002) The World Distribution of Income (Estimated from Individual Country Distribution), NBER Working Paper, May 2002, www.nber.org/papers/w8933.

Sandbrook, R. (1996) Democratization and the Implementation of Economic Reform in Africa, *Journal of International Development*, Vol. 8, No. 1: 1–20.

Schady, N. (2005) Do Macroeconomic Crises Affect Schooling and Child Health? Evidence from Peru, World Bank Website, accessed December 2005.

Schubert, B. (2005) The Pilot Social Cash Transfer Scheme. Kalomo District, Zambia, mimeo, Berlin, presented at CPRC conference Social Protection for Chronic Poverty (February) www.sed.manchester.ac.uk/idpm/research/events/february2005/protection-papers.htm.

Scoones, I. (1995) Investigating Difference: Applications of Wealth Ranking and Household Survey Approaches among Farming Households in S Zimbabwe, *Development and Change*, Vol. 26: 67–88.

Seidman, A., and R.B. Seidman (1994) *State and Law in the Development Process. Problem-solving and Institutional Change in the Third World*, New York: St. Martin Press.

Sen, A. (1981) *Poverty and Famines: An Essay on Entitlement and Destitution*, Oxford University Press.

Sen, A. (2000) *Social Exclusion: Concept, Application and Scrutiny*, Social Development Paper No. 1, Manila: Asian Development Bank, www.adb.org/Documents/Books/Social_Exclusion/social_exclusion.pdf.

Sen, A. (2006) The Man Without a Plan, *Foreign Affairs* (March/April).

Shaffer, Paul (1998) Who's Poor? Comparing Household Survey and Participatory Poverty Assessment Results from the Republic of Guinea, *World Development*, Vol. 26, No. 12.

Shaffer, P. (2002) Poverty Naturalized: Implications for Gender, *Feminist Economics*, Vol. 8, No. 3: 55–75.

Shah, P., and D. Youssef (2002) Voices and Choices at a Macro Level. Participation in Country-Owned Poverty Reduction Strategies, Action Learning Program Dissemination Series, No. 1, Social Development Department. Washington DC: World Bank.

Shariff, A., P. Ghosh and S.K. Mondal (2001) State Adjusted Public Expenditures on Social Sector and Poverty Alleviation Programs in the Light of the Budget 2001, New Delhi: National Council of Applied Economic Research.

Shepherd, A., and E. Gyimah-Boadi (2004) Bridging the North–South Divide in Ghana, Background Paper for WDR 2006, www.worldbank.org/socialpolicy.

Shin, D-M. (2000) Economic Policy and Social Policy: Policy-linkages in an Era of Globalisation, *International Journal of Social Welfare*, Vol. 9: 17–30.

Shiva, V. (2005) Two Myths That Keep the World Poor, posted on info. interactivist.net, accessed November 2005.

Siebrits, F.K. (1998) Government Spending in an International Perspective, in I. Abedian and M. Biggs (eds), *Economic Globalisation and Fiscal Policy*, Cape Town: Oxford University Press, pp. 305–36.

Silver, H. (1994) Social Exclusion and Social Solidarity: Three Paradigms, IILS, Discussion Papers No. 69, Geneva.

Silver, H., and F. Wilkinson (1995) Policies to Combat Social Exclusion: A French-British Comparison, IILS, Discussion Papers Series No. 83, Geneva.

Smeeding, T.M. (2005) Public Policy, Economic Inequality, and Poverty. The United States in Comparative Perspective, *Social Science Quarterly*, Vol. 86, No. 1: 955–83.

Smith, W.J., and K. Subbarao (2003) What Role for Safety Net Transfers in Very Low Income Countries?, Social Protection Discussion Paper No. 0301, Washington, DC: World Bank.

Söderbäck, M., and E. Dohlman (2006) Promoting Pro-Poor Growth: Key Policy Messages, paper presented at the UNU-WIDER Conference on 'Aid: Principles, Policies and Performance', 16–17 June, Helsinki, http://www.wider.unu.edu/conference/conference-2006-1.

Son, H.H. (2006) Assessing the Pro-Poorness of Government Fiscal Policy in Thailand, Working Paper No. 15, Brasilia: International Poverty Centre, UNDP, www.undp-povertycentre.org/newsletters/WorkingPaper15.pdf.

South Africa, Department of Agriculture (2001) The Strategic Plan for South African Agriculture, http://www.nda.agric.za/docs/sectorplan/sectorplanE.htm (accessed June 2006).

Standing, G. (2003) The Right to Basic Income Security, Presentation at Chronic Poverty Research Centre Conference, Manchester (April).

Stern, N. (2002) Dynamic Development: Innovation and Inclusion, Munich Lectures in Economics, Munich, 19 November.

Stewart, F. (2006) Do We Need a New 'Great Transformation'? Is One Likely?, UNU-WIDER Research Paper 2006/36, Helsinki: WIDER (www.wider.unu.edu/publications/publications.htm).

Stewart, F., and M. Wang (2003) Do PRSPs Empower Poor Countries, and Disempower the World Bank or Is it the Other Way Around?, Queen Elizabeth House Working Paper Series, Oxford University, www.qch.ox.ac.uk/pdf/qehwp/qehwps108.pdf

Stiglitz, J.E. (2002) *Globalization and Its Discontents*, New Delhi: Penguin Books.

Subbarao, K., A. Bonnerjee, J. Braithwaite, S. Carvalho, K. Ezemenari, C. Graham and A. Thompson (1997) Safety Net Programs and Poverty Reduction: Lessons from Cross-Country Experience, The World Bank, Directions in Development, Washington DC.

Sundaram, K., and S.D. Tendulkar (2003) Poverty among Social and Economic Groups in India in the 1990s, CDE Working Paper 118, Delhi: Delhi School of Economics.

Suwannarat, G. (2003) Southeast Asia: Learning from Crisis, in Cook et al. (2003), pp. 200–60.

Sweetman, C. (2003) Editorial, *Gender and Development*, Vol. 11, No. 3: 2–7.

Tangcharoensathien, V., W. Teokul and L. Chanwongpaisarn (2005) Challenges of Implementing Universal Health Care in Thailand, in Kwon (2005), pp. 257–82.

Tanzi, V. (2000) Globalization and the Future of Social Protection, IMF Working Paper 00/12, Washington DC: IMF.

Tanzi, V. (2002) Globalization and the Future of Social Protection, *Scottish Journal of Political Economy*, Vol. 49, pp.116–127.

Taylor, L. (2001) Outcomes of External Liberalization and Policy Implications, in Taylor (2001b) pp. 1–10.

Taylor, L. (ed.) (2001b) *External Liberalization, Economic Performance, and Social Policy*, Oxford University Press.

Taylor, M. (2006) From National Development to 'Growth With Equity': Nation-building in Chile, 1950–2000, *Third World Quarterly*, Vol. 27, No. 1: 69–84.

Taylor-Gooby, P. (2005) Is the Future American? Or, Can Left Politics Preserve European Welfare States from Erosion through Growing 'Racial' Diversity?, *Journal of Social Policy*, Vol. 34, No. 4: 661–72.

Tendler, J. (1999) The Rise of Social Funds: What Are They A Model Of?, mimeo, MIT for UNDP.

Tendler, J. (2000) Why Are Social Funds So Popular?, in S. Yusuf, W. Wu. and S. Evenett, *Local Dynamics in the Era of Globalization*, Oxford University Press for the World Bank.

Tendler, J. (2004) Why Social Policy is Condemned to a Residual Category of Safety Nets and What to Do about It, in Mkandawire (2004), pp. 119–42.

Ter-Minassian, T., S. Gupta, B. Clements, M. Guin-Siu and L. de Mello (2001) Debt Relief in HIPCs: Fiscal Policy Issues, Washington DC: IMF.

Thin, N., et al. (2001) Sub-Saharan Africa's Poverty Reduction Strategy Papers: Social Policy and Sustainable Livelihoods Perspectives, Paper for DFID, Oxford Policy Management, Oxford.

Thobani, M. (1983) Charging User Fees for Social Services. The Case of Education in Malawi, World Bank Staff Working Paper 572 Washington DC: World Bank.

Thompson, L. (2005) Social Security and Economic Growth, International Social Security Association, Regional Conference for Africa, Zambia.

Tilly, Ch. (1998) *Durable Inequality*, Berkeley, CA: University of California Press.

Timmer, P. (2004) Operationalizing Pro-Poor Growth. A Case Study on Indonesia, paper for the multi-donor research programme Operationalizing Pro-Poor Growth, London: DFID.

Titmuss, R. (1950) *Problems of Social Policy*, London: HMSO.

Tostensen, A. (2004) Towards Feasible Social Security Systems in sub-Saharan Africa, WP 2004:5, Bergen: Chr. Michelsen Instititute.

Townsend, P. (2004) From Universalism to Safety Nets: The Rise and Fall of Keynesian Influence on Social Development, in: Mkandawire (2004), pp. 37–62.

Toye, J. (2000) Fiscal Crisis and Fiscal Reforms in Developing Countries, *Cambridge Journal of Economics*, Vol. 24: 21–44.

Tzannatos, Z. (1998) Women and Labor Market Changes in the Global Economy: Growth Helps, Inequality Hurt and Public Policy Matters, SP Discussion Paper 20051, Washington DC: World Bank.

United Kingdom Government (2006) *White Paper on International Development, 'Eliminating World Poverty: Making Governance Work for the Poor'*, London: The Stationary Office.

United Nations (1999) *UNDAF Guidelines*, United Nations, http://rescoor.undp.org.tt/initiatives/English-UNDAF.pdf (accessed 25 April 2006).

UNDP (2005) *Human Development Report 2005: International Trade and Security in an Unequal World*, New York: UNDP.

UN Millennium Project (2005) *Investing in Development: Millennium Development Goals*, London: Earthscan.

USAID (2005) Pro-Poor Economic Growth. A Review of Recent Literature, prepared by Development Alternatives and the Boston Institute for Developing Economies.

Vandemoortele, J. (2004) Inequality and the Millennium Development Goals, Presentation at DFID, London, 7 October.

Van der Hoeven, R. (2000) Into the Twenty-First Century: Assessing Social and Political Concerns, in *On the Threshold: The United Nations and Global Governance – the New Millennium*, proceedings of the conference at Tokyo, 19–21 January 2000, http://www.io.org/public/french/employment/strat/macropol/pdf.htm

Van Ginneken, W. (2000) The Extension of Social Protection: ILO's Aim for the Years to Come, in Conway *et al.* (2000).

Van Ginneken, W. (2003) Extending Social Security: Policies for Developing Countries, *International Labour Review*, Vol. 142, No. 3: 277–93.

Véron, R. (2001) The 'New' Kerala Model. Lessons for Sustainable Development, *World Development*, Vol. 29, No. 4: 601–17.

Vélez, C. (2004) Determinants of Income Inequality in LAC: Some Lessons from Brazil and Colombia, presentation at DFID, London, 29 October.

Voitchovsky, S. (2004) The Effect of Inequality on Growth: A Review of the Recent Empirical Material, paper presented at DFID, London.

Von Hauff, M., and A. de Haan (eds) (1997) *Social Security in the International Development Cooperation*, Bonn: Friedrich Ebert Stiftung.

Wagstaff, A. (2001) Poverty and Health, Paper WG1-5, WHO Commission on Macroeconomics and Health, http://www.worldbank.org/research/bios/awagstaff.htm.

Walby, S. (2003) The Myth of the Nation-State: Theorising Society and Polities in a Global Era, *Sociology*, Vol. 37, No. 3: 529–46.

Watkins, K. (1998) *Economic Growth with Equity: Lessons from East Asia*, Oxford: Oxfam Insight Publications.

Watkins, K. (2001) Cost Recovery and Equity in the Health Sector: The Case of Zimbabwe, in Mwabu et al., (2001), pp. 186–210.

Wei, Shang-Jin, and Yi Wu (2001) Globalization and Inequality: Evidence from Within China, NBER Working Paper No. 8611.

Whaites, A. (ed.) (2002) *Masters of Their Own Development? PRSPs and the Prospects for the Poor*, Monrovia, CA: World Vision International.

White, H. (2001) Pro-Poor Growth in a Globalized Economy, *Journal of International Development*, Vol. 13: 549–69.

White, S. (2002) Thinking Race, Thinking Development, *Third World Quarterly*, Vol. 23, No. 3: 407–19.

White, H., and E. Anderson (2000) Growth Versus Distribution: Does the Pattern of Growth Matter?, Mimeo, IDS Sussex.

Widner, J.A. (ed.) (1994) *Economic Change and Political Liberalization in Sub-Saharan Africa*, Baltimore and London: Johns Hopkins University Press.

Wilhem, V., and I. Fiestas (2005) Exploring the Link between Public Spending and Poverty Reduction: Lessons from the 90s, paper for research programme Operationalizing Pro-Poor Growth, Washington DC: World Bank.

Wilkinson, R. (1998) Unhealthy Societies: The Afflictions of Inequality, *IDS Bulletin*, Vol. 29, No. 1.

Winters, L.A. (2002) *Trade Liberalisation and Poverty: The Empirical Evidence*, Nottingham: CREDIT.

Wolf, E. (1982) *Europe and the People Without History*, Berkeley: University of California Press.

Wood, A. (2004) Making Globalization Work for the Poor: The 2000 White Paper Reconsidered, *Journal of International Development*, Vol. 16: 933–7.

Wood, G. (2003) Governance and the Common Man: Embedding Social Policy in the Search for Security, in P. Mosley and E. Dowler (eds), *Poverty and Social Exclusion in North and South. Essays on Social Policy and Global Poverty Reduction*, London and New York: Routledge, pp. 83–121.

Wood G., and I. Gough (2006) A Comparative Welfare Regime Approach to Global Social Policy, *World Development*, Vol. 34, No. 10: 1696–712.

World Development Report (various years) World Bank, Oxford University Press.

World Bank (1994) *Averting the Old Age Crisis: Policies to Protect the Old and Promote Growth*, New York: Oxford University Press.

World Bank (1997) *Sharing Rising Incomes. China 2020. Disparities in China*, Washington DC: World Bank.

World Bank (1999) Principles and Good Practice in Social Policy, mimeo, Washington DC: World Bank.

World Bank (2000) *The Quality of Growth*, Washington DC: World Bank.

World Bank (2002) Review of the Poverty Reduction Strategy Paper (PRSP) Approach: Early Experience with Interim PRSPs and Full PRSPs, Washington, DC: World Bank.

World Bank (2002a) EFA: The Lessons of Experience. The Impact of Policy in 20 Case Studies, paper for the Accelerating Action towards EFA Conference, Amsterdam (April).

World Bank (2003) Inequality in Latin America and the Caribbean: Breaking with History? Washington DC: World Bank.

World Bank (2004) Responsible Growth for the New Millennium: Integrating Society, Ecology, and the Economy, Washington DC: World Bank.

World Bank (2005) Vietnam Poverty Reduction Strategy Paper Annual Progress Report (July 12), http://siteresources.worldbank.org/INTPRS1/Resources/Vietnam-PRSP_APR2(July12-2005).pdf.

World Bank (2006) Repositioning Nutrition as Central to Development. A Strategy for Large-Scale Action, Directions in Development, Washington DC: World Bank.

World Bank (2006) Republic of Kenya: Country Social Analysis, Draft, ESSD, Africa Region (March), Washington DC: World Bank.

World Bank, Africa Region (1997) Status Report on Poverty in Sub-Saharan Africa 1997. Tracking the Incidence and Characteristics of Poverty, Washington DC: World Bank.

World Bank Development Economics (2002) The Role and Effectiveness of Development Assistance. Lessons from World Bank Experience, mimeo, Washington DC: World Bank.

World Bank, Independent Evaluation Group (2006) Debt Relief for the Poorest. An Evaluation of the HIPC Initiative, Washington DC: World Bank.

World Bank, Infrastructure Network (2006) Infrastructure: Lessons from the Last Two Decades of World Bank Engagement, discussion paper, Washington DC: World Bank.

World Bank, Institutional and Social Policy Poverty Monitoring Team (1997) Africa Household Surveys Data Bank, draft, Washington DC: World Bank.

World Bank, Operations Evaluation Department (2002) Social Funds. Assessing Effectiveness, Washington DC: World Bank.

World Bank, Operations Policy and Country Services (2001) Adjustment Lending Retrospective. Final Report, Washington DC: World Bank.

World Bank, Quality Assurance Group (I. Husain et al., Working Group for Social Funds Portfolio Review) (1998) Portfolio Improvement Program: Review of the Social Funds Portfolio, Quality Assurance Group, Mimeo, Washington DC: World Bank.

World Bank, Social Development Department (2004) Social Development in World Bank Operations: Results and Ways Forward, Discussion Draft, February, Washington DC: World Bank.

World Bank, Social Protection Sector (2000b) Social Protection Strategy: From Safety Net to Spring Board, Sector Strategy Paper, Draft Final Report (August).

World Bank, South Asia Region (PREM) (2003) India. Sustaining Reform, Reducing Poverty, Report No. 25797-In, Washington DC: World Bank.

World Bank and IMF (2005) Review of the PRS Approach: Balancing Accountabilities and Scaling Up Results, Washington DC: World Bank.

World Bank, AFD, BMZ, DFID (2005) *Pro-Poor Growth in the 1990s. Lessons and Insights from 14 Countries*, Washington DC: World Bank.

World Commission on the Social Dimension of Globalization, 2004, *A Fair Globalization: Creating Opportunities for All*, ILO, Geneva.

World Health Organisation (2001) Health in PRSPs, WHO Submission to World Bank/IMF Review of PRSPs.

Yeates, N. (2001) *Globalization and Social Policy*, London: Sage.

Yeates, N. (2005) 'Globalization' and Social Policy in a Development Context. Regional Responses, Social Policy and Development Programme Paper No. 18, Geneva: UNRISD.

Yi, I., and B-h. Lee (2005) Development Strategies and Unemployment Policies in Korea, in Kwon (2005) pp. 143–69.

You, J.-I., and J.-H. Lee (2001) South Korea: Economic and Social Consequences of Globalization, in Taylor (2001b) pp. 283–315.

Yusof, Z.A. (2006) Affirmative Action. Malaysia, Inter-Regional Inequality Facility, Policy Brief 13, www.odi.org.uk/inter-regional_inequality.

Zhang, X., and R. Kanbur (2003) Spatial Inequality in Education and Health Care in China, http://www.arts.cornell.edu/poverty/kanbur/ChinaSocialInequality.pdf

Notes

Introduction: Why Focus on Social Policy?

1 The term 'the South' is used to refer mainly to countries of 'low-income' (as used in World Bank statistics, for example), 'developing' countries or 'non-OECD', but includes middle-income countries too.

2 Polanyi emphasizes the pressure exerted by a wide variety of people for social protection, understood in a broad sense, with reference to the social fabric. Some analysts have compared the liberalization period of the 1980s/1990s to the nineteenth century period of liberalism (for example, Stewart, 2006).

3 Granovetter, borrowing from Polanyi, emphasizes that action is not merely shaped by the institutional context but is *embedded* in it, hence actors may not be able to conceive of alternatives (in Lecours, 2005: 10, who describes the 'new institutionalism' in social sciences).

4 LSE, Department of Social Policy, www.lse.ac.uk, accessed 2000.

5 www.ilo.org, accessed 2000; the ILO's social security department highlights work on both social security and social protection as fundamental human rights.

6 This is thus broader, and in my view more appropriate, than the definition used in the related research programme at IDS Sussex, which defined social policy as concerned with the public provision of (public or private) goods and services to meet human needs, thus stressing the role of the state – see section 1.4 below.

7 Chapter 4 uses a terminology of social policy regimes rather than welfare regimes; the last is used mainly for the social policies that have dominated in OECD countries since the Second World War; social policy here is used in the broader sense of collective political action and principles of solidarity or social integration. In Esping-Andersen's analysis the focus is on management of social risk, while here the provision of health and education is included in the analysis.

8 As described by Hill (1996), for whom social policy is simply about 'the role of the state in relation to the welfare of its citizens'.

9 This interesting collection of articles highlights marked differences in the impacts of and policy reaction to liberalization, but puts little emphasis on understanding underlying policy processes.

10 At least in the North, countries with active labour market policies tend to have more extensive social security policies.

11 Peden (1991) stresses the need to study economic and social policy in their interrelationships in the context of Britain, from Victorian ideas till the Thatcher period. It was a central theme of the UNRISD research programme (Mkandawire, 2000, 2005), and *World Development Report 2006* makes a similar argument about the potential complementarity of policies for efficiency and for equity. See Chapter 3.

12 This is now recognized as a priority by International Financial Institutions, where a range of analytical instruments have been developed around Poverty

and Social Impact Analysis (Coudouel et al., 2006). It is a central concern of work on social policy for example in Hall and Midgeley (2004), and at the Arusha Social Policy conference: December 2005 (www.worldbank.org/socialpolicy).

13 Pritchett emphasized the importance of distinguishing between 'policy', 'policy action' and 'policy outcome'; Max Everest-Phillips helped to point this out; see also Cook and White (2001) on approaches to welfare policy analysis (new institutional economics, politics and political economy).

14 Kanbur (2005), in a discussion of economic and social policies, distinguishes outcome/objectives, policies and mechanisms (or disciplines of analysis) – his questioning whether there is a separate field of social policies underlines a main argument of this book, that the instruments of social policies have received insufficient attention.

15 Aryeetey and Goldstein (2000) describe different phases of de facto social policymaking in Ghana since Independence, which we return to in Chapter 4.

16 See also Adesina (2006). For the African Union (2006a: 12) '[s]ocial policy is a set of actions, programmes and projects designed by governments in collaboration with relevant stakeholders to promote social development through improvements in the quality of life of citizens irrespective of class, gender, race, ethnicity, religion, political beliefs, national origin and geographic location.' A cross-sectoral approach and partnerships between state and civil society feature strongly in the AU approach developed since the 2004 Ouagadougou summit (also African Union, 2006b).

17 In their terms, the crucial distinction between the two focuses on whether countries have waited to grow rich before extending large-scale public support; this book emphasizes different ways in which solidarities can be articulated, including through labour market policies.

18 The World Bank's (1999) 'Principles and Good Practice in Social Policy', drawing on the declaration of the Copenhagen Summit, summarized these around four objectives: universal access to basic social services; secure and sustainable livelihoods and decent working conditions; promoting social protection and safeguards against shocks; and fostering social integration.

19 Norton and Conlin (2000) describe five similar objectives, linked to Millennium Development Goals: universal basic social services; sustainable livelihoods and decent working conditions; robust systems of social protection, safeguards against shocks and declines in assets; social integration, safe and just societies, through open and accountable governments, combating discrimination and exclusion; and empowerment of men and women, enabling them to participate in decision-making, and claim civil, political, economic, social and cultural rights.

20 The distinctive feature of the welfare states that emerged in the North after the Second World War, according to Marshall (1950, in Esping-Andersen, 1999: 34) was the recognition of citizens' social rights, alongside a promise to bridge class divisions. A feminist perspective is presented by Lister (1997) and in the special issue of *Gender and Development* of November 2003 (Sweetman, 2003).

21 Differences can be illustrated by the evolving ideologies of the British Poor Law of 1834 and the collectivist approach of the 1948 National Assistance Act, challenged since the 1970s; see also Moore (2000).

22 Herbst (2000) describes this as a critical difference with state formation in Africa, where the international system provided legitimacy to a large number of nation states which historically had a very weak basis.

23 Mishra emphasizes the commonalities in response to globalization in the very different welfare states of Sweden, Germany and Japan.

24 In Zimbabwe, as late as 1972–6, the ratio of government expenditure on education for black and white children was 1:12 (Osei-Hwedie and Bar-on, 1999: 93).

25 In Africa, public employment growth may have reached 10 per cent or more per year (Lienert, quoted in Addison, 2003: 56). According to Addison, the social contract was based on increasing employment, benefiting mostly urban areas, with some benefits for rural areas through remittances. In Kenya, even in the late 1980s, public sector employment formed 50 per cent of total formal sector employment (Kulunde Manda, 2003: 153).

26 Raczynski also highlights the factors that discredited the earlier model: fiscal imbalance, lack of capacity, inefficient administration and centralized decision making.

27 Adesina, who draws on the research project with UNRISD on social policy in a developmental context, emphasizes the sharp break in trends – in ideas, and health and education service provision – around 1980.

28 For example Appleton (2001) with respect to education and changes in World Bank policies in the early 1980s; see further Chapter 3.

29 Sen's (1981) concept of capabilities emphasizes rights and command over goods, and opportunities in various spheres. His paper on social exclusion (2000) distinguishes between the constitutive relevance of exclusion (deprivation of intrinsic importance), and instrumental importance (in itself not impoverishing but can lead to impoverishment).

30 Gough (in Esping-Andersen, 1997: 75) shows that targeted social assistance was almost 100 per cent of total social protection spending in Australia and New Zealand, 40 per cent in Ireland and the US, 20–30 per cent in Canada and the UK, and 12 per cent in Germany.

31 According to Taylor (2006) 'the social transformations engineered through neo-liberal restructuring have infused multiple contradictions into the "Third Way" practices of the post-dictatorship Concertación governments'.

32 Wood (2003: 90), reflecting on the research program Social Policy in Development Contexts, notes that "colleagues at Bath were, early on, accused in effect of contextual ignorance and intellectual imperialism by poor country specialists."

33 2003 World Development Indicators; also, there is as much variation among OECD countries – for example, the US with government spending of 19 per cent of GDP as against the UK with 36 per cent – as between countries in the North and in the South.

34 Also Poku and Whiteside (2002), which emphasizes the declining role of WHO vis-à-vis the IFIs, and a similar point can be made with regard to the role of the ILO, including in the area of pensions.

35 See, for example, Deacon (2003: 23–29), with reference to debates in Geneva in 2000 that highlighted opposition from the South. Ferguson (1999) discusses the UK social policy principles initiative.

36 On the other hand, welfare state research has remained restricted to a relatively small number of OECD countries, though this has been broadening recently (Hort, 2005).

37 This is of course a generalization, and much good experience exists. The statement is based on my own experience with adjustment lending in India (Orissa in particular), and draws on reviews of PRSPs. The review by Grindle (2002) indicates that the new governance agenda is unrealistically ambitious, suggesting that in final lending negotiations room necessarily exists for selective emphasis.

38 An example of such a technocratic focus is Kaul and Conceição's description of the 'new public finance', which emphasizes that 'public finance is expected to help provide public goods and to foster equity ... [and] allocative efficiency is the main rationale for government interventions to support public good provisions' (Kaul and Conceição, 2006: Overview, p. 8), as opposed to seeing these as the outcome of political processes and public pressure. During the period of greater fiscal stability in the poorest countries, since the mid-1990s, the debate has been broadened, and more attention is paid to orientation and composition and the impact of spending (Addison et al., 2006).

39 The UNRISD social policy research programme has recently started a sub-project on 'Financing Social Policy in a Development Context', coordinated by Katja Hujo.

40 The literature on the importance of institutions for economic growth has emphasized that the economic growth literature had focused on the *proximate* causes of growth: innovation, capital accumulation *are* growth, not causes of growth (Acemoglu et al., 2004: 1, quoting North and Thomas).

41 A similar critique of quantitative poverty studies is formulated in Chapter 5; also De Haan (2004a), which argues that a link exists between the predominant form of poverty analysis and the residual approach to social policy that emerged during the 1980s.

42 See the special issue of *World Development*, Vol. 28, No. 7, including the contributions by Elson and Çagatay (2000).

43 See, for example, Budlender (2000 and 2003), Commonwealth Secretariat (1999), and documentation by the International Budget Project (www.internationalbudget.org).

44 Recent work by the DAC Network on Poverty Reduction shows the donor community's emphasis on the multiple dimensions of poverty (Söderbäck and Dohlman, 2006), but with little attention to what this implies for cross-sectoral policy-making.

45 Debates on quantitative versus qualitative approaches to poverty (Kanbur, 2003) continue to centre on differences in approaches to poverty analysis, and not on policy-making. Methodologies of participatory poverty analysis have become influential, as illustrated in *World Development Report 2000/2001*, following the research *Voices of the Poor*.

46 Brett (2003: 11) argues that participatory theorists often make unrealistic assumptions about the ability of the poor to access joint decision-making processes, and that rapid development is often not associated with participatory structures.

47 Project approaches have influenced approaches to social policy, as emphasizing technical solutions tends to make invisible the political nature of interventions (Ferguson in Manji, 2000: 14).

48 Marshall and Butzbach (2003) provide a wealth of case studies in different contexts, but do not develop a framework or approach to social policy.

49 During the Arusha social policy conference in December 2005, a participant stressed that Western social policy experiences are irrelevant for an Indian context; while in fact the history of SEWA (one of the case studies under discussion) shows that interaction with the formal sector, and hence the set of social policies that structures the labour market in the Indian context, is central to SEWA's advocacy efforts.

50 Boltodano (1999) emphasizes that concepts of social policy are intimately linked to the historical evolution of Western societies, the evolution of sovereign states, and the creation of social order, thus making the concept less useful in a period of globalization. However, Aina (1999) in the same volume does use a notion of social policy and argues it is an intrinsic dimension of development, as do recent publications by the African Union (2006).

51 Emphasizing the a-historicity of applications of notions of social policy, the IDS programme showed little awareness of the diverse histories of development and crises of OECD welfare states, and did not seriously engage with its literature. The quote of Baltodano is selective, as his emphasis is on reinterpreting the welfare state as reshaped under forces of globalization, rather than rejecting the notion altogether.

52 See the IDS Bulletin 'Social Policy in the South: Revisioning the Agenda', Kabeer and Cook (2000) and Devereux and Cook (2000). The textbook *Social Policy for Development* by Hall and Midgley (2004) also proposes a cross-sector livelihoods analysis as basis for social policy study, and the link between social policy and assets is explored as part of the World Bank programme New Frontiers of Social Policy (www.worldbank.org/socialpolicy).

53 Lloyd-Sherlock (2000) whose research has focused on provisions for the aged has also emphasized the need for an inter-sectoral approach.

54 Osmani (2002) provides a cogent argument concerning why employment should be key to growth–poverty debates, focusing on employment elasticity as one explanation of the variation in growth–poverty elasticity, and 'integrability', or the ability of poor workers to avail themselves of new opportunities.

55 Deacon (1997, 2000, 2004), the journal *Global Social Policy*, and the work of the Globalism and Social Policy Programme (www.gaspp.org). *Global Social Policy*, Vol. 6, No. 3, discusses whether the World Bank Arusha Conference shows a change in World Bank thinking on social policy. Deacon (2001, and 2003: 29–32) and Yeates (2005) describe social policy initiatives by regional organizations.

56 As highlighted by Yeates (2001), different frameworks have been proposed for the integration of a global perspective in social policy analysis.

57 This is well summarized in the ODI *Development Policy Review* of November 2002; see also work published by the Asian Development Bank (2002), and perspectives of various agencies documented earlier in Conway et al. (2000).

58 This research project resulted in a range of UNRISD Working Papers (www.unrisd.org), an international conference in 2001, and a series of publications by Palgrave Macmillan.

Globalization, Inequality and the Demise of the State?

1 In response to Sachs, Vandana Shiva (2005) highlights the modernist assumptions in his analysis, ignoring the links between accumulation of wealth in the North and underdevelopment in the South under colonialism.

2 Ravallion (2004b) describes competing concepts and their applications: absolute vs relative inequality (the growth–inequality debate stresses relative inequality); vertical vs horizontal (deviation at given income level) inequality; and interpersonal vs inter-country inequality.

3 Population and wealth data over the last 20 centuries are analysed by Maddison (in Sachs, 2005: 27ff). Income poverty data are available on a global (comparable) scale only for the period since the 1980s (Chen et al., 1993), and analysis usually relies on the database prepared by Deininger and Squire (1996) or by WIDER.

4 There is likely to be considerable measurement error in changes in inequality over time; findings that there is no change in overall inequality can be consistent with considerable 'churning' under the surface, with gainers and losers at all levels of living standards; and an unchanging Gini index with growth can mean large increases in absolute income disparities.

5 Sala-I-Martin (2002) estimates a world distribution of income, by integrating individual income distributions for 125 countries between 1970 and 1998, using 9 indexes of income inequality: all show substantial reduction in global income inequality during the 1980s and 1990s.

6 Atkinson and Brandoloni (quoted in WDR, 2006: 63), and van der Hoeven (2000). Cornia (1999b) highlights that after a period of declining inequality until the 1970s the trend reversed; during the 1980s, wage and income inequality increased in a majority of countries (see also Cornia, 2004: 6ff).

7 See further UNDP *Human Development Report 2005*; see also Vandemoortele (2004) on inequalities in education in particular.

8 *The Economist* (11 October 2003, p. 13, and 10 June, 2006, p. 25). *The Economist* of 17 June 2006 focused on increased inequality in the US, caused by increased returns in the global market.

9 According to the author, while explaining differences in levels and trends of inequality is difficult, the higher levels of income inequality in the US are due to the large number of low-skill workers, wage distribution, and inadequate (and not – as in the UK – improving) safety nets.

10 The 'secular decline in inequality' is attributed to declining inflation, declines in returns on education, rural–urban convergence, an increase in social transfers targeted on the poor and possibly a decline in racial inequality.

11 The economic crisis of the late 1980s led to significant losses, for example in infant mortality, particularly among less educated women, but since then these inequalities may have been reduced; Paxson and Schady, quoted in WDR 2006: 34. The impact of crises on human development is not straightforward: while in Peru economic crisis did lead to losses in terms of infant mortality, it did not lead to losses in education, as wage reductions reduced the opportunity costs of going to school (Schady, 2005).

12 *World Development Report* 2006, Okojie (2006), Anderson and MacKay (2004) and Nel (2003). Notwithstanding two decades of support for poverty measurement in Africa, data are still more limited than in Latin America, particularly regarding trends. Comparisons are difficult, and in the case of Africa data have been based on consumption rather than income, which is more predominant in Latin America (*World Development Report 2006* contains strong warnings against comparisons of income and consumption inequality).

13 The grouping of these three countries is interesting, as in Tanzania the low income has been accompanied by social peace, while Rwanda's low income inequality in the 'high-quality' data set was not at all a predictor of social cohesion (country specific research suggests very rapid growth in inequality during the 1990s, see Cramer, 2003: 407).

14 World Bank March 2006; see also the 2004 PRSP; it is not clear that the data for income poverty are comparable over time.

15 Ahuja et al. (1997) was one of the early reports focusing on inequalities during East Asia's miracle; see also Watkins (1998).

16 Kanbur and Zhang's (2004) time series indicates that inequality has peaked three times; during the Great Famine, at the end of the Cultural Revolution and in the current period of global integration.

17 A special section on China in *The Economist* of 25 March 2006 (p. 5) notes that Chinese officials are aware of the country's vulnerability, and of the causes of the collapse of other former communist countries. The official media has discussed the 'Latin Americanization' of China, referring to the possibility that growing income inequalities could lead to upheaval.

18 Motonishi (2003) shows that the impact of the sectoral shift is larger than the impact of financial development (which tends to reduce inequality), education level disparity, and aging.

19 Suwannarat (2003: 205) highlights the parallels between the opening up of the Vietnamese and Chinese economies.

20 World Bank, Vietnam Poverty Reduction Strategy Paper Annual Progress Report, 12 July 2005, p. 17.

21 Datt and Ravallion (2002), Deaton and Drèze (2002), de Haan and Dubey (2003), Jha (2004), Purfield (2006).

22 Though this implied reductions in defense and economic services, not the social sectors (Dutt and Rao, 2001).

23 WDR 2006: 204, which discusses four types of strategies to address regional inequality: fiscal incentives (which can be distorting); public investment, particularly in infrastructure; facilitating labour mobility; and enhancing agency, including addressing discrimination.

24 See also the OPPG study on India (Besley et al., 2004) and Purfield (2006); both studies highlight the policies that affect the cross-state patterns of growth, for example, relating to private sector investment, smaller government and better institutions.

25 Calculations of coefficients of variations of poverty incidences show increased disparities during the 1980s and 1990s; Drèze and Srinivasan (1996); de Haan and Lipton (1998); de Haan and Dubey (2003).

26 Researchers emphasize the absence of estimates of ethnic groups (Saavedra et al., 2002; Figueroa and Barrón, 2005).

27 Mamdani (2001) with a focus on Rwanda but with implications for other countries in the region; Moncrieffe (2004) for Uganda, including the intersection with gender differences.

28 http://www.chronicpoverty.org; in particular the first major output, the *Chronic Poverty Report 2004–2005*.

29 Cornia in Nissanke and Thorbecke (2005), p. 3; Taylor (2001) indicates that the social impacts of globalization and liberalization were unfavourable in 8 out of 11 case studies.

30 This is based partly on Petrella, quoted in Yeates (2001, 5) and Brawley (2003). While many of these processes of integration have accelerated in recent decades, the processes themselves are far from new, and as Eric Wolf (1982) emphasized, economic, political and socio-cultural developments interacted on a world scale throughout the colonial period.

31 Development of information technology and telecommunications has been a catalyst of globalization, and has enabled much more intensive contact with consumers, as well as globalization of production processes (for example, highlighted by the outsourcing of administrative operations by companies in the North).

32 A.T. Kearny and Foreign Policy (2004) – this ranks countries for 14 variables related to globalization, in four clusters of economic integration, personal contacts, technology and political engagement.

33 There is considerable variation in rankings of the different factors, also within the cluster of economic integration: the United States is the most globalized country technologically but ranks 56 out of 62 in terms of economic integration; Malaysia ranks eighth in terms of economic integration, second in terms of trade, but forty-second with respect to portfolio flows.

34 Exports form 30 per cent of GDP for Sub-Saharan Africa, and only 19 per cent for OECD countries (Human Development Report, 1999, p. 2; also HDR, 2000, pp. 79ff.).

35 Relatively small numbers of international workers outside the national system can have a disproportionate impact on welfare provisions (Deacon, 2004).

36 De Ferranti et al. (2000, Chapter 2). Volatility of GDP increased during the 1990s in East Asia, but not in other regions. Sub-Saharan Africa has the highest volatility, but this was highest during the 1970s and declined thereafter. Volatility rose in Latin America until the 1980s, but during the 1990s this rising trend was partially reversed. South Asia has relatively low volatility, and declined after the 1970s.

37 Adelman (2000: 1053), in a *World Development* editorial introduction to 'Redrafting the Architecture of the Global Financial System'; these crises were triggered by massive outflows of short-term foreign capital.

38 Ferreira et al. (undated); Adelman (2000); IMF (2003) 'Fund Assistance for Countries Facing Exogenous Shocks', quoted in Gottschalk (2005, 422).

39 For example, a special issue of *Third World Quarterly* (Vol. 27, No. 1) emphasizes the difference between the post-1945 'nation-state system' and 'global capitalism' (Berger and Weber, 2006).

40 Milanovic (2003) compares the periods of 1960–78 (marked by 'import substitution') and 1978–98 and shows that growth rates in GDP and GDP per capita were much higher in the first period, and that in the first period there was more convergence between regions than in the second.

41 Lessons from structural adjustment (Killick, 1999) show why adjustment may not have been *enough* to enhance growth and poverty reduction. For example, Zambia has done more than many countries to open up its economy, but this has not generated much economic response.

42 Dutt and Rao (2001). It should also be stressed that rates of foreign investment in India remained low, while trade expanded markedly. Berry's (2006) review of the Latin American literature suggests that free capital movement

(rather than freer trade) may be the cause of the growth slowdown since the 1980s.

43 As in Peru, where infant mortality particularly among less educated women increased with the economic crisis; quoted in WDR 2006: 34, based on research by Paxson and Schady.

44 Ravallion and Chen (1997), Ravallion (2001), Dollar and Kraay (2002); and Kraay (2004) finds a very strong growth–poverty correlation.

45 Ravallion and Datt (1999), Datt and Ravallion (2002), Besley, Burgess and Esteve-Volart (2004).

46 Quoted in Lopez (2004). Berry (2006) concludes that a "reasonable guess is that increased openness has been at least partly to blame for increased inequality" (p.61), partly because of labor-displacing technologies, but finds it harder to assess whether capital account liberalization has contributed to rising inequality.

47 Altimir, Beccaria and González, quoted in Medrano et al. (2006). Argentina liberalized and froze interest rates in 1991, grew till the crisis of 1995, recovered but contracted again in 1998–9 (Berg and Taylor, 2001: 39), and experienced a major crisis in 2001. The restructuring during the 1990s led to increased unemployment and rising utility prices following privatization, and additional bankruptcies following the collapse in demand (Önis, 2006: 248).

48 Lundberg and Squire (1999) in a then controversial paper suggested that openness to trade (measured by the Sachs-Warner index) was correlated negatively with income growth of the bottom 40 per cent of the population.

49 See further Hoekman and Winters (2005), focusing on labour market outcomes, emphasizing that many questions remain, and that the literature has largely ignored trade in services.

50 Kabeer et al. (2003), Fontana et al. (1997); *Gender and Development* of May 2003 contains a series of articles on the impact of globalization on women's rights and gender relations (Kerr and Sweetman, 2003).

51 Wei and Wu (2001) argue that globalization led to reduced rather than increased rural–urban disparities; see also Ravallion (2003b).

52 De Haan (2006) summarizes the evidence arguing that clear research findings exist, but that outcomes are heavily context-dependent.

53 Lopez (2004), who also emphasizes the importance of context in determining impacts of openness, distinguishes policies where a growth–inequality conflict emerges (for example, government size, financial development, trade openness), and policies that do not present such a conflict (education, infrastructure and inflation).

54 In China, taxation of farmers (and inflation) was probably more important from a distributional point of view than opening up to external trade (Ravallion and Chen, 2004).

55 Hirst and Thompson, quoted in Brawley (2003: 36); Mishra (1998, 1999); Thompson (2005) on social security.

56 For example, Martin and Schumann, in Brawley (2003: 44); Brawley also quotes Cerny emphasizing that globalization limits states' potential to provide services because of the integration of financial markets (and globalization reconfigures political activity).

57 Also, as highlighted by Sassen, states may have chosen to limit their sovereign powers. The argument about the race to the bottom is an example of this position (Walby, 2003).

58 Deacon (2001) describes the emergence of a global market in health, education and social insurance, and how this may contribute to undermining national welfare provisions. Global institutions like the World Bank and the IMF promote private welfare for a global middle class; 'globalisation is unravelling the social bond' (Deacon, 2000).

59 As noted in Chapter 1, while the pace or period of globalization may not be exceptional, it is still unique for the way it has impacted upon the welfare state that has developed since the Second World War (Mishra, 1999).

60 Maxwell (2006) on the '20 per cent and 0.2 per cent clubs' of aid dependent countries versus large countries, which are now also becoming donors.

61 Aizenman and Jinjarak's (2006) cross-country regressions show how under globalization countries are collecting more 'difficult taxes'.

62 Quoted in Brawley (2003: 113). Increasing levels of trade and capital market liberalization did not lead to lower taxes on capital. An IMF study, however, showed that poor developing countries had difficulties in dealing with the revenue consequences of trade liberalization (Clements et al., 2004: 13).

63 Resnick and Birner (2006: 27) quote Arimah and Dollar and Kraay with differing results.

64 Social expenditure as a percentage of GDP increased in 19 out of 21 OECD countries during 1980–2001; while the variation across countries shrank; Rothgang et al. (2006: 255).

65 There is very little literature on expected or recommended size of states. W. Arthur Lewis in 1978 estimated that the public sector in the South should be spending 20 per cent of GDP on services, excluding defense and debt repayment (quoted in Herbst (2000: 118), who emphasizes the concerns about an upward trend in spending during the 1960s).

66 Pierson (2004: 15) noted that while changes in the global economy impact upon ranges of policy options, they do not undermine the viability of welfare regimes.

67 Rodrik (1998) confirms this link. De Grauwe and Polan (2003) conclude that there is no necessary trade-off between social spending and international competitiveness, but with an important role for efficient governments.

68 Gough (2005). In Spain during the 1980s 'implementation of universalistic social policies in health, unemployment, education and pensions minimized the losses that the industrial and economic transition carried for important sectors of the Spanish labor force... [and] ... the expansion of compensatory programs (as well as of policies directed toward education and human capital formation) extracted a much higher level of popular compliance with the general strategy of "modernizing" the Spanish economy than what might have been possible otherwise' (Boix, 2004).

69 *The Economist* (May 2002) describes the Netherlands as an example of a small country with successful adjustment during the 1980s and 1990s, how the national 'polder model' (that is, consensus politics, the role of trade union leaders, then Prime Minister Wim Kok) was crucial in this, and how social policies were key and linked to increasing international competitiveness.

70 The process of liberalization in many cases is associated with economic crisis, which adds complexity to understanding trends in social expenditure.

Integrating Social and Economic Policies

1 UN General Assembly, Report of Secretary General, 1 September 2000; www.un.org/esa/socdev/csd/2002.htm; www.un.org/esa/socdev/csd/csd40docs/ Resolution40agreedconclusions.pdf; www.iisd.ca/download/pdf/sd/sdvol104 num1e.pdf.

2 Holtz (1998), summarizes a series of studies for IDRC, with reference to environmental as well as economic and social policies (as did the 2004 World Bank publication *Responsible Growth for the New Millennium*).

3 Lucas, cited in Appleton (2001); Barro (1997); Barro and Lee (2000) also emphasize positive impacts on social outcomes (child mortality, fertility, education, income distribution). Barro (1997) also shows a positive correlation between democracy and economic growth, at the low end of the political liberalization spectrum.

4 See, for example, http://www.imf.org/external/np/exr/facts/prgf.htm (accessed February 2006). The PRSP approach which is an overarching approach for PRGF and PSIA will be discussed in Chapter 6.

5 Emphasis on social development (or economic) outcomes tends to neglect policies. Kanbur (2005) stresses that donor social policy literature insufficiently distinguishes objectives, instruments and mechanisms. He stresses that societies neither have wholly economic nor social objectives, but tends to ignore that the policy processes connected to these outcomes are clearly separable and in practice separated (often reinforced by donor practices).

6 The following is based on a summary by Alex van den Heever, (then) member of the Committee of Enquiry on Social Security in South Africa, in de Haan, Huber and van den Heever (2001). He highlights that small countries may have increasingly small margins in their monetary policies to set interest rates and exert control over capital flows.

7 An IMF study on the introduction of VAT in Ethiopia showed that VAT is progressive, but not as progressive as sales tax and as such VAT introduction had a negative impact on the poorest 40 per cent (Clements et al., 2004: 13).

8 Clements et al. (2004: 6). Reduction of deficits under structural adjustment does not usually lead to a reduction in the relative size of social sectors, but the impact of reductions in other sectors may have an equally large impact on the poor.

9 Over time, according to Peng (2004) and not unlike the development in South Korea (see Chapter 4), the Japanese welfare state has moved from selective to more inclusive during a period of economic crisis and mounting public pressure.

10 The separation of the two may be stronger in an Anglo-Saxon (laissez-faire, Victorian) tradition than, for example, in the Netherlands, where the SER (Sociaal Economische Raad, or socio-economic council) provides a platform for discussing the two in conjunction.

11 Quoted in Lewis (1996: 96). Bates' work on markets and states in Africa is usually seen as a marker of the theoretical shift of the 1980s. Rocha Moncal (2004) provides an interesting comparison of Bates' work with Peter Evans' concept of 'embedded autonomy' which stresses the central role of the developmental state in industrial development in Korea, India and Brazil, against Polanyi's analysis of counter-movements to the self-regulating market.

12 Seidman and Seidman (1994: 24). World Bank analysis relied heavily on American political science and saw the African state as 'a machine concerned only with extending its reach in order to maintain short-term political order in a context of generalized "legitimacy deficit" ... through the centralized development/extension of patronage institutions and networks, via the disbursement of state resources' (Gibbon, 1996: 764),

13 Birdsall (2005: 9) summarizes findings of the 1993 World Bank study *The East Asian Miracle: Economic Growth and Public Policy*, but adds that these countries were also characterized by low initial levels of inequality.

14 Significantly for the argument about the need for a better cross-sectoral view, it appears that within the IMF and the World Bank the collection of data has by and large been left to sectoral experts (Erwin Tiongson, personal communication).

15 For example across the 19 countries that reported such spending in 2005; (World Bank, IEG, 2006: 2). Focus on pro-poor spending is manifested, e.g., in a recent review of the Malawi PRSP (Government of Malawi 2006) or the World Bank/IMF Joint Staff Assessment of the Kenya Economic Recovery Strategy of April 2004.

16 There seems to be little research on the question of whether spending is pro- or counter-cyclical. Evidence from Latin America suggests that social spending is often pro-cyclical (De Ferranti et al., 2000), though the cases of South Korea and Indonesia (discussed in Chapter 4) show expansion of funding following the crisis of 1997–8.

17 In many African countries in particular, much of this has been deficit spending, and the capacity for revenue generation has increased little over time (Herbst, 2000: 121–6). Relatively high spending does not necessarily imply state authority over the entire country, or the accountability that would be enforced with higher direct taxation of citizens (Herbst, 2000: 133 argues why African states' accountability is low by comparison). A trend of increased deficit spending appears illustrated by Kenya since 2000, as highlighted in its PRSP (Republic of Kenya, 2004), and the subsequent Joint Staff Assessment (http://povlibrary.worldbank.org/files/cr0510.pdf).

18 The variation in public health spending is partly the result of variation in total (public and private) health spending, and the proportion of public in total health spending – the last of which is very low in India, Indonesia and Vietnam but not Uganda (data in Musgrove et al., 2002).

19 While in India a large part of public spending on health is provided by states, and in China much funding was provided by state-owned and collective units, South Korea spends a very large share of government spending on education, and most education is centrally financed (You and Lee, 2001: 306).

20 Barrientos suggests a positive association between economic development and public expenditure on social protection, but political economy is important in explaining demand for social protection expenditures, revenue collection capacity is a key factor explaining supply, and (quoting Smith and Subbarao, 2003) donors play an important role in financing social protection expenditure and in setting poor countries' policy priorities.

21 The literature on the effects of adjustment is voluminous; links with health and nutrition outcomes are summarized in Breman and Shelton (2001), noting that the literature suggests worsening nutrition outcomes under adjustment.

22 According to 1991 IMF guidelines staff should be explicitly concerned with the effects of economic policies on the poor, and in 1997 it issued guidelines on social spending trends and targets. Board discussion in 1999 highlighted divergent views, and subsequently operational problems have continued, including in collaboration with the World Bank (IMF, 2000: 53–4). The current IMF position is still that social spending should be a central concern, but that the IMF have no expertise on the composition of public spending and this is left to the World Bank (within the World Bank, as noted, this has been left to individual sectors), and subject of discussion in a 2007 Board Paper. Heller et al. (2006: 9) emphasizes the long-term funding implications of donor-funded social spending, for example, for treatment of AIDS.

23 Paternostro et al. (2005); and highlighted in World Bank evaluations of the HIPC in 2003 and 2006 (World Bank, IEG, 2006). In Tanzania, the adoption of the PRSP (and during a period of liberalization) is thought to have had such an impact, increasing the share of spending on education between 1998/99 and 1999/2000 suddenly, and in health more gradually between 1995/96 and 2002–3 (Lipumba, 2006: 21).

24 Analysis of British aid to Africa by Killick (2005: 668–9) shows trends in investment in 'directly productive' activities (economic plus rural livelihoods) as a percentage of 'social' spending (education plus health plus social plus governance), which declined from 371 per cent in 1988/9–1989/90 to 45 per cent in 2003/4. There is evidence that this trend is not unique to DFID (Tony Killick, personal communication). Changes in lending to infrastructure, and its pendulum swings, is discussed in the World Bank's Infrastructure Network discussion paper of 2006.

25 Kraay found total government consumption negatively associated with both growth and with growth in incomes of the poor. Kraay also found a negative correlation between government consumption and growth, but government consumption improves distribution (in Resnick and Birner, 2006: 26).

26 Pattillo et al.'s (2005) review of the literature on fiscal policies emphasizes that the impact of fiscal policy on growth is different in low-income from that in richer countries.

27 Addison et al. (2006: 5) find 'mostly a positive relationship between public investment and private investment – the so-called 'crowding-in' effect.' But there are limits, and public investment eventually starts to have a negative impact.

28 Patillo et al. (2005), using World Bank indicators of quality of governance, level of social sector spending, and education and health outcomes showed that countries that scored high on both governance and education or health spending also did well in education or health outcomes.

29 Drèze and Sen (2002), pp. 38ff describe the interrelationships between 'social variables' and economic growth, as well as the interdependence between markets and governance.

30 Mackintosh and Tibandebaga (2004), p. 156; similarly, education is key to the construction of citizenship, a theme taken up in a recent paper by the Inter-American Development Bank (Cox et al., 2005).

31 Easterly, quoted in Hillman and Jenker (2004: 258).

32 Schultz (2002): female education is associated with a range of positive development outcomes, including nutritional ones.

33 In turn, lack of income or bad working conditions and long hours of work contribute to bad health and under-nutrition; see, for example, Frankenberger et al. (2002), or Mason et al. (2002: 15) with reference to Asia.

34 Nemer et al. (2001) stresses links between under-nutrition and cognitive development; the *4th Report on the World Nutrition Situation* highlights effects of nutrition deprivation throughout the life cycle, and argues that under-nourishment at birth is so crucial that it could be considered a vital summary indicator of human development.

35 Wagstaff (2001) shows this with respect to differences in inequality of health outcomes. The *Update on the Nutrition Situation 1994* (p. 5) plots changes in underweight prevalence and economic growth, showing a moderate fit.

36 Jonsson (1997) explores the reasons for high levels of child malnutrition in South Asia, emphasizing the form of subordination and exploitation of women. Issues of malnutrition have been extensively explored in ADB papers by Gillespie and Haddad (2001) and Mason et al. (2001).

37 Glewwe et al. (2002), using data on household expenditure and stunting between 1992–3 and 1997–8. The impact of household expenditures on children's nutritional status was positive, but small; other factors like community level health services and parents' (mothers') health knowledge played an important role.

38 4th Report World Nutrition, p. 43; see also Chopra et al. (2002), quoting work by Horton that suggests that the costs of malnutrition may exceed 2 or 3 per cent of GDP.

39 Mayer's (2001) analysis of 18 Latin American countries shows that the impact of health on economic growth is over the long term (for example, through increased investment in education, female participation and healthier grandparents).

40 Baldacci et al. (2004). See the summary of research by de Mello (2002).

41 Musgrove et al. (2002): this is based on national health accounts, and includes all sources of public and private spending. It notes that the WHO estimates of national account do not match IMF estimates of health expenditure when much expenditure passes through national governments, as in Brazil, China and India.

42 Davoodi et al.'s (2003: 31) review of benefit incidence studies shows that incidence of education and health spending tends to be more pro-poor in richer than in poorer countries, in more unequal countries, and in countries with better governance indicators.

43 This is illustrated by Aryeetey and McKay (2004) with respect to Ghana, where government budgets are considered to be high at least by the World Bank, and spending is dominated by health and, particularly, education: 'There may indeed be strong arguments against the growth in such expenditure, but it is also obvious that the demand for it is overwhelming.' This discrepancy is present in ideas about the role of aid as well: 'A conflict exists between the basically state-based and state-supporting aspects of official ... cooperation on the one side and the widespread resistance to the state as the major actor in the development process on the other' (Degnbol-Martinussen and Engberg-Pedersen, 2003: 4).

44 Jamison and Radelet (2005) discuss donor support to education, the increase in funding since 1990, but in their view the still low priority (7.7 per cent of total ODA), particularly for primary education (1.9 per cent).

45 Public financing increases as a share of GDP, and converges at high incomes. Within public spending, there is no convergence in the type of finance (general revenue versus social insurance). Private insurance is usually insignificant except in some rich countries (Musgrove et al., 2002).

46 See, for example, Appleton (2001) for education. Mwabu et al. (2001) for health and Watkins (2001) on Zimbabwe. OXFAM labelled charges for education a 'tax on human development'. Hillman and Jenker (2004) review user payment in education (existing in a large majority of poor countries) and experience of their abolition in Malawi in 1994 and Uganda in 1997.

47 Birdsall may have been the first to articulate a more positive view of user fees, signaling a breakdown in consensus for free education (Appleton, 2001). A World Bank staff working paper (Thobani, 1983) seems one of the first, arguing for charging in education as governments cannot afford the total subsidy required, that rationing would hurt the poor more than the rich, and user fees would help expand access for the poor.

48 This reflects a neo-classical paradigm, suggesting one can assess globalization without taking account of institutions, and that one can separate 'making globalization work for the poor' from a detailed assessment of social protection needs, and social protection as a core part of sustainable growth models.

49 Besley et al. (2003) summarize the literature on whether and to what extent publicly provided social expenditures crowd out private transfers: empirical evidence for (partial) crowding out was found by Barro, Andreoni, Jimenez and Cox (who found that social security payments in Peru reduced private transfers from young to old by 20 per cent).

50 Besley et al. (2003). 'In addition, many of the forms of intervention that safety nets take are responding to the existence of some form of market failure, such as the presence of externalities or public goods. These elements are usually not captured in benefit incidence studies.' Barrientos (2004) also emphasizes that the benefits of social security spending in terms of addressing market failures can off-set the costs to the economy of taxation.

51 In South Africa the self-reported health status of women improves dramatically when they become eligible for the social pension, and in households that pool income.

52 Pensions in southern Africa help to get grandchildren into schools; Barrientos and Sherlock-Lloyd (2001); Heslop (1999). The cross-sectoral relevance of specific interventions has been shown also in targeted nutrition intervention in Bangladesh: this did not improve nutrition levels as much as it contributed to helping children into schools.

53 Rodrik quoted in Besley et al., 2003), using cross-country evidence to show efficiency gains to be had from government provision of social services, indicates that those economies with good institutional frameworks are most able to deal with external shocks in the long run, while economies with weak institutions tend to delay price and fiscal adjustments in response to shocks. The 'free lunch' of the welfare state is free only under specific circumstances, including democratic control, accountability, competition of interests (Lindert, 2004) – as with health, we need to see these policies as deeply embedded in the political economy and institutions of particular countries.

54 Critical reviews have highlighted the problems of cross-country regressions (Forbes, 2000; Voitchovsky, 2004), and in comparing data on inequality (*World Development Report 2006*: 38; Cramer, 2003).

55 Nel (2006) reviews recent research projects, asserting the importance for public policy of national-level inequality.

56 *World Development Report 2006* (Chapter 5) describes links between inequalities and investment, for example quoting (p. 97) research in Mexico that shows how returns to capital vary with firm size.

57 Also Deininger and Olinto (2000) and Carter (2004); Sabates-Wheeler (2004) emphasizes the interlinkages of forms of inequalities for understanding the impact of land inequality.

58 In industrialized countries inequality has been shown to be damaging for health as well (Wilkinson, 1998).

59 Besançon (2005) uses this analysis to show how different forms of inequality can influence ethnic wars and revolutions.

60 Seguion in Cramer (2003); Naila Kabeer's presentation at DFID, September 2004.

61 The focus of the Centre for Research on Inequality, Human Security and Ethnicity (www.crise.ox.ac.uk/) is on 'horizontal' or group inequalities, and a recent paper by Brown and Stewart (2006) emphasizes the implications of this for aid, with particular reference to Ghana and Nepal.

62 A 1997 World Bank report on China argued that access to land has the function of reducing the need for costly public transfers.

63 Milanovic (1999), Ravallion (2003), de Mello and Tiongson (2003) and earlier articles by Alesina and Rodrik, Persson and Tabellini and Bénabou (in de Mello and Tiongson, 2003: 4) argue that if capital and insurance markets are imperfect and individuals heterogeneous, inequality leads to less popular support for redistribution.

64 Boix (2003) uses game theory to describe links between political transitions, and economic assets, their distribution and the balance of power between social groups. Falkinger and Grossmann's (2005) model highlights interaction between unequal distribution of power and openness to trade, with evidence regarding the role of landed elites in South America.

65 Social expenditure forms 33 per cent of GDP in Sweden, 15 per cent in the USA and 12 per cent in Australia.

66 Brazil and South Africa are interesting extremes in this respect: the state most likely reinforced inequalities, but over time pressure for redistribution did arise.

67 In Lindert's analysis, a range of other factors influence the development of welfare states, including degrees of mobility between bottom and middle ranks, and ethnic homogeneity. Lindert makes some reference to development in East Asia, which he considers as fitting into the general pattern of expansion of social policies.

68 This is partly because of the fragmented and disciplinary nature of social sciences (though challenged in problem-oriented fields like 'development' or 'women's studies'), partly because of the fragmented way in which international development practices operate, and partly because of the dominance of Anglo-Saxon and neo-liberal traditions that posit a fundamental trade-off between efficiency and equity.

69 In the UK too social and economic policies have been studied in isolation from each other (Peden, 1991). Teaching in the UK has tried to move away from 'its close identification with social work and to recognise that ... analysis of those policies needs to deal with interactions between social and economic policies' (Hill, 1996).

70 The Robin Hood paradox is formulated by Lindert (2004: 15–16): redistribution from rich to poor, through social security, is least present when and where it seems most needed (partly because poor people are less likely to be able to advocate redistribution); the paradox here is 'double' as *total* social spending is also lower where most needed.

Evolving Social Policies: The Importance of National Contexts

1 Therborn defined welfare states as those states where more than half of government expenditure was on social policy, as opposed to the economic, military, law and order, infrastructure, and other traditional functions of the state (Gough, 2004: 19).

2 This is highlighted in the common concern regarding the crowding-out effects of public provisions as mentioned in Chapter 3. It appears feasible to analyse welfare mixes, including for different income categories, on the basis of (some) household surveys.

3 Esping-Andersen (1999: 40–1). Societies have different interpretations of equality or fairness: a study showed that in Scandinavia popular assessment regarded a top-and-bottom income ratio of 4-to-1 as just, compared to 12-to-1 in the US (Esping-Andersen, 1999: 7).

4 The category 'productivist' appears different from the categories of solidarity in the welfare regime context, and cuts across the three main categories of solidarity; it will, however, be used below, taking account of the fact that each welfare regime also relates to ways in which social and economic policies are interrelated (the inclusive social policies of the Nordic and newly independent countries were productivist, too; Andersson and Gunnarsson, 2004 for Sweden).

5 In Taylor-Gooby's statistical analysis, the impact of ethnic or racial fragmentation is reduced once left-wing politics are taken into account.

6 Gough (2004: 28–33) lists nine contrasts: the limited importance of a capitalist mode of production, the importance of exclusions and coercion, broader livelihoods rather than wages and salaries, forms of political mobilization, weakly differentiated states, a wider set of actors responsible for the welfare mix, limited 'de-commodification', the international community's role influencing path-dependency, and a limited role of social policy as countervailing force.

7 Quoted in Yeates (2001), p. 18: her book emphasizes the importance of seeing social policy in a globalization perspective.

8 This is consistent with Esping-Andersen's analysis, which emphasizes that solidarity principles pre-date the welfare states and allows for different levels of 'de-commodification'.

9 There is no space here to discuss the concept of the informal sector, but it is important to note that the concept, 'discovered' in 1970, has deeper roots in a colonial tradition that categorically distinguished a modern from a traditional sector without analysing the interaction between the two (Breman, 1980).

10 Models of citizenship across Europe have also varied greatly, and rules of access seem to have been tightening with citizenship rather than need becoming more important.

11 Brown (2005) compares the management of political identities in Malaysia, where identity became central in the political structure, and Indonesia, where regimes sought to suppress such forms of identity.

12 Pierson (2004: 15), also Yeates (2001: 18) highlighting how development of social policy has been influenced by colonial links, Japan, Taiwan and Korea importing models and/or thinking from the West, and the influence of the Marshall Plan on the development of the welfare state in Western Europe.

13 Gough (2004); Mackintosh and Tibandebage (2004: 144) state that 'the health policy and development literature lacks an overarching theory of policy', and that policy analysis needs more of the 'thicker methodologies' that characterize studies of public policy in the North.

14 Kwon (2005) emphasizes differences between Taiwan and Korea where social development was seen as a priority, and Singapore and Hong Kong where it was subordinated to the overall economic development strategy (and more so after the East Asia crisis of the late 1990s). The first two countries introduced mainly insurance-based welfare arrangements, while Singapore followed the British model of Provident Funds.

15 Brett (2003) describes how success in East Asia may be attributed to embedded autonomy, ability to shelter officials from social groups with vested interests, rather than 'participation'.

16 Gough (2004b: 186), this assessment is in line with the characterization of the East Asian model as 'authoritarian developmentalism', of pro-active economic development with emphasis on integration into the East Asian market (the term used by Watanabe, quoted in Ohno, 2003).

17 According to Pierson (2004: 15) welfare states of late industrializers have been smaller and less redistributive.

18 Substantial investments during the 1970s depended on revenue from oil and donors: 'Indonesia was unusual in being able to invest heavily in both infrastructure and human capital in the early stages of its development because of financial support from donors and then from oil revenues' (Timmer, 2004).

19 The Minimum Living Standard Guarantee was introduced in 2000, and during 1998–9 public works were put in place, forming the largest single budget item.

20. Earlier data from Klump and Bonschab (2005), and more recent data from the government and World Bank, provided by Gita Sabharwal, DFID Vietnam.

21 Suwannarat (2003), p. 228 notes only 19 per cent of the workforce was covered by social security.

22 Stakeholders in these selective provisions have to a large extent been unable to resist reforms, partly because of the way these provisions fragment interest groups – though exceptions exist, such as pensions in Brazil (Barrientos, 2004).

23 See Gasparini and Bertranou's (2005) discussion of information derived from household surveys in various Latin American countries.

24 An extensive description of the changes in Chile can be found in Mesa-Lago et al. (2000).

25 According to Berg and Taylor (2001: 3) Mexico also abandoned its policies supporting the rural poor.

26 Jaramillo and Parodi (in Medrano et al., 2006) evaluate the impact of pro-
    grammes on equity. Implementation of insurance had a positive effect on cov-
    erage, but incidence analysis shows targeting error and benefits biased
    towards the richest.

27 Presentation by the Vice Minister at a UNDESA session of the UNESCO con-
    ference in Buenos Aires, February 2006.

28 I am not aware of research that studies the colonial social policy links, and
    the differences between, for example, Anglo- and Francophone social policies,
    though Manji (2000) provides a short sketch for Africa.

29 After that the size has remained fairly stable, but is still seen by the IFIs as rel-
    atively large (in Aryeetey and McKay, 2004).

30 Bevan (2004: 248) is concerned that a social policy notion is a Western concept,
    and continues pursuit of the Enlightenment project, which is inadequate to
    understand insecurity in Africa (e.g. Sierra Leone in the 1990s, humanitarian
    aid in Sudan in the 1980s). See Adesina 2006.

31 This argument is probably less true for the health and education sectors, where
    sector-wide approaches have done much to support capacity (see Chapter 6).

32 In Malawi, significant variations in percentage shares to poverty reducing
    activities have been observed, which have been attributed, partly, to levels of
    donor funding (Government of Malawi, 2002: 15).

33 The long-standing debate on urban bias is, of course, relevant here; this is
    well summarized and critiqued by Corbridge and Jones (2005).

34 The Malawi PRSP notes this bias continues to exist, with substantial inequality
    (bottom 20 per cent of population has only 6.3 per cent of national income)
    and predominance of small landholdings (Government of Malawi, 2002).

35 For example, Kakwani et al. (2006) report that only 3 per cent of Kenya's elderly
    population receives any pension benefits, and 5 million of a total of 7 million
    workers have no coverage at all.

36 For example, Mkandawire (verbal communication) points out that there are
    no recorded histories of countries that developed without expansion of higher
    education.

37 See Watkins (2001) for a description of the rapid progress in Zimbabwe ('a
    human development success story') in the decade after independence in
    1980, and the sharp reversal during the early 1990s.

38 Historically, in Europe, national social policies built on, and often kept
    intact, civil society organizations, particularly mutual funds that were often
    organized on a professional basis.

39 See the official government website http://ssa.nic.in/.

40 The expression was coined by Skocpol (quoted in Mkandawire, 2005), in the
    context of US social policies, and building *inter alia* on William Julius Wilson's
    arguments against racially targeted programmes, as well as programmes
    restricted to the poor.

41 This section draws partly on the joint work at PRUS (de Haan, Lipton, et al.
    1998a) on targeted anti-poverty programs, and particularly Michael Lipton's
    insights into the earlier history of targeting.

42 As Sarah White (2002) has argued 'development … may be regarded as a
    process of racial formation', and social categories are 'actively constituted in
    and through development intervention'. The importance of categories is
    highlighted in a recent volume by Moncrieffe and Eyben (forthcoming).

Structural Adjustment, Poverty Analysis and the Safety Nets Paradigm

1 Moser (1992) and Devereux and Cook (2000) describe a continuum of social policy approaches: a residual welfare mode, in which social welfare institutions come into play only when market and family structures fail; a sector-based institutional model, with a shift towards statutory provisions by the state; an incremental model in which a gradual increase in budgetary allocations is envisaged; a basic needs approach, developed primarily as a project-level strategy for poverty alleviation; and a structural model in which satisfaction of needs on the basis of equality is central.

2 This section draws on de Haan with Koch Laier (1997), de Haan et al. (1999), and de Haan (2004a). The argument put forward in earlier work stressed the need for more attention to the institutionalization of poverty analysis, emphasizing continuing poverty monitoring to trace changes in well-being and effects of policies, and attention to the place of poverty analysis or monitoring in national policy-making processes and debates (as it does in India, for example).

3 Related surveys include: *Integrated Surveys* with detailed information on household responses to adjustment; *Priority Surveys* providing rapid information on key socio-economic indicators and target groups; and the *Community Data Collection Program* providing baseline data, and monitoring markets and infrastructure (Grosh and Glewwe, 1995, and Grootaert and Marchant, 1991, describe data initiatives at the World Bank).

4 Alternative types of surveys have tried to address this: the self-rating of poverty in the Philippines to measure policy impact and as an instrument of policy monitoring; the *Core Welfare Indicators Questionnaire* (CWIQ) as a rapid and relatively cheap monitoring tool measuring key indicators with the potential to monitor and directly inform policies; and monitoring initiatives like UNDP-supported work in Cambodia.

5 However, surveys have broader objectives than poverty assessment, and are relevant for a range of planning purposes, including the expenditure patterns of the richer segments of the population.

6 Overviews of PPAs are provided in Norton et al. (2001), Robb (1999, 2000), Booth et al. (1998). Participatory approaches were core to Voices of the Poor (Narayan et al., 2000), and greatly influenced the World Development Report 2000/2001. During the 1990s more than 100 countries carried out PPAs with international assistance.

7 With the emphasis on accountability and service delivery, a range of other instruments such as citizens score cards have been discussed in the literature (including in World Development Report 2004).

8 The now voluminous literature on comparing and combining methods includes Carvalho and White (1997), Christiaensen et al. (2001), Ravallion (1996), Scoones (1996), Shaffer (1998), and international workshops organized by Ravi Kanbur and Paul Shaffer (related to the IDRC-funded MIMAP project, and including projects to strengthen national capacity in Vietnam and Kenya; http://www.q-squared.ca/).

9 According to the World Bank and IMF review (2002) all PRSPs included targets for economic growth as well as for the reduction of the number of poor

people, and improvements in health and education. It noted that poverty reduction policies had been 'upgraded' from their residual status in social sectors and welfare ministries, and had become more central to debates with ministries of finance, and more closely linked to resource allocation decisions.

10   Burkina Faso has two fairly recent comparable household surveys, and some limited participatory research, when it finalized its PRSP poverty analysis included analysis of links between growth and poverty – but links with policies remain unclear.

11   In Tanzania as elsewhere (Mozambique, Mali), the PRSP process led to renewed planning for the collection of such data and analysis.

12   Poverty analysis was not the only weak link, but, for example, public expenditure management and data were also noted as constraints on PRSP processes.

13   In the context of PRSPs, the instrument Poverty and Social Impact Analysis (PSIA) was developed to provide a basis for considering policy options and appropriate sequencing of policies, and to include compensating measures in the reform programme.

14   '[T]hey are embedded so deeply that a willful act of discrimination is not really necessary to maintain gender inequality' (in Tilly, 1998: 32). Inequality can be conceived both as difference in position with respect to similar variables, and as a characteristic of relationships between people. Individualistic accounts of mobility, according to Tilly, 'deliberately start off by talking as if people promoted themselves instead of being promoted by employers...'.

15   This is based on the joint work with Claudia Fumo, Jeremy Holland and Nazneen Kanji, documented in Fumo et al. (2000) and de Haan, Holland and Kanji (2002). Insightful reviews from outside the Bank include Cornia (1999), Reddy (1998) and the very critical work of Tendler (1999, 2000). The cross-country analysis by the Human Development Network and PREM is the most extensive internal review, focusing on how well social funds reach poor areas and people, quality of investment, impact on living standards and cost-efficiency (Rawlings et al., 2004). A little earlier social funds were evaluated by the World Bank Operations Evaluation Department (2002).

16   Data on social fund financing presented in McLeod and Dudzik (2000). This compares to a World Bank social protection portfolio, in fiscal 1999, of 92 social protection loans with commitments of $6 billion (and another 183 loans containing social protection components worth $8.9 billion).

17   The 1998 Portfolio Review of Social Funds by the World Bank Quality Assurance Group defined social funds as 'quasi-financial intermediaries that channel resources, according to pre-determined eligibility criteria, to small-scale projects for poor and vulnerable groups, and implemented by public or private agencies'.

18   As an increasing number of countries move to decentralize, social funds are finding ways to increase the involvement of local governments (for example, in Bolivia, Honduras and Zimbabwe; Parker and Serrano, 2000).

19   Covey and Abbott (1998: 75), discussing the emergence of social funds with long-term objectives, commented that the analytical and methodological adaptations to respond to this transition had not taken place on the same scale.

20   By 1996, a third of social fund projects had the 'short-term objective of rapid employment creation in response to a shock. The majority ... had longer-term objectives of delivering services and building local capacity for sustainable service provision' (Quality Assurance Group, World Bank, 1997, viii–ix).

21 Expansion of social funds has been associated with the expansion of community-based development, for which World Bank lending rose from $325 million in 1996 to $2 billion in 2003 (Mansuri and Rao, quoted in Gaspart and Platteau, 2006: 3).

22 Narayan and Ebbe (1997) describe the organizational features to increase demand orientation, community participation and local organizational capacity. De Silva (2000) emphasizes political will in favour of community management, and community cohesion and previous experience, as conditions for success.

23 Supply-driven schemes tend to have better records of targeting. Review of cross-country experience with safety nets showed that demand-driven approaches have not ensured that the poorest regions and groups receive resources (Subarrao et al., 1997).

24 Effective demand orientation exists when people are offered a range of options and impartial information to assist them in making choices – in conditions usually of asymmetries of information and power – and when evidence of commitment is required through cash or in-kind contributions and labour.

25 Gaspart and Platteau (2006) criticize the practice of providing cheap aid money for poor communities, as this leads to corruption and may strengthen or create unequal power relations. Capacity differentials among communities impact disbursement. The requirement of community contributions can favour projects where contributions can be more easily quantified and projects approved (such as school-building), but disadvantage poorer communities, and those for whom the opportunity costs of in-kind contributions is too high.

26 Holland (1999), describing in some detail the poverty approach in Egypt's social fund. The following is based mainly on his analysis, presented in section 4 of Fumo et al. (2000).

27 Criticism of geographical targeting often stems from a concern that communities are not homogenous but conceal high levels of inequality and exclusion.

28 A review of budget allocation in four social fund projects (Subbarao et al., 1997) found a negative correlation between geographic poverty levels and per capita social fund expenditure. Actual expenditures lagged behind allocation in higher income-poverty regions while they far exceeded allocations in lower income-poverty regions.

29 Certain types of programmes, such as public health services or infrastructure, are less easily targeted.

30 This section is based on section 3 of Fumo et al. (2000), written largely by Nazneen Kanji, which summarizes a number of evaluations of the organizational characteristics of social funds.

31 This assessment is in line with the World Bank OED evaluation (2002), though receiving less attention in Rawlings et al. (2004). The first international conference on social funds (Bigio, 1998) emphasized that social funds should seek better integration in national policies, pay more attention to developing sustainable communities and capacities of the local community, and mainstream innovations and techniques throughout the public sector.

32 Egypt's central government allocations to local government were cut back because of expected inflows for the social fund. Allocations for the ministries of health and education in Honduras declined at the same time as local

government was receiving resources from the social funds (World Bank, 1997, cited in Tendler, 1999, p. 19).

33 This section builds on work undertaken by DFID since 2000 (Conway et al., 2000), and at ODI (*Development Policy Review*, Vol. 20, No. 5, 2002). A recent paper by Barrientos (2006) discusses the concept of social protection (illustrated with reference to Chile Solidario)

34 In World Bank terminology, this includes policies for risk *reduction*, for example through enhancing skills, risk mitigation in areas of old age and unemployment, and risk *coping* involving safety nets for the poorest. Other kinds of programmes listed as social protection (for example, by Norton et al., 2000), include policies for labour markets, decent employment and labour standards; support for goods produced or consumed by the poor. It is possible to list micro-finance under a social protection heading, as such services can enable the poor to save and create a buffer against shocks, and to access loans to invest or meet consumption needs in times of hardship.

35 http://www.eldis.org/gender/socialprotection_genderdimensions.htm.

36 Ortiz (2000), Strategy and Policy Department, Asian Development Bank emphasizes how economic crises and transition during the late 1990s underscored the need for greater attention to social protection.

37 Bonilla Garcia and Gruat (2003) emphasize social protection as a 'life cycle continuum investment', with globalization and its impact on employment and state financing providing new challenges.

38 Earlier discussions of safety net programmes include Subbarao et al. (1997).

39 It may be relevant to emphasize here, too, that social protection within the World Bank continues to be embedded within a sectoral organizational set-up.

40 DFID's Private Under Secretary of State in a speech to the Global Partners Forum, Lancaster House, on 9 February 2006 highlighted the need for social investment in the poorest countries.

41 1 April 2006, Belo Horizonte, IDB Annual Meeting, http://www2.iadb.org/events/file/do605.doc.

42 The rationale of these programmes is different from public works, such as within social funds, TRABAJAR in Argentina, or the employment scheme in Maharashtra, which involves payment for work in a 'self-targeting' manner.

43 Apart from Mkandawire, critical views are expressed in Tendler (2004) and Deacon (2000) (who includes the ILO as an agency in which targeting has gained popularity). Arguments in support of targeting draw on de Haan and Lipton (1998).

44 Using a modelling exercise focusing on political feasibility, Gelbach and Pritchett (1997) argue that targeting reduces social welfare.

45 The term coined by Skocpol (in Echeverri-Gent, 1993: 197ff), highlighting a strategic selection of policy tasks through which universalistic policies are to be applied (education, health, employment programmes).

46 In the case of the India World Bank office, I encountered very little knowledge of the Washington social protection agenda, despite substantial Bank engagement in programmes like ICDS (see Ratna Sudarshan's report of a survey among donors, in de Haan, 2004c).

47 Van Ginneken (2003) emphasizes the need to ensure linkages between different approaches to social security (statutory social insurance, contributory schemes, particularly community based and tax-financed social benefits).
48 Recent publications, such as by Graham (2002a) for the social protection sector at the World Bank, and work by IDS on 'transformative' social protection (http://www.ids.ac.uk/ids/pvty/socproinfocus.html) are moving in this direction.

New Poverty Reduction Strategies and the Missing Middle

1 See Dijkstra and van Donge (2001) for a discussion of developments in Uganda, often seen as the show-case of the success of structural adjustment.
2 As well as strong critiques, notably by former World Bank economist Bill Easterly (2006), who in turn was criticized by a large number of economists at the 2006 Annual Wider Conference, and Amartya Sen in *Foreign Affairs*.
3 Report of the International Conference on Financing for Development Monterrey, Mexico, 18–22 March 2002: http://www.un.org/esa/ffd/aconf198-11.pdf. It argued for strengthening coherence between the United Nations, the Bretton Woods institutions, the World Trade Organization and financial institutions.
4 The following is to a large extent based on the joint work with Max Everest-Phillips (2006), and the discussion of the evolution of governance work and the Monterrey Consensus draws largely on his insights.
5 Moore's (1994) early review of the good government donor literature identified no fewer than twelve components of what good government is thought to entail: participation; accountability; predictability of government action; transparency; free information flow; rule of law; legitimacy; constitutionality; socio-political pluralism; decentralization; market-oriented policies; concern for socio-economic equity and poverty.
6 Grindle (2002) quotes a survey of expert opinion in 20 countries that revealed very critical perspectives on government performance, but also a perception that improvements had been made in civil service reforms, privatizations, reduction of the public sector wage bill, improved performance of state enterprises and service delivery, and restructured relationships between central, provincial and local governments. The GDN research project on reforms also indicates reforms have generally been implemented, though definitions of reform changed over time (Fanelli, 2004).
7 The following draws heavily on this and related (Brown et al., 2001) publications. Walford (2003) provides an overview of definitions used in different agencies, and Lavergne and Alba (2003) a good overview and comparison with other approaches, from a CIDA perspective.
8 Brown et al. (2001: 25) refer to the Bangladesh health and population programme and the Pakistan social action programme. In the case of DFID support in Orissa, a project unit existed, too, but was seen as a stepping stone towards a health sector programme, which was very difficult to establish.

9   HIPC-II to be accurate; the original HIPC debt initiative by the World Bank and International Monetary Fund had been launched in the autumn of 1996. HIPC was not the first effort to reschedule debt, but the first one involving the International Financial Institutions (IFIs).

10 See Alemayehu (2002) for an historical description of the origins of the debt crisis (and arguments why the HIPC initiative may not be sufficient to solve Africa's debt crisis).

11 The report led to discussion around the question whether aid has been effective (at the macroeconomic level), including critique of the World Bank's (Burnside and Dollar) analysis; see the special issue of *Journal of Development Studies*, and the introduction to that volume by Hermes and Lensink (2001). A 2002 World Bank study reinforced the message that aid can work (and that effectiveness has improved), particularly as a 'catalyst for change' (World Bank DEC, March 2002). The discussion continued, including during the 2006 annual WIDER conference.

12 Ahmed et al. (2001); World Bank, Operations Policy and Country Services (2001).

13 The review also focuses strongly on experience in and with IFIs, and does not pay much attention to the slightly older UN experiences with UNDAF (UN, 1999), and the National Strategies for Sustainable Development (NSSD) which emerged out of the Rio UN Conference.

14 Robb (2001) describes a series of arguments for civic engagement in PRSPs, including enhancing ownership, accountability and civil society capacity building. Though participation was no requirement for I-PRSPs, in many cases participation was strongly encouraged.

15 Stewart and Wang (2003: 10–11), emphasize that the process of participation was strongly led by government and not by civil society.

16 Gottschalk (2005) highlights that the macroeconomic framework of PRSPs tends to be too narrowly focused on fiscal balance and price stability, paying too little attention to economic fluctuations and external shocks. According to Owusu (2003) the Comprehensive Development Framework, alongside NEPAD, has settled a long-standing debate over development strategies, in favour of neo-liberalism and global integration.

17 To establish such links has not proven as easy as some may have expected, and some of the more traditional adjustment measures, for example, related to inflation, was shown not to have the anti-poor effects that some had suggested – though debates about appropriate levels of inflation continue.

18 Problems with budgeting include the still-common practice of off-budget financing (ibid: 363), which may be on the increase with new vertical aid initiatives, as discussed in the section on sector-wide approaches.

19 The experience in Latin America has given rise to a debate about whether the PRS approach should be abandoned (Dijkstra, 2005, 2006; Holmqvist and Metell Cueva, 2006); in the view of Booth et al. (2006) emphasis should be put on donors' alignment and harmonization, a central part of a PRS approach, in a way that allows strategic support to specific initiatives.

20 A Bank–Fund review paper (7 Jan 2002), following IFI's directors' call for a joint assessment, acknowledged that the PRSP approach was extremely demanding, and with hindsight its objectives too ambitious. Consensus building around a poverty strategy was found to be difficult. It was noted that a

comprehensive strategy itself is a complex undertaking, that there was a risk of overloaded agendas.

Conclusion: A Framework for Social Policy

1 This builds on the practical guidance provided by Moser (1992), Norton and Bird (1998), Cook and Devereux (2000), Davis (2000), Hall and Midgley (2004), Wood (2004), and Christiansen (2004).

Index